(continued from front flap)

a dual portrait of courage on the part of U.S. airmen who flew into the teeth of Luftwaffe defenses, and of an entire nation that resolved to resist, if necessary, the full might of the Wehrmacht.

The story of U.S. airmen in Switzerland is filled with examples of heroic resolve, occasional cultural conflict and serious mistakes that were committed by the militaries of both nations. At the same time it explodes many myths that have gestated since the war about Switzerland and the American airmen who sought refuge there.

Carefully researched, with a multitude of firsthand accounts of "near-death" in the air war, *Refuge from the Reich* finally brings to light the relationship between American airmen and the small democracy that stubbornly held out in Europe through the darkest days of World War II. It is a fascinating story of fighting men from the world's greatest democracy finding shelter within the borders of a far smaller one, when there was no other safe haven in the proximity of Hitler's Reich to be found.

Stephen Tanner is a New York-based writer specializing in military history. After editing numerous well-received works from Julius Caesar's campaigns to the Gulf War, he became the leading contributor to *Great Raids in History: From Drake to Desert One* (1996), and the author of *Epic Retreats: From 1776 to the Evacuation of Saigon* (2000).

SARPEDON PUBLISH.
An Imprint of Combined Publishing
ISBN 1-885119-70-4

REFUGE FROM THE REICH

REFUGE
from the
REICH

American Airmen and Switzerland During World War II

STEPHEN TANNER

SARPEDON
Rockville Centre, NY

Published by
SARPEDON
An Imprint of Combined Publishing

© 2000 by Stephen Tanner

ISBN 1-885119-70-4

For sales information, please contact Combined Publishing,
P.O. Box 307, Conshohocken, PA 19428.
E-Mail: combined@combinedpublishing.com
Web: www.combinedpublishing.com

Library of Congress Cataloging-in-Publication Data

Tanner, Stephen, 1954–
    Refuge from the Reich: American airmen and Switzerland during World War II /
by Stephen Tanner.
    p. cm.
    Includes bibliographical references and index.
    ISBN 1-885119-70-4
    1. World War, 1939–1945—Prisoners and prisons, Swiss. 2.
Neutrality—Switzerland—History—20th century. 3. World War, 1939–1945—
Switzerland. 4. World War, 1939–1945—Aerial operations, American.
5. Airspace (International law)
I. Title.
D805.S78 T36 2000
940.53'494—dc21   00-058784

10 9 8 7 6 5 4 3 2 1

MANUFACTURED IN THE UNITED STATES OF AMERICA

Contents

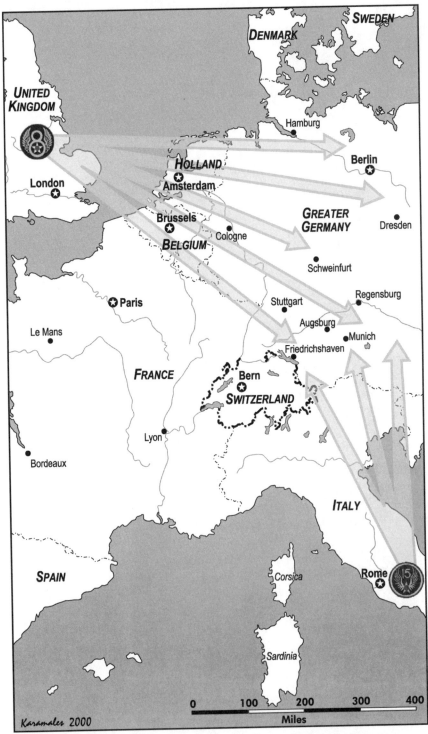

At the height of the U.S. strategic bombing campaign, 1944–45, Germany came under simultaneous assault from the Eighth Air Force, based in England, and the Fifteenth Air Force, based in Italy.

ACKNOWLEDGMENTS

While writing this book I was continually gratified by the level of interest and expertise I encountered from those who participated in the events of World War II. As a result, I owe a debt of gratitude to a number of individuals who have assisted or contributed to this work. Foremost, the Swiss Internees Association, its current president, Robert A. Long, and its membership of ex-USAAF flyers have been an essential resource. Particular thanks go to Cyril Braund, Jack McKinney, Christy Zullo, who also supplied a number of photographs, Clinton Norby and Martin Andrews, who graciously contributed a foreword, for their interest and assistance. Mr. Long, whose knowledge of the subject, as well as of flying a B-24 ("like a wrestling match!"), is encyclopedic, continues to shepherd and enhance the Association's archives, a veritable treasure trove for World War II historians.

There was a moment of disappointment when I discovered early in the writing process that the following would not be the first U.S. publication on American airmen in Switzerland during the war. That pang soon gave way to pleasure and I owe a special thanks to two Swiss authors, Hans-Heiri Stapfer and Gino Künzle, whose book *Strangers in a Strange Land, Volume II: Escape to Neutrality* was published by Squadron/Signal Publications in 1992. Copiously illustrated and meticulous in its chronology, this work became a much-valued secondary source. I trust that Messrs. Stapfer and Künzle will appreciate the instances where I differ from their analyses because of information that has since come to light. For specific details of each USAAF plane

vii

(including serial numbers), and on each date, that flew into Switzerland during World War II, their intensely researched book remains unsurpassed.

I deeply appreciate the hospitality of Mr. and Mrs. Paul Rothenhäusler, who welcomed me on a recent visit to Switzerland, and to Geoffrey von Meiss, a former Swiss fighter pilot who, during the war, welcomed a number of U.S. aircrews into the country from his post high above the clouds. Dr. Jürg Stüssi-Lauterburg, The Librarian, Federal Military History and Historical Service, in Bern, displayed both patience and insight with my requests for specific data and his personal perspective. I'm honored that he found the time to answer my queries, and in such enlightening detail.

I am very grateful for the learned advice and suggestions of Dr. Douglas Sears, Boston University, and of Thomas Ryan, who kindly reviewed this work during its early stages. Thanks go, too, to Heather Barry, whose research was of enormous help, and to my editors at Sarpedon Publishers, Daryl Horrocks and Sam Southworth, for their expertise with the manuscript. The assistance of Professor Douglas Anderson of Penn State University, the foremost American authority on USAAF flyers in Switzerland, was invaluable. His own forthcoming work on the subject is keenly anticipated. To those I may have forgotten to name, my sincere apologies; to everyone who so generously offered their expertise and firsthand experience to the work, my heartfelt thanks.

FOREWORD

Stephen Tanner's aptly named book chronicles the experiences of American airmen whose planes were forced to land in neutral Switzerland during World War II. More than that, it describes a tiny nation and her people who maintained an island of sanity and freedom in the middle of a continent controlled by evil.

Most combat veterans are reluctant to talk about their wartime experiences. The reason is simple. They were survivors, and survivors feel guilt. "Why me? All the good guys got killed." As one of more than 150 pilots of the U.S. Army Air Force in World War II who were forced by battle damage to land with their crews in Switzerland, I still feel dismay that so many comrades died and I survived. My solace is that I preserved the lives of the members of my crew, which was made possible by the existence of Switzerland. We remain forever grateful to that little country and her people.

Switzerland has long been considered of small consequence by those who view history only through the lens of conquest with its attendant subjugations, ruin and liberations. But the people who would diminish Switzerland totally ignore the political genius and common will that have made and kept a country of multi-ethnicity and different religions a cohesive and democratic whole. When one considers the murderous and endless ethnic and religious strife rending other countries all over the world, one has to marvel at what the Swiss have been able to achieve.

Switzerland, alas, was not an option for the far more numerous bomber pilots of the Royal Air Force. They flew at night, when

Switzerland was blacked out. Heaven only knows how many of their airmen died in planes that couldn't get home and had no place to go. We Americans were luckier in that respect. Bombing Nazi Germany in broad daylight was dangerous duty, but we could see the earth and sky.

A poet wrote:

> If I sense dread,
> It is of things not done, not said.

Now this story has been told.

For their size and place in history, the great air battles over Europe —with fleets of American bombers and German fighters locked in mortal combat—were a once and only thing that will never happen again. Mr. Tanner has done a great service in illuminating and re-creating a significant part of that aviation story and in explaining the importance of Switzerland, not just as a refuge for stricken American bombers, but as a model of democracy for the world.

Martin Andrews
Port Jefferson, NY
August 7, 2000

INTRODUCTION

The word "courage," when applied to the World War II generation, can encompass an enormous range of experiences. Even as we enter the new century, there are aspects of history's greatest war that continue to unfold and portraits of heroism that have for decades been neglected. The relationship between the nation of Switzerland and the U.S. strategic air campaign against Nazi Germany is one such drama. Perhaps understandably, the record of American aircraft severely damaged by German fire and forced to seek refuge in a neutral state has been sidestepped by chroniclers of the air war who prefer to report on our ultimate victory; likewise, the struggle of Switzerland to maintain its national integrity in Nazi-held Europe has remained largely unexamined. Together, however, the story of U.S. airmen and Switzerland reveals a fascinating panorama of heroism from the personal to the national level. Amid the cataclysm of global war, a small democracy was able to offer safety to individual fighting men of a larger one. How this came to be is a story worth telling.

Of all the soldiers who fought in World War II, a special respect is due the air warriors, who fought miles above ground and who, if hit by enemy fire, could only face a greater danger, from the terrifying pull of gravity as their ship plummeted to earth. In many cases the only remaining hope would lie with a silk parachute or with split-second decisions by a bomber pilot, nine men depending on the tenth to crashland safely. The scale of the battles in the skies that took place in World War II was unique in history, not preceded and never to be equaled. The young waist gunners, radiomen, turret gunners and bom-

1

bardiers of World War II stand alone as representatives of the only generation in history thrust en masse into combat amidst the clouds.

The tremendous vulnerability of citizens-turned-aircrew rushed into service during World War II did not, of course, stop governments from launching ever-increasing numbers of them into high-altitude warfare. Fear of flying assumed a new dimension when enemy fighters and anti-aircraft guns opened fire, expending every ounce of their lethal energy to knock one's aircraft out of the sky. During some stages of the air war, the survival rate for bomber crewmen across their projected 25 missions was calculated at nearly zero. By the end of the war the United States had lost 80,000 airmen (as had the British), often in the most gruesome ways imaginable. The combat loss rates of these U.S. airmen—especially those who flew bombers in Europe—far exceeded that of any other branch of the U.S. armed forces.

The crews in crippled planes that managed to reach Swiss airspace lived through and could later describe a "near-death" experience. Hit by enemy fire and unable to return to base, their options were grim. They could land or parachute into enemy-held territory and pass into German captivity, where 10 percent of prisoners died. In many cases, parachuting airmen were reached by murderous civilians before authorities could take them into custody. Another possibility was that their plane would suddenly explode or lose power and dive into the ground, the last few seconds of life a passage through sheer terror. During the years when the strategic air campaign raged above a continent almost completely covered by the swastika, there was, in fact, no good option for a crew whose plane had become a serious casualty of the air war. No option, except one.

Switzerland, which is seldom mentioned in histories of American ground triumphs in World War II, comes up more often in histories and firsthand accounts of the air war. The phrase "made it to Switzerland" indicates that a crew was able to trade life for death or refuge for capture by the enemy. The number of U.S. aircraft that tried to head for Switzerland but didn't succeed, falling prey to German fighters, flak or engine failure en route, can never be ascertained. Many other planes that were guided to safety by the Swiss air force would probably not have survived if they had lost altitude so helplessly over the Third Reich. But enough U.S. airmen—over 1,700—made it to the "safe haven option" to provide a fascinating look at what it meant to be shot down in the strategic air campaign and subsequently experience wartime life in the Continent's oldest democracy—the only nation to successfully deter the Nazis from invasion and occupation.

While the bravery of American flyers during the war inspires awe, another kind of courage was displayed by an entire nation—men, women and children—during the aggressive war launched by the Third Reich. When every other nation in mainland Europe, from Franco's Spain to the Soviet Union, had fallen to the Nazis or become allied with them, the Swiss stood alone in the very center of the Continent, unbowed and defiant. Switzerland's experience during World War II was so far from any scenario that could possibly develop for the United States that it has often been overlooked, if not completely misunderstood, on these shores. Suffice to say that if America ever found itself completely surrounded and outnumbered forty to one by a belligerent, aggressive enemy, it would do well to emulate the intrepidness shown by Switzerland during the five years when it survived as an oasis of democracy in the center of the Third Reich.

A visit to modern-day Switzerland can provide clues, if not answers, to how this ancient people was able to remain a unique case in Nazi-held Europe. What one encounters is a rather plain people: handsome but not ostentatious in clothing or behavior; scrupulously honest but always exact in transactions; hardworking but unaggressive. The economy, at least compared to New York, is a curious hybrid: trolley cars dating from the 1920s skid through city streets past shops with electric sliding doors, in buildings that predate indoor plumbing. The architectural motif, especially in the countryside, remains rooted in the latest styles of the 16th century. The prevailing impression is utilitarian, without excess or apparent signs of status.

From a military history point of view, Switzerland is somewhat more revealing. At the Zurich train station, groups of men in camouflage tunics walk by or congregate at kiosks. In the United States, camouflage dress has become a fashion affectation, but in Switzerland it indicates the army. Police are seldom seen, but young soldiers in groups of six to a dozen—some wearing red berets, others gray or black ones—are ubiquitous. Some have submachine guns slung across their backs; others carry long, narrow bags that indicate a rifle with the barrel folded over for storage. At the ticket booth, young men lean on black assault rifles which look similar to an enlarged version of the

U.S. M-16. Between Zurich and Bern, there are long trains of flatcars mounted with scores of military trucks and armored personnel carriers. A few miles further along there is a goods train: gravel cars and boxcars and then, incongruously, two dark green self-propelled guns with 155mm cannon. On first impression, Switzerland appears to be a nation mobilized for war; yet, I am assured, this is only how the Swiss have practiced neutrality—for years, decades and centuries.

The terrain of Switzerland is itself instructive when seen firsthand. The southern half of the country is covered by the Alps, the great historic barrier bifurcating Europe (both north and south, east and west) and Switzerland's special domain. The surprise is that the rest of the country resembles something no less forbidding than New York's Adirondacks, or, on the Swiss plateau, southern Pennsylvania with a multitude of "round tops." Everywhere are steep hills and ridges, cut by rivers or divided by lakes. The occasional flatland is suddenly interrupted by a massive height, too formidable for motor vehicles. It is clear that an invader would have limited road access to the interior of the country, only to face serious flank problems from wooded heights on every side. On reaching the Alps, an attacker would find any challenge he had surmounted in the north multiplied to an enormous degree. It was, in fact, beyond my imagination to picture how the Swiss Alps could be seized from an army that was resolute in defense. The overriding impression of modesty one receives from the Swiss people is somewhat belied by the majestic strength of their mountains; but then, perhaps there is a cause and effect. In Swiss towns, the white cross on red background flies overhead, next to church steeples that appear to be hundreds of years old; in the cities, statues of great warriors from the Middle Ages rise above parks. And this from a nation intent on staying out of European wars.

I asked a Swiss woman who was a teenager during World War II whether she thought the Swiss Army could have coped with a German invasion. She thought for a moment as if this were an odd question, and then replied, "We really would have hurt them quite badly." Her answer was matter-of-fact, as so much of the country appears to an American observer.

With World War II fading rapidly into the annals of time, the firsthand experiences of participants can supply a corrective to distortions of fact that often creep into the actual record. Although participants seldom shared identical experiences, collectively their stories provide a strong defense against the twin evils of revisionism and romanticism that inevitably seep into history that is written long after the fact.

During World War II, to U.S. airmen and the proud public that followed their exploits, the word "Switzerland" came to mean welcome refuge in a country that defied Hitler. In years since, however, the word has sometimes been connected with a tempting option, on the part of aircrew, to drop out of the war. To this day, the public is largely unaware that the American flyers who made it into Switzerland, with very few possible exceptions (perhaps none), had no other choice. Their bravery in combat was unsurpassed by aircrews whose intact craft allowed them to return to base. For the crews of smoking, burning planes that careened amid the Alps seeking the option of haven from death or Nazi capture, there is no alternative sentiment but respect. The hundreds of subsequent escapes and attempts to escape internment, too, reveal the indomitable spirit of the U.S. flyers who came down on Swiss territory. Despite the excruciating danger of the air war, most men wanted to rejoin their units.

The Swiss nation's role in World War II, in addition, has remained a matter of vague conjecture on the part of the general public. Many Americans still believe that Switzerland didn't even *have* an army, much less the largest one, relative to its population, on the Continent. Many assume that Switzerland conducted business as usual during the war or that Swiss neutrality meant not knowing or caring about the cataclysm the Nazis had unleashed on Europe. Contemporary Swiss voices, in addition to accounts from American airmen, provide a firsthand view of a small country that was able to stand bravely when all its neighbors had caved in to German arms or Nazi philosophy.

In the following pages I have not sought to convey a sense of victory or triumph, although World War II provides ample material for both. I have instead attempted to bring to light a story of survival: of American soldiers who participated in the greatest air war in history, and of a small nation that braved dangerous odds of its own. For those of us who enjoy the freedom for which they fought, the airmen who made it to Switzerland deserve our deepest respect. As for the Swiss, they have always relied on their own resources to preserve their freedom, and I suspect they will continue to do so in the future.

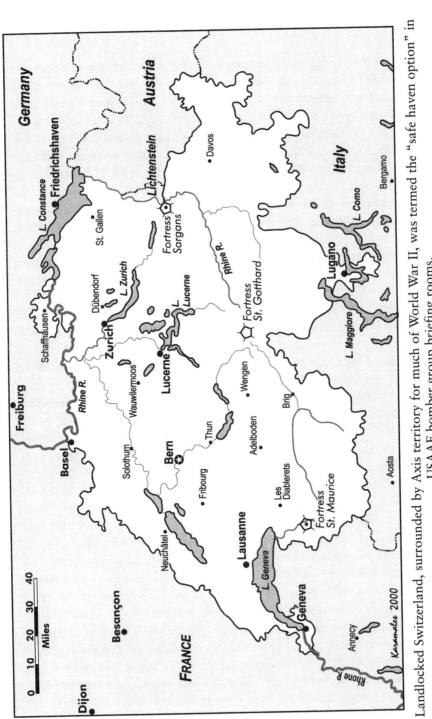

Landlocked Switzerland, surrounded by Axis territory for much of World War II, was termed the "safe haven option" in USAAF bomber group briefing rooms.

1

CRASHLANDING

Darkness had just begun to yield to daylight on July 21, 1944, when thousands of engines roared to life across scores of airfields in southern England. It was to be a "maximum effort" by the "Mighty Eighth"—everyone and everything that could fly would fly. Eleven hundred four-engine bombers—B-17 Flying Fortresses and B-24 Liberators—accompanied by 800 fighters would penetrate deep into the Third Reich to lay a pattern of death and destruction across the industrial centers of southern Germany.

One Liberator, *Ginny Gal,* waited for its turn on the runway, shutting down its number three engine while a ground crew topped off its right wing gas tank. The plane's pilot, 1st Lieutenant Key Caldwell, wanted every last drop of fuel he could get. Fully laden with bombs and ammo, the ungainly looking B-24 could make it to the center of Europe; the problem was getting back. On its return trip the ship would be lighter by nearly all its 3,000 pounds of fuel and over eight tons of bombs, but on a deep penetration raid such as this there was little room for error, or the unexpected. The gunners positioned throughout the aircraft could only hope that by the time they returned to base they wouldn't have had to lighten the craft by firing off all their 50-caliber machine-gun ammunition at marauding German fighters.

After roaring down the runway at 30-second intervals, the Eighth Air Force bombers assembled into formation in the sky, each squadron joining its group over its base. Then the groups formed into wings and then divisions over East Anglia, northeast of London near the British coast. The intricate choreography required to weave over a thousand heavy planes simultaneously into a unified formation was astonishing considering that two years earlier a majority of the pilots had never even set foot in an aircraft; the ground controllers had never handled nearly so many planes; and that one mistake—a collision—over the often fog-shrouded land would probably mean instant death to twenty men. The sun had just risen fully over the horizon when the vast American air armada, 15 miles wide and 60 miles long, headed east across the English Channel.

It was the 17th mission for *Ginny Gal*'s crew, which was already minus its original co-pilot, bombardier, engineer and tail gunner. *Ginny Gal* was the crew's third plane, the first having been badly holed by German flak on their first mission and the second reduced to near scrap on their tenth, a raid on the east German town of Halle. After Halle, bombardier Jack Dobson was buried in the American cemetery at Cambridge. Turret gunner/engineer Arlin Neill had barely survived. During the return from Halle, Neill had performed his duties so well that the rest of the crew didn't realize how badly he had been injured by shrapnel.

After the three air divisions of the Mighty Eighth crossed the Channel, navigator Strickland Holeton recalled, "We soon encountered a cloud-covered continent. And then we hit towering cumulus about halfway to target, running us up to 26,000 feet, near our maximum altitude, and burning fuel by the ton." *Ginny Gal* was in the lower, rear echelon of its group, following the "lead" plane at the front of the formation. At that point they had traversed the green countryside of France at about 200 mph and had crossed the Rhine into Germany. The lead was assigned to steer the formation on a precise, zigzag route intended to deceive German radar about the bombers' true destination while avoiding enemy anti-aircraft concentrations along the way. "Then 'lead' started to cut corners to save fuel," Holeton said, "and we got caught in a sharp left turn near Saarbrucken. Mushy as we were at that altitude with a full load, the whole lower echelon stalled out and spun down into the soup."

As the plane twirled downward, centrifugal force pinned the crew against their seats or the fuselage. After a 6,000-foot spiral, pilot Key Caldwell somehow regained control of the craft and swung it back into a pure dive. "With a lot of creaking and groaning we leveled out around 19,000 feet, ice all over the plane, barely controllable, 7,000 feet under and who knows where from the bomber train." While flying blind in the clouds with other disoriented ships nearby, the biggest fear was collision. Pilots wouldn't see each other until it was too late; the roaring noise thrown up by the engines made it impossible to hear other aircraft nearby.

Ginny Gal salvoed its bombs near Saarbrucken and turned southeast toward what it hoped was the safety of the bomber stream and its protective screen of fighters. According to Holeton, "We had just begun to climb when we started to get hit by everything but slingshots. Under 22,000 feet the German flak was really murderous. They could get us with their 75mm anti-aircraft guns which, when added to their 88s and 105s and highly accurate radar, made a deadly combination. They were hitting us, one plane, through at least six to eight thousand feet of cloud cover! Number one engine went out fast, number three suddenly got all dirty with oil streaming out. We quickly lost our hydraulic pressure, but three kept running as we started slowly climbing."

"It was then that I noticed a light still lit on the bomb panel. We had one hung up! I frantically triggered and retriggered the bomb release levers, doing a little praying on the side, until after a seeming eternity the light went out, indicating the bomb had dropped. I've often wondered what it may have hit but have no idea due to the thick cloud cover below us and our informal position fix at the time. One recurring thought is that there is a German farmer somewhere, minus his favorite cow, still asking 'Why me, why me?'"

Ginny Gal got lucky, and after heading southeast encountered the bomber stream north of Munich heading due east, from where it would turn and attack that city from behind. Holeton said, "We came bursting out of the clouds right into the middle of another group. Why they didn't shoot us down, I'll never know, since the Germans were in the habit of using captured bombers to track our formations to give speed and altitude to their flak units. Guess they figured no Germans could be so stupidly obvious, and they allowed us to pull up into a 'Tail End Charlie' position of the nearest group."

"Key Caldwell poured on the inches and we were almost keeping up. As we turned west onto the bomb run, however, we were treated to the most impressive display of murderous thick-boxed anti-aircraft fire I'd ever seen. Whole groups would disappear into this continuous big black cloud over the city and then come staggering out the other side in a motley formation with assorted beat-up stragglers."

The greatest concentrations of German anti-aircraft around Munich were north and west of the city, so the pilots had been briefed to overfly the target and attack from the east, then turn sharply left, to the south, west again for a short 30-mile stretch, and then northwest for home. According to Holeton, "With no bombs, low fuel, two bad engines, and a well-bruised piece of equipment, we decided to take a southwesterly heading and pick up the train south of the city. Worked great. Right heading, right spot, great navigation. One problem—'lead' was still cutting corners and made a sharp right turn to due north immediately off the target! We were hung out to dry all by ourselves, directly over the Junkers factory and airfield just south of Munich."

Ginny Gal was by itself, a magnetic prey for Luftwaffe fighters. The pilot and co-pilot made a quick check of remaining fuel versus planned fuel consumption, and discovered they had no chance at all of making it back to base. There were then no Allied "lines" to make it back to, except across the English Channel. By July 21, Allied ground troops had won only a precarious toehold in France. On that day the U.S. First Army, six weeks after D-Day, was in the middle of a raging battle with the Wehrmacht for St. Lo in Normandy. Patton's Third Army had not yet begun its breakout from the beachhead. Even if *Ginny Gal* reached the American front, there was nothing for the crew but to bail out over the battlefield because there were still no Allied airfields on the Continent.

As navigator Holeton put it, "We were as deep in Germany as we could get. We had no chance of rejoining or even keeping up with the now rapidly disappearing bomber train and its covering fighters. There were lots of German fighters and flak between us and any sort of safety. Number one was dead and feathered. Number three was getting dirtier, and hotter, and losing power by the minute.

"Switzerland was about an hour south of us, if we could stay in the air. We attempted to contact base or group without success, finally just going on the air in the clear, advising of our intentions and why. We then turned south again directly over the Junkers airfield, on a heading to the Swiss border.

"It was then that I became aware of two German Me-109s having taken off from that field and coming up fast with us in mind. Damn, they could climb! They both climbed above and to our rear and turned into a diving pass at our tail. Then, suddenly, two beautiful, silver P-51s came screaming down on them from the north. The 109s never fired a shot—just kept diving with the 51s doing a job on them. Where those Mustangs came from, or what they were doing there, I'll never know, but they sure were a welcome sight."

Ginny Gal continued south across almost solid undercast. Another stroke of luck occurred when a small break in the clouds revealed Lake Constance, which straddles the Swiss-German border. The Liberator was on the right track, but not yet out of danger. "We spiraled down through the break to 5,000 feet above the lake, then zigged and zagged westward up the valley, between 12,000-foot mountains, their peaks hidden in clouds. The scenery was beautiful, but our admiration was strained because the foothills often came close to our wingtips as we struggled, unable to climb. We were trying to make the briefed safe haven option at Dubendorf airbase near Zurich, with me and my charts running a course while squatting between the pilots. We inexorably lost altitude even with the crew frantically jettisoning everything that wasn't bolted down or removable by ax, including the waist guns."

Just then, two more Messerschmitt 109 fighters appeared out of the clouds, their barracuda-like silhouettes instantly recognizable to every flyer in Eighth Air Force. And this time there were no guardian Mustangs to chase them off. The bomber's crew held its breath until, finally, man after man let go a sigh of relief. The fighters were Swiss. Holeton said: "As we staggered out of the mountain valley, onto the rolling plains southeast of Zurich, we were suddenly joined by a gleaming Me-109 on each wing! They came sliding in to us in gentle curves, though, and when they were alongside they raised their wings to display the Swiss cross. They carefully slid closer, in case of a nervous gunner, and then indicated they wished us to land, pointing toward the fighter base ahead.

"Key dropped the gear and dipped the nose in acquiescence, and as we neared the field lumbered into the righthand pattern suggested by the Swiss fighters. I'll never forget that grassy knoll south and west of the base since we literally trimmed that grass, just barely clearing it, as we were unable to climb. As we made our slow righthand turn we could see that we were at least the eighth or ninth ship into the field that day and couldn't use the main runway due to the other planes in assorted positions bracketing the end of it. We touched down at about 130 knots without flaps or brakes, having exhausted our hydraulics."

Caldwell shut off the only two working engines, two and four, at touchdown, but the B-24 careened across the slick field, unable to stop. A camouflaged Swiss anti-aircraft emplacement, covered with logs, was on the far side of the field, and the Liberator, its bomb bay doors opened to create drag on the ground, crashed into it with a screeching cacophony of tearing, crushing metal. The right wing broke upward and back, and the fuselage broke just behind the command deck. Then came the equally disturbing sound of dead silence.

The crew of *Ginny Gal* had suffered bumps, cuts and bruises, but fortunately no one was seriously injured. As the airmen cautiously took stock, they heard a crash on the plane and then a violent hissing. Everyone hastily scrambled from the bomber, the aft crew surprised to find they were already on grass. On getting a few feet away the crew realized that the 10-man life raft emplaced in the right wing had automatically activated on impact. The bright yellow device had popped up on the wing and was just noisily filling itself with air.

Another surprise was in store. Holeton said: "The radioman, Johnny O'Neal, and I literally dived head first from the command deck onto the curved surface of the collapsed bomb bay doors, which acted as a slide, catapulting us out onto the grass which I hit scrambling, trying to distance myself from the hissing monster. I then became aware of a line of gray-clad soldiers with helmets and rifles, and I had a brief ridiculous urge to return to the ship to recheck my charts!"

The soldiers wore unfamiliar helmets and their rifles were fixed with bayonets. The panting American navigator stopped running at a vehicle at the end of the line of soldiers and clambered onto its right seat. He was physically tired, mentally exhausted, and not quite sure what would happen next. At that point, one of the soldiers calmly offered him a cigarette. He said, "Is OK, is OK. Ich bin Swiss. You get flight pay!"

Of the 1,110 bombers the U.S. Eighth Air Force launched against Germany on July 21, 1944, 31 were lost. Of these, 23 were destroyed in the air, ditched in the Channel, or their crews were forced to bail out over Nazi-held territory, consigned, if they survived, to the grim fate of a German stalag. *Ginny Gal* and seven other American aircraft found refuge in Switzerland, the "safe haven option," and a nation which emerged from World War II with its own dramatic story to tell.

By the end of the war, 1,704 American soldiers had entered Switzerland, the vast majority arriving via crippled bombers that had no other protective destination within range. So it happened that during the last two years of World War II, while the titanic American strategic bombing campaign raged in the skies over Germany, and while the Swiss faced the greatest foreign threat in their 700-year history, the soldiers of the United States and Switzerland came into direct contact for the first time.

It is ironic that Switzerland, whose democracy predated America's by nearly 500 years and whose policy of armed neutrality had been in place since 1515, was still largely a mystery to Americans during World War II. At one time, the two countries were thought to be intimately linked. The American Founding Fathers studied Switzerland closely during the late 18th century because it was the only democratic state in Europe at the time, having already institutionalized, in the shadow of immense foreign power, the conviction not to live under the rule of kings. In the debates of 1787 that raged over the the new U.S. Constitution, the Swiss example was cited on every side. James Madison and Alexander Hamilton, in favor of a strong central government, vied with Patrick Henry and Richard Henry Lee, who admired the Swiss concept of a loose confederation. Others, such as John Adams, simply analyzed the cantons' history in published writings. But once the United States was established and began to far exceed Switzerland in size and strength, the "Sister Republics," as they were termed in George Washington's day, had little direct contact.

Part of the reason was cultural, because even though the Swiss population spoke four official languages, none of these was English. While learned Americans were familiar with Switzerland's unique democratic system as well as its reputation for martial prowess, most people in the United States knew little about the country. By the time Hitler declared the Third Reich, most Americans associated Switzerland with yodelers, cheese, chocolate and the story of a charming young girl named Heidi.

The second of the Sister Republics had by then burst into great-power status with a robust vitality. The New World nation had rapidly expanded westward, terming its mission "manifest destiny." En route, it had paused to fight a war that pitted its northern states against its southern ones, leaving behind 600,000 dead while affirming its essential founding principle: freedom for individuals. The Swiss, adhering with equal fervor to the same principle, also fought a civil war, in 1848, but it concluded with a revised federal constitution and few casualties. Both countries produced prominent individuals in science and the arts, but Switzerland never approached great-power status. American citizens subsequently assumed world leadership in business, heavy industry and two uniquely 20th-century fields: mass entertainment and aviation.

The greatest cultural divide that increasingly separated the Sister Republics stemmed from their starkly different geopolitical positions. To Americans, freedom meant opportunity, an evidently unlimited concept whether applied to land, personal wealth or national power. In tiny Switzerland, geographically confined between Germany, Austria, Italy and France, freedom, aside from its literal definition as applied to individuals, equated more closely to national independence: not being conquered or controlled by a larger foreign state.

The concept of unlimited possibilities was never part of the Swiss psyche, even as it was uniquely integral to the American one. The Swiss, like all peoples, sought material prosperity, but the country lacked natural resources. In foreign policy, the multi-ethnic democracy formally undertook, at the time Michelangelo was painting the Sistine Chapel, to refrain from taking an active role in European wars. In return, other consenting parties undertook not to attack Switzerland, a provision the Swiss safeguard by continuing to train each succeeding generation of their male population as soldiers. The United States could occasionally suspend its semi-traditional policy of neutrality (or perhaps more accurately, isolationism) with great bursts of crusading fervor and the dispatch of troops abroad who invariably returned home victorious. The Swiss were committed not to engage in general European wars. In World War II, Americans, who were imbued with the concept of freedom as a vessel brimming with possibility and, indeed, as an exportable commodity, would be confounded by the instinctive Swiss view that freedom in the shadow of larger, autocratic states was tenuous and could only be earned, or, if need be, defended.

When, in August 1914, the great European powers launched armies of unprecedented size into a conflict that for approximately 20 years was justifiably known as the "Great War," the United States came to the rescue of France and Britain near the end of the conflict, tipping the balance fatally against the German Kaiser. Throughout that long, horrible conflict, Switzerland remained neutral. Few outside the small Alpine nation realized that the Swiss had buttressed their policy with hundreds of thousands of troops who would have fought only if foreign soldiers had set foot on Swiss territory. By the time World War II broke out, many Americans assumed that Swiss neutrality was a given, as if some ancient European edict which even Hitler's Nazi state was compelled to obey ensured that Switzerland needed to be sidestepped in the event of Continental conflagrations. Many Americans assumed that the neutral state was pacifist, or that Switzerland, due to some overriding sense of consideration, or even sympathy, on the part of larger powers was deliberately excused from major European conflicts.

In the Old World, of course, Switzerland's nature was less ambiguous. The country was sometimes called the "porcupine of Europe." It was a pure democracy so averse to one-man rule, or what Adolf Hitler would eventually term the "Führerprinzip," that it did not even elect presidents. The nation was governed by a council vested with powers strictly confined so as not to infringe on the prerogatives of more local representatives at the cantonal, town or village level. No man would ever "rule" Switzerland, not even a Swiss. The Swiss foreign policy of neutrality was, in part, a recognition that the multi-ethnic, multi-lingual land could never be unified for the purpose of alliance with another ethnic power. Neutrality was also rooted in Swiss determination to retain a democratic system regardless of what territorial wars might be waged among their more imperially minded neighbors. It was only in the event that Swiss territory itself was violated that the "herdsmen" (as the Swiss were called in late medieval times) would rise en masse to the defense of their democratic way of life. During World War II, of course, few Americans knew anything about the history of the country their airmen were describing as a safe haven. The flyers only recognized that for some reason a "white spot" existed in the center of the maps they were shown in their briefings before missions. All they knew for certain was that there was one country that the Germans had not attempted to invade.

The great constant in the equation of Swiss independence, including the country's status as a safe haven, was the abiding vigilance of the Swiss Army—the only one in Europe which, in a system dating from medieval times, called upon every able-bodied man to be a soldier. Because marksmanship was the national sport, the Swiss militia infantry was formidable. Many American airmen in Switzerland would criticize the zealousness Swiss soldiers showed when performing their duties, but others recognized that if the Swiss had not been tough, well drilled and ready to fight, given their location on the doorstep of Hitler's Reich, the country would not have existed at all.

A common misperception of Switzerland during the war was that it was an oasis of plenty in the midst of a continent otherwise suffering under the weight of total-war economies. A typical view was voiced by U.S. airman Leroy Newby in his memoir *Target Ploesti*. Newby, terming Switzerland "a little neutral country caught in the middle of a big war," went on to say:

> Throughout our tour of duty, it was an inside joke among all of us that if we ever got anywhere near Switzerland, we would feather an engine and wing it for the promised land. We had heard tales of downed fliers living in swanky resort hotels, drinking fine wines, eating good food, and dating bad girls. They would ski every day in their spare time.

American airmen such as the crew of *Ginny Gal* were among the first to learn that, internally, the safe haven from Hitler's Third Reich was not what it was perceived from abroad. In reality, the young U.S. flyers found they had landed in a fortress nation where food, heat and other necessities of life were rationed and outside communications were controlled by aggressor forces that loomed over the border on every side. American airmen were indeed put up at hotels, but these were abandoned summer resorts, ill-heated at best and supplied with wartime rations. Good food and fine wines had been more plentiful in England, Italy or even North Africa than in the safe haven. The "promised land" was cold and its people were thin.

While many American airmen were dismayed that their haven was not an "Eden," bountiful with food and comforts, others were surprised at the strict nature of neutrality practiced by the nation which had, as a result of successive international concords, essentially invented the concept. Swiss neutrality, as the American airmen found, did not mean apathy, nor did it mean weakness. To Hitler, as the entire world had learned by mid-1940, neutrality meant nothing at all, and his attitude, more than any other factor, validated the Swiss concept of *armed* neutrality. The stress was on "armed," because if the Swiss had not been ready to fight and die for their confederation, it would surely have disappeared. (After World War II, the Swiss declined to join NATO, although the Soviets appeared to be just as ruthless as the Nazis, and no less ambitious.) Switzerland's centuries-old foreign policy, along with its even older commitment to democracy, had become an article of faith to the Swiss public, ingrained through successive generations. Its policy of defensive self-reliance, combined with respect for international law, was adhered to in practice as precisely as possible. During World War II, Switzerland's strict, even militant, application of the rules governing its geopolitical stance nevertheless seemed odd to many freedom-loving, freewheeling American internees who had no real understanding of historic armed neutrality.

The advent of air power added a new dimension to European warfare, resulting in new circumstances for noncombatant states in their dealings with belligerent soldiers. The Hague Convention of 1907, reinterpreted in the following decades to include arrivals from the sky, provided guidelines for how the Swiss or other neutrals should receive combatants who sought refuge in their territory. The airmen who landed or parachuted into Switzerland became "internees," effectively prisoners of war in a neutral country, and were to be sheltered and fed, and also guarded to prevent escapes. There were different rules for "escapees," who had fled belligerent foreign POW camps, or for "evadees," who were, for example, U.S. airmen who had landed in France and then made their way to Switzerland on foot. Internees, according to international law, were the only group that couldn't leave the country any time they wished, since they had entered armed and in the midst of combat.

A paradox of the American internees' stay in Switzerland was that while they were in the custody of a Swiss Army that, perhaps especially on the small-unit level, was determined to be as vigilantly tough as possible, the airmen were surrounded by a Swiss public that was overwhelmingly pro-Allied. Despite the fact that three-quarters of Swiss shared a common ethnic and language connection with Germany, well over 90 percent of Swiss viewed Nazism with abhorrence and were prepared to fight against it, just as American internees had been doing before they were shot down. Among the Swiss, too, it can be said that "flyboys" tended to be viewed as glamorous, as they were in every nation. Many Swiss, not underrepresented among the female gender, viewed their American guests as heroes.

The result was that American airmen faced two separate attitudes on the part of the Swiss: strict adherence to the rules of neutrality enforced by an active military on the one hand; and an empathetic, often admiring, public on the other. When the American Seventh Army reached the Swiss border in late summer 1944 and internees began trying to escape by the hundreds, the airmen were often assisted by Swiss civilians, even as they were simultaneously forced to evade Swiss soldiers. Interestingly, not a single American airman was killed in any of the internees' 948 recorded escape attempts, though a few suffered leg wounds from the accurate shooting of border guards. These guards were, of course, both citizens and soldiers, so their empathy and accuracy could bridge any gulf between duty and conscience.

It's significant that the two nations that came into wartime contact for the first time during World War II—Switzerland and the United States—are two of the three oldest democracies in the world. The third, Great Britain, was not only America's closest ally, providing the staging ground for the bulk of the U.S. air campaign, it also shared common ground with Switzerland during the war. During the dark days immediately after the fall of France, when the Soviet Union was still allied with Nazi Germany and the American public was still resolved to avoid "entangling alliances," Britain and Switzerland stood alone against what appeared to be an irresistible Nazi tide. Aside from the courage of their people, the best protection each country could claim was, for the British, a thin barrier of water called the English Channel, and, for the Swiss, the Alps.

The German invasion of Russia, followed by the Japanese attack on the United States, changed the equation. Britain found powerful new allies whose participation in the war would prove decisive. Switzerland, on the other hand, remained alone throughout the conflict, adhering to neutrality while striving to ensure that any invader would pay dearly for attempted invasion. The Swiss, situated in the center of Europe without the geographic advantages afforded the alliance that from the periphery of the Continent eventually brought Germany to its knees, required a special kind of courage simply to keep their borders inviolate. Near the end of the war, buttressed by the emerging superpowers that were gradually crushing Nazi Germany between their east-west vise, British Prime Minister Winston Churchill remembered the other democracy that had once stood defiant against Germany when the future of Britain itself seemed forlorn. "I put this down for the record," he wrote. "Of all the neutrals Switzerland has the greatest right to distinction." After the war was won by the combined might of the Allies, it was all too easy to forget the smaller European nation that had held its ground during the period when the "Thousand-Year Reich" appeared to be a fait accompli. Churchill's statement stands as testimony to the more realistic contemporary view. It also reflects the sentiments of many United States Army Air Force enlistees who, if not for Switzerland, would have died or fallen into Nazi captivity.

As for the brave crew of *Ginny Gal*, and the hundreds of other American airmen who preceded or followed them into Switzerland, perhaps they can provide the clearest picture of all. The portrait is of two free nations—one large and one small, one surrounded by oceans and one surrounded by Axis tyranny. During World War II, the Americans projected their might into Nazi-held Europe while the Swiss simply endeavored to protect their freedom along every inch of their border. It is fortunate that the Swiss were able to do so, because their actions enabled the Sister Republics to once more come into contact.

2

THE HERDSMEN

The story of American airmen and Switzerland in World War II cannot be told without first looking at the history of that small European nation which would eventually be termed by USAAF mission planners a "safe haven." From a New World perspective, nearly every European country conceals beneath its modern exterior a panorama of history that stretches far beyond the American experience, with a national character resting on a foundation constructed over many centuries. Even in the rich European historical context, however, there is a uniqueness about the history of Switzerland that goes far toward explaining how U.S. flyers were eventually able to consider it a refuge from, rather than a part of, the Third Reich.

Switzerland, which still terms itself "Helvetia," was first identified for the record by Julius Caesar in Book I of "The Gallic Wars." After Caesar had singled out the Belgae in the far north as the fiercest of barbarian tribes, because of their remoteness from "merchants, bringing those things that tend to make men soft," he wrote, "It is the Helvetii who are the bravest of all the other Gauls because they have almost daily skirmishes with the Germans, either keeping them out of Helvetian territory or else starting hostilities on German land themselves." In 58 B.C., Helvetii leaders organized a great migration from their confined territory, intending to cross the Rhone River into modern-day France. They assumed that they could seize any land they wished from weaker Celtic tribes, but they failed to consider that by so doing they would be treading upon Roman imperial ambitions.

Caesar, in his first military campaign as a general, defeated the Helvetii in a series of battles and forced the tribe to return to its home, modern-day Switzerland. He needed them to act as a buffer for Rome against the German tribes that were constantly threatening to cross the Rhine.

Long after Caesar's death, around A.D. 260, a Germanic tribe called the Allemanni did cross the Rhine, and erased much of the Celtic, or Gallic, civilization of which the Helvetii had been a part. Nevertheless, the Allemanni grafted their own traditions of independence and freedom onto the remote land. The territory was bordered by the Rhine on the north, the Alps to the east and south, and the Jura Mountains to the west, and the communities of hardscrabble herdsmen and farmers in the territory began to adopt a way of life distinct from that of their neighbors. Europe evolved through its feudal era during which hereditary kings and nobles ruled peasants who in turn worked to support their masters. During the Middle Ages, the House of Savoy dominated western Switzerland while the Habsburgs formally ruled the east. In the rugged Alpine valleys in the center of the territory, however, the poor farmers and herdsmen developed their own system of local rule largely unbothered by royal decrees. Within the borders of ancient Helvetia, in fact, the people who we now know as Swiss became determined not to live under the rule of kings.

In 1291, representatives from three Swiss cantons met at a spot called the Rütli Meadow by the Lake of Lucerne to pledge mutual support against threats from a foreign monarchy, at that time personified by the Austrian Habsburgs. These roughhewn "Companions of the Oath" are credited with founding the modern Swiss nation. A crossbow-wielding warrior named William Tell is the most famous of early Swiss freedom fighters, though the tale of his shooting an apple off his son's head, as well as the man himself, may only be a legend. More historically reliable is archaeological evidence in central Swiss cantons of Austrian towers and castles destroyed during this period.

In November 1315, Archduke Leopold of Austria invaded the canton of Schwyz in order to reestablish Habsburg rule. His army of 20,000 men was led by mounted knights in armor with a greater density of foot soldiers back in the column. At one point the Austrians had to march through a narrow pass between a steep hillside called Morgarten and a lake. The Swiss were waiting for them on the heights and began the battle by rolling boulders and tree trunks down the slope. Then a contingent of Swiss attacked the van from in front, trapping the column in the narrow defile. The knights and horses panicked and some, attempting to flee, began trampling their own infantry. At that point, the main body of Swiss, said to be 1,400 men, rushed down the hill and wreaked havoc on the congested column. Many Austrians were driven into the lake and drowned; hundreds more were slaughtered where they stood. The Battle of Morgarten validated in emphatic fashion the oath of independence made by the Companions at the Rütli Meadow.

The original confederation of three cantons—Uri, Schwyz and Unterwalden—grew with the addition of Lucerne, Zurich, Bern, Zug and Glarus by the mid-14th century. In the process, more battles against feudal lords from outside the Confederation enhanced the Swiss reputation for ferocity in combat.

At Laupen in 1339 a Swiss victory not only resonated through the cantons but across the Continent: for the first time after centuries of feudalism, infantry defeated armored cavalry in an open-field battle. Burgundian nobility from what is today eastern France advanced on the cantons with 12,000 men, placing their mounted knights on the right to turn the Swiss flank. The Swiss, together numbering 6,500, met the invading army by the village of Laupen in three wedges. On the left were men of the original three cantons, armed mostly with halberds; in the center were the Bernese, armed with pikes; on the right stood Bern's other allies. When the armies came to grips, the baronial infantry collapsed before the onslaught of the center and right Swiss divisions. The knights, meanwhile, were unable to subdue the halberd-swinging Confederates on the left. When the victorious Swiss wedges swung around to the flank and rear of the attacking cavalry, coming to the rescue of their leftmost wedge, the battle was decided. The Burgundian knights fled, leaving their dead behind.

"For the continent," Charles Oman wrote in *The Art of Warfare in the Middle Ages*, "Laupen was the first revelation as to the power of good infantry." The battle also had the effect of tempting the Swiss into an era of territorial aggrandizement. As they increasingly adopted the long pike as their weapon of choice, they found that no feudal army could resist their onslaught and armored cavalry could not break their formations. The approach of a Swiss pike square bristling with iron-barbed poles, wedded to the reputation for ferocity of their bearers, could strike fear into the hearts of opposing knights and footmen before it even made contact. On the battlefield, Swiss character and tactics had combined to resemble an irresistible force.

Ironically, in view of 20th-century events to come, a parallel answer to the supremacy of mounted knights was being formulated during that same 14th century in England. As opposed to using the two-handed pike to combat cavalry, the English had come up with a weapon of far greater range: the longbow. The determined Swiss pike square and the row of powerful English archers were not destined to meet each other in combat, but each, separately, offered a solution to the dominance of armored horsemen. As Oman stated, "The knight, who had for so long ridden roughshod over the populations of Europe, was now to recognize his masters in the art of war. The free yeomanry of England and the free herdsmen of the Alps were about to enter on their career of conquest."

At the Battle of Sempach in 1386, Duke Leopold III of Austria died, along with 2,000 of his men, after colliding with a Swiss force of 1,300. A fighter named Arnold Winkelried entered Swiss folklore by holding onto a number of Austrian lances that had pierced his body, thereby enabling his compatriots to break through the enemy line. Two years later, at Näfels, another Austrian army was routed with heavy losses by 400 Swiss rolling stones down a hill, and by other contingents from the countryside rushing to the battle.

During the latter half of the 14th century, the Habsburgs were expelled from Switzerland, as it was then constituted, and the Confederation expanded by attracting more cantons. Though the Confederates remained nominally under the sovereignty of the Holy Roman Empire, new institutions began to replace aristocratic rule. In rural areas these were called *Landsgemeinden*, public assemblies, at which decisions would be debated by citizens and put to the vote. In towns, merchants and guilds assumed political authority for the common interest. Even as the Swiss developed their system of councils to ensure domestic harmony and rule of law, however, they continued to wage war against the baronial armies of their neighbors.

At Arbedo in 1422, an invading force of men from Lucerne was overwhelmed by a larger force of Italians. In that case, Count Carmagnola of Milan had astutely ordered his armored cavalry to dismount to face the Swiss on foot. Twenty years later, at St. Jakob an der Birs, a force of Confederates, estimated at 1,500 men, resisted an invading French army of 15,000. The Swiss refused to retreat and were killed to a man, yet before they fell inflicted such carnage on the French that the invaders withdrew to Alsace.

More commonly it was living Swiss who held the field. In February 1476 they met and defeated an invasion by Charles the Bold, Duke of Burgundy, at the Battle of Grandson. The Swiss held off two charges by heavy cavalry and then relentlessly chewed their way into the Burgundian lines. Charles planned to allow his center to give way and envelope the enemy with his wings, as Hannibal had planned for the Romans at the Battle of Cannae. But then two more Swiss divisions came marching over a hill to join the battle. The Burgundians, though still holding a numerical advantage, panicked, and the Swiss wreaked havoc on the retreating army, inflicting thousands of casualties while losing only 412 of their own men.

Charles then assembled an even larger army, only to suffer a greater defeat, at Morat. Of his 23,000 men, 10,000 were killed. A decade later, the Swiss joined allies from Lorraine to face the Burgundians one last time. At the Battle of Nancy, a two-pronged Swiss assault overwhelmed the enemy lines, killing 7,000 and forcing the remainder of the army to flee. Charles the Bold attempted to protect the backs of his retreating men and was later found in a ditch, the victim of a halberd blow to the head. This battle ended the power of Burgundy as an independent state, and it was subsequently incorporated into France by Louis XI.

The Swiss reputation for battlefield ferocity had by now become widespread in Europe. Lacking nobility of their own, the Swiss did not distinguish between high-born nobles and low-born peasant opponents in combat. Knights who might have honorably surrendered to their opposite numbers in more conventional battles seldom had that option against the Swiss, who would just as soon have obliterated an invading army as negotiate or trade selected nobles for ransom. When the herdsmen gained a tactical advantage in the field the consequences could be fearsome, as the lopsided casualty figures in many late medieval battles between the Swiss and baronial armies attest.

In 1499 the Swiss faced a formidable challenge from the southern German province of Swabia, which was controlled by the Holy Roman

Emperor, Maximillian I. The Swabians fielded disciplined heavy infantry (called *Landsknechte*), armed with pikes and whose tactics mirrored the successful, and now famous, Swiss pike square. The battles featured no maneuvers beyond a headlong charge at the outset. The subsequent grappling of tightly packed wedges of men could seem interminable until one side or the other broke. Nevertheless the Swiss finally overcame the Swabians in a series of engagements and Maximillian sued for peace. A Swiss victory over the Swabians at Dornach was the last battle fought on Swiss soil for 300 years.

The Swiss during the late medieval period evoked comparisons with the Romans of the early Republic, not only for their victories won through a formation that resembled an ancient phalanx, but for their system of calling on a free citizenry to arms. Uniquely, Swiss armies did not fight under generals but under councils—no leader from one canton could tell the men of another what to do. Their success relied on force rather than maneuver, and the unity of purpose of the disparate cantons, especially in collective defense, was as great a phenomenon of the period as the unstoppable pike square. Niccolo Machiavelli toured Switzerland in 1508 and described how every man was compelled to have weapons and how each canton was required to provide 4,000 men for common defense, as well as a lesser, voluntary, number for foreign expeditions. The overriding principle was "the love of liberty and the need of self defense against princes." Foretelling a confrontration that would eventually come, Machiavelli wrote:

> the Swiss are enemies, not merely of the Emperor and princes, but also of the nobility of Germany; since in their own country there is none, neither any distinction among men, saving of those acting as magistrates, and all enjoy complete freedom. Thus it comes about that the German nobles do their utmost to keep their communities divided from the Swiss.

The sands of time, however, were running out on the era of Swiss dominance of the battlefield. Just as the Swiss had ended the thousand-year reign of armored cavalry two centuries earlier, a new development was about to make their pike squares obsolete: gunpowder. In the early 1500s, war broke out in northern Italy between the French and Papal forces and the Duchy of Milan. The Swiss

Confederation was involved, first fighting against one side and then the other. At the Battle of Novara in 1513, the Swiss were able to break a French army that featured battalions of arquebusiers and artillery. But then, in 1515, came the Battle of Marignano.

The Swiss, deployed in their standard formation of echeloned squares, attacked a French army of 60,000 that included 100 cannon and 6,000 men with the arquebus (a precursor of the musket). The 26,000 Swiss came under galling fire from artillery and small arms shooting into their packed columns; still, they came on. This epic battle lasted for two days, and French king Francis I led a number of frantic counterattacks against his obstinate foe. In his history of France, Thomas E. Watson describes the scene:

> [The Swiss] relied upon their close array, and their pikes eighteen feet long, and they advanced upon the French artillery with the utmost courage. Thirty times in succession the French charged them without checking their advance. [Swiss] seized the first batteries, and it required the most desperate efforts of the king and all his generals to save the day. Night came on, but the fight raged till the moon went down. . . . The contending forces were all intermingled, and so remained till daylight again made it possible to know whom to kill. Between nine and ten o'clock in the morning, the French received a reinforcement of Venetian troops, and the Swiss retired. They did not scatter, they did not flee, they were not demoralized; they simply marched back home, in good order.

Young King Francis exulted, "I have conquered those whom only Caesar has overcome!" About 6,000 on each side had been killed. An even more profound result was that the Swiss realized they could no longer force decisions on the battlefield. For two centuries the independence of the Confederation had been guaranteed by the pikemen's ability to wreck any opposing feudal armies with simple weapons, courage and single-minded determination. Now the larger powers of the Continent were advancing beyond them in technology. The following year the Swiss made peace with France. Internally, they resolved never again to venture outside their borders. The Swiss Confederation by now included cantons of different languages and religion, each attracted by the principle of independence from auto-cratic rule and safety from foreign invasion. Cantonal unity, while essential for defense, was jeopardized by foreign expeditions, which in any event often took place for no greater purpose than plunder. The dawn of the gunpowder age put the seal on a conviction that had already been gestating in the cantons: that the Confederation should be a defensive alliance, not an aggressive one.

The Swiss Confederation began its policy of neutrality after Marig-nano in 1515, whereupon, for the next three hundred years, Swiss sol-diers became the most renowned mercenaries in Europe. Fighting for foreign princes, as opposed to eking out a living from their own poor country, was often the quickest, or only, means for a young man to advance himself. In turn, it became a status symbol for European roy-alty to have their persons protected by Swiss guards. The climax of the Swiss mercenary era would come at Versailles in 1793 when 600 fell while standing alone to protect Louis XVI against a French Revo-lutionary mob. The last vestige of the tradition is evident today in the Vatican, where Swiss guards continue to guard the Pope.

The Swiss cantons' first great test as a freestanding alliance occurred during the Thirty Years' War, 1618–48, when Europe was set aflame by the Protestant Reformation. Great armies traversed the Continent for their respective causes, and countless communities were torn apart along the lines of religious faith. The Hanseatic League, an alliance of German states similar to the Confederation, was engulfed by the conflict and destroyed. In Switzerland, the various cantons' commitment to respect for individuals without ceding to higher authority was able to surpass the fervor of its Protestants and Catholics. Even as its fighting men served as mercenaries on all sides of the conflict, the Confederation itself was able to weather the storm. These years saw the genesis of Switzerland as a refuge for intellectuals and thinkers who came to live, work and publish in the country, after fleeing from religious or political persecutions. In 1648, the multina-tional Treaty of Westphalia, which officially ended the war, affirmed Switzerland's separation from the Holy Roman Empire and its status as an independent confederation. To the degree that Switzerland was a state, it was the only one in Europe not subject to royalty or to any man's rule.

Switzerland did have the advantage of its natural barriers—the

Rhine, the Jura range and, most formidably, the Alps—in addition to the fearsome reputation of its fighting men. Within the Confederation, strife between Protestants, the majority, and Catholics, who had strong foreign support, continued sporadically until in 1712 the cantons arrived at a formula that called for a commission of equal numbers of Protestants and Catholics to mediate disputes. In the decades that followed, the era of "Cabinet Wars," Europe was divided between warring monarchies and principalities, while the democratic enclave in the center of the continent was left alone. The Swiss practiced self-rule on first the village and then canton level, and the cantons themselves were only bound by loose agreement, most concertedly when the issue was common defense. Just as the maurauding Swiss armies of prior years had not bothered to appoint generals, the Confederation dismissed the idea of assigning a national leader. Each canton within the alliance governed itself.

In 1775 the British colonies in America revolted against the rule of the King of England. Upon winning their war against the armies of the Crown the statesmen of the new nation hotly debated the constitution that would henceforth guide their democracy. Many orators referred to the citizens of ancient Athens or early Rome as their forebears but others pointed to Switzerland, whose confederation had by then endured in the center of Europe for centuries. Constitutional scholar Stephen P. Halbrook wrote, "From its beginnings, the United States had a healthy regard for the Swiss example of a decentralized federal state, guarded from invasion by a well-armed and well-trained citizens' army." He cited Patrick Henry's ringing oration during the Virginia Constitutional debates of 1787:

Switzerland consists of thirteen cantons expressly confederated for national defense. They have stood the shock of 400 years. That country has enjoyed internal tranquility most of that long period. . . . Their attachment to their country, and to freedom— their resolute intrepidity in their defense; the consequent security and happiness which they have enjoyed, and the respect and awe which these things produced in their bordering nations, have signalized them republicans. . . . Their heroism is proverbial. They would heroically fight for their Government, and their laws . . .

The thirteen American colonies indeed followed the example of Switzerland's then-thirteen cantons by establishing a central government that was institutionally prevented from overriding the will of the states, and, through the mechanism of elections, that of the individual. The Civil War, among other factors, would eventually lead America to assign more powers to its central government than it might have originally planned, while Switzerland to this day does not even elect a president directly. Meanwhile, the American Revolution helped to unleash a further movement toward individual freedom in Europe.

The Swiss Confederation could claim to be the oldest continuous democracy in the world were it not for one man: Napoleon Bonaparte. In his rise to power, Napoleon rode the wave of French Revolutionary ardor, itself fueled by the American example, and harnessed it to a combination of ambition, political acuity and breathtaking military skill. Immediately after decapitating their king, Louis XVI, the French found themselves at war with the remaining monarchies of Europe, who were determined to crush the dangerous French concept of "liberty, equality, fraternity" before it could pour over their borders.

In Switzerland, the new French philosophy had adherents, particularly in the French-speaking westernmost cantons. In the loosely governed land, the ancient *Landsgemeinden* had sometimes given way to patrician hierarchies of merchants or landowners whose political control had become almost indistinguishable from aristocracy. By one estimate, prior to Napoleon's attack, fewer than one-sixth of Switzerland's 1,200,000 men had access to political power. (Women did not receive the vote until 1971.) Though this was still a better percentage than found in other European countries, the one exception that pointed toward even greater individual freedom was France. The French were by then trumpeting their thrilling message of political power to the common people of Europe, and combining the message with the military might to make it happen.

Northern Italy became the setting for Napoleon's initial campaigns against the Allied coalition seeking his defeat. After wresting that region from the Austrians, he viewed Switzerland as essential because of its strategic location that connected France with Italy, Austria and the German states. In late 1797, French Revolutionary forces seized the canton of Vaud, then Basel, and in 1798 spread throughout the country. Many Swiss greeted French troops as liberators who would elevate their social or economic status. It was left to a few deeply patriotic communities, centered on the city of Bern, to resist the French onslaught. Their weapons and battlefield tactics were no match for Napoleon's troops, and the nation was forced into submission. When the Second Coalition—Russia, Britain, Austria, Portugal, Naples, the Vatican and the Ottoman Empire—took the field against Napoleon in December 1798, Switzerland became a battleground. French Marshal André Massena was able to defeat an Austrian invasion in the east of the country just before a Russian army came marching from northern Italy through the Alps. The Russians, under Aleksandr Suvarov, fought their way through the mountains in an epic, high-altitude battle at the Devil's Bridge, but by then were too weak to hold the cantons. Beset by continual French ambushes from surrounding heights, the surviving Russians marched north to Bavaria.

As often noted, history has produced far worse megalomaniacs to be conquered by than Napoleon, and the French First Consul proceeded to give Switzerland the first central government in its history, based on the French Revolutionary model. Self-rule by individual cantons was eliminated and the Confederation became a unified political entity called the Helvetic Republic. Napoleon instituted educational reforms, standardized the systems of currency, weights and measures, and initially granted freedom of the press. This last reform soon had to be withdrawn after the press became too critical. Swiss soldiers, of course, were incorporated into Napoleon's forces, the central component of which was now called the Grande Armeé.

While Napoleon went on to redraw the map elsewhere at the expense of Europe's great powers, the Swiss seethed under their new constitution and foreign rule. Fighting broke out not only between Swiss and French but among Swiss themselves. Federalists who favored the old cantonal system were pitted against partisans of a stronger central government. In 1803 Napoleon reentered the country and adjusted the constitution in an act called "The Mediation." Certain powers were returned to the cantons, lending a semblance of continuity to earlier Swiss traditions of self-governance. As for his own democratic dispositions, the following year Napoleon vacated his post of First Consul and declared himself Emperor, taking the crown from the Pope's hands and arrogantly placing it on his head himself.

Across Europe, the promises of the French Revolution began to fade in the face of Napoleon's personal ambitions and the abrasiveness of foreign military domination. After Bonaparte's defeat at Leipzig, following his disastrous venture into Russia, the Swiss mounted the only military expedition outside their borders since 1515. During the "Hundred Days," culminating in the climactic French defeat at Waterloo, Swiss troops sallied out to join the multinational coalition that exiled Napoleon once and for all. At the 1815 Congress of Vienna, where the outlines of pre-Bonaparte Europe were restored, Swiss independence and neutrality were reaffirmed. Switzerland, before the assembled nations of Europe, was officially accorded neutral status in the event of further European wars. As a confederation of democratic cantons encompassing three language groups—German, French and Italian, plus a fourth in one Alpine canton, Romansh, a Latin-based vestige of ancient Roman rule—the Confederation could logically, if idealistically, expect to be excluded from future continental conflicts. The underlying truth, however, was that the only guarantor of Swiss neutrality would continue to be the Swiss people—their courage and ability to resist an aggressor.

Two further events are important in describing the foundation of the modern nation of Switzerland. Somewhat humbled by their experience with Napoleon and mindful of their older tradition of martial skill, the Swiss strengthened their militia system with the requirement that every man in the country be expert in the latest model of firearms. Instead of skiing or soccer, marksmanship became—and still is—the Swiss national sport. Every man in the country is required to serve in the army beginning at age 20 (an age lowered during World War II), in a system that became the model for Israel's military after 1948.

The second event is that, prior to the American crucible of 1861–65, the Swiss endured a civil war of their own, in 1847–48, one facet of a general political upheaval in Europe. In Switzerland the conflict was concluded with little bloodshed (though for the first time a general was named to command the army) and the ceding of more powers to a centralized government. For foreign policy and other common endeavors—trade policy, social welfare, transportation and other issues—the Swiss tied the cantons together by creating a Federal seat in Bern. The executive power of the Swiss Federal government was invested in a seven-man council, with the presidency of the country rotated among the members. Swiss abhorrence of living under "one man's rule" was thus accommodated by a system of temporary presidents so that no one could ever claim to be solely in charge. In the process of strengthening the Confederation, the Swiss drew upon Napoleon's 1803 Mediation, parts of which they had too hastily thrown out along with French occupying troops, and upon the United States Constitution, which, ironically, had originally been influenced by the earlier experiences of the Confederation.

During the rest of the 19th century, while America pursued its Manifest Destiny to the west against assorted Indian tribes, the most important development in Europe became the unification of Germany, led by Prussia. The Germans, perpetually divided into separate principalities, had always been viewed as a formidable people, but under Bismarck were forged into a great nation. The worry of other European states, during the industrial age that was rapidly eclipsing the colonial one, was that the German state was looming as more powerful than any of its neighbors. In 1866, the Germans employed the relatively new invention of railroads to mass forces quickly against their neighbor, the Austro-Hungarian Empire. The Austrians fell quickly and conceded vast stretches of territory to the growing German state. In 1870 the Franco-Prussian War broke out, and in six weeks effectively ended with a humiliating defeat for France. Germany gained more land, primarily the province of Alsace-Lorraine. By then it was clear that the Germans were capable of dominating Europe.

The Swiss stayed neutral during both the Austro-Prussian and Franco-Prussian Wars, though during the latter they took the step of naming another general to command their army. Only one general had been named throughout Swiss history, Henri Dufour, in 1847. In 1870 Johannes Herzog was promoted to commander-in-chief. In two instances French armies, each numbering about 100,000 men, retreated to the Swiss border, where they were disarmed and allowed to cross as internees. The Swiss Army, by then equipped with the latest model of repeating rifles, was arrayed along the border to prevent German pursuit. After Napoleon III's surrender at Sedan, followed by Prussian mopping up and the drama of the Paris Commune, the Continent remained peaceful for over 40 years, although during that period France, Britain and other states fought numerous colonial wars.

In 1914, the volatile combination of European political rivalry and massive arms build-ups exploded into a multi-front war. France, Britain, Russia and Italy united to combat the German behemoth which, combined with the Austro-Hungarian and Ottoman Empires, threatened to overturn the hierarchy of great powers that had endured on the Continent for centuries. The Swiss, once more, stayed neutral, though Ulrich Wille was named the third general in Swiss history and hundreds of thousands of militia were mobilized to forestall potential cross-border thrusts from either Germany or France. The Germans violated Belgian neutrality, not Switzerland's, in their attempt to out-flank the French, however, and the war in the west subsequently took place on northern French soil and in Flanders. The war became a static slugging match, waged by infantry dashing mere hundreds of yards between trenches, sacrificing themselves for minute tactical gains. There were no great maneuvers that followed the initial massive thrust at the beginning of the war, and in the end neither side opted to vio-late Swiss territory. The Swiss, in any case, remained prepared to counter any incursions throughout the conflict.

In 1917 the Germans spirited a Russian emigre, Vladimir Lenin, from Zurich, where he had lived in exile, back to his home in Russia. Lenin's subsequent success in commandeering a revolution that had already begun against the Tsar's government helped to drive Russia out of the war. Its eastern front secure, for a brief period it appeared as if Germany could bring superior force against France and Britain. But then the United States entered the war on behalf of the Allies. The Germans were unable to counter the fresh men, material and enthusi-asm that the United States introduced into the conflict beginning in late 1917, and in November 1918 the Germans sought an armistice. The triumphant Allies chopped off slices of German territory, both east and west, and placed severe reparation obligations and military restrictions upon the defeated state.

Germany subsequently spiraled into deep decline, due to econom-ic hardship and the effects of their former tool, Lenin, who had put into practice a revolutionary concept that promised to equalize wealth and political status. Lenin's system, appearing so successful in Russia, found millions of adherents among the working classes and intellectu-als of western Europe, causing turmoil and a diminution of support for traditional governments. In exporting his revolution, Lenin paid particular attention to his former hosts, the Swiss, partly on the assumption that their weak central government would be vulnerable to a rising of the "masses." The Swiss Army was called upon to put down a series of unruly strikes, after which Switzerland broke off diplomatic relations with the Soviet Union. Switzerland subsequently voted against Soviet membership in the League of Nations, headquartered in Geneva, in part to prevent Soviet agents from having diplomatic immunity in the country.

As the Swiss stood down and Europe licked its deep wounds from the war, American doughboys returned to their homes, flush with victory despite the price they had paid of 115,000 lives, 300,000 more wounded. As the joy of victory faded, the outcome of the war was increasingly seen as unequal to the cost it had taken to achieve. Henceforth in America there would be increased resistance to the idea of taking part in new European conflicts. It was hoped that the recent one would live up to its name, "The War to End All Wars," since a repeat of the broad, largely pointless massacre of young men in the mud and trenches was too awful to contemplate.

Although the Great War would indeed have sufficed as crowning proof of the folly of European states going for each other's throats, unfortunately it spawned an even greater menace. An Austrian, Adolf Hitler, had served with distinction in the German Army in the west, 1914–18. Three times wounded, he emerged from the war with a fanatical commitment to reverse the humiliation of the German capitulation embodied in the Treaty of Versailles. A talented orator and skilled political leader, his first animosity was toward the Communists, that international brotherhood he felt was undermining the German nation. His second was toward the decadence and lack of purpose he believed had overcome Germany after its defeat.

Ultimately, however, his antagonism would be aimed at foreign states and peoples. Hitler planned to surpass Bismarck and Kaiser Wilhelm by uniting all the ethnic Germans of Europe—and only them—into a conquering power that would at long last fully realize the ancient German claim to greatness. Thereafter, the government in Berlin would rule a larger and more unified empire than even Napoleon had dreamed of. Hitler's would be the "Third Reich," surpassing Charlemagne's (Karl der Grosse) and Bismarck's. In historic terms, France was the ancient enemy. In economic terms, the east, where Josef Stalin had supplanted Lenin in 1929, was the key to ensuring the Reich's enduring power. As Hitler's Nazi movement grew, its simplistic symbol, a twisted cross called the swastika, proved valuable in rallying Germans behind the new resurgence. Stark black uniforms and intricately orchestrated torchlight parades helped enforce the Nazis' image as a core of purposeful strength for the "Volk." To a significant degree, the new surge of power that began with Hitler's rise to the Chancellory in 1933 was intoxicating for Germans and for others who feared the more subtle pan-European movement represented by the hammer-and-sickle. At that time the major democratic powers, France and Britain, were uninspiring: threadbare and more concerned with holding onto their sources of wealth in Africa, Asia and the Indian subcontinent. Under Hitler, meanwhile, the German state would not long remain prone. Despite the temporary verdict of the Great War, it still had a great destiny to fulfill.

After 1933, the Swiss began hearing the muscular bombast and Wagnerian anthems coming from across their northern border. Predictably, the Swiss found the entire Teutonic cacophony ludicrous. Their state had been founded on democratic, not ethnic, principles and had proven throughout the centuries that it did not need an all-powerful "leader." The Swiss also had their unique military system in place, which assured that every man in the country was trained and equipped to defend the collective independence of the cantons. Ironically, German-speaking Swiss, who comprehended from the beginning the racist, totalitarian creed espoused by the new German government, were more ardently anti-Nazi than French-speaking Swiss, who were slower to realize the threat, and, after French capitulation at the war's onset, somewhat more resigned.

In May 1933, just four months after Hitler had taken office, the Swiss Federal Council banned the wearing of uniforms by political demonstrators, as well as "Hitlerite" insignia. In July, Rudolf Minger, the head of the Military Department, gave a speech at the ancient Roman fort of Windisch. "Never will our people agree to weaken our democracy," he said. "It will defeat dictatorial ideas from whichever side they come. . . . For this purpose we do not need extra shirts nor extra flags; the white cross in the red field will suffice." At the end of the year Minger pushed through appropriations to modernize infantry weapons, machine guns and artillery. By 1934, when most nations were still assessing Nazi Germany with little more than curiosity, the Swiss were already rearming and fortifying their border. They were the first to recognize the Nazi threat and respond with military measures accordingly.

Germany's strength increased steadily during the 1930s as the Nazis reinvigorated the German economy, initiated a vast rearmament program and grabbed every vulnerable piece of territory within reach. In February 1938 Austria voted overwhelmingly to accept the "Anschluss"—absorption into the Reich. A union between Germany and Austria had been specifically forbidden at Versailles, but Hitler had repudiated the document in 1935, correctly assessing that there was nothing the Allies would do. He then set his sights on the Sudetenland, that part of the new nation of Czechoslovakia which bordered Germany and was populated by German ethnics.

On September 28, 1938, at Munich, an international conference between the leaders of Germany, Italy, Britain and France took place to consider Hitler's demands. The German Army massed along the Czech border; France and Britain faced the quandary that the Sudeten Germans themselves wished to join the Reich while the Allies were neither prepared nor willing to go to war over the issue. The democracies conceded to Hitler in the hope that by doing so another major war could be avoided. British Prime Minister Neville Chamberlain returned to London and announced his belief that the conference had achieved "peace in our time."

After 1938, maps appeared in German newspapers depicting the Third Reich as a vast, expanded territory with Berlin at its center. Missing from the map, along with the names of Czechoslovakia, Poland, Denmark and the Low Countries, was Switzerland, most of which was shown incorporated into Germany with a few cantons ceded to Italy and France. The Swiss thus had no illusions about their giant neighbor's designs, or about the challenge they would soon have to face. The Swiss press ridiculed Germany's pretensions while the Federal government began monitoring German nationals in the country as a potential fifth column. Meanwhile, the Swiss Army continued building fortifications along the Rhine.

For the Western powers, the new German threat combined with the problem of additional totalitarian states springing up throughout

Europe. Italy had been seduced by a Fascist with imperial ambitions, Benito Mussolini; Hungary, Romania and Portugal were ruled by dictators, and Yugoslavia's king was favorable toward Hitler. A long civil war in Spain concluded with the ascension to power of General Francisco Franco, who had been assisted by the Germans and Italians against Republicans supported by the Soviet Union. The latter, then busy with vicious enforcement of its rule in the Ukraine and other regions, was an unknown quantity. If Hitler's racist Germanic philosophy was distasteful, the emanations from Moscow, unbounded by ethnic lines, appeared even more dangerous to Western states in the long term. Already, the Communist Party in France was undermining support for the government of Edouard Daladier, inhibiting its task of preparing for a new war.

The biggest question was whether Germany's sudden rearmament could result in another potentially overwhelming menace to Europe's remaining democracies. Until Hitler repudiated the armistice agreement in 1935, the German Army had consisted of only 100,000 men. Armored vehicles, U-boats and capital ships had been expressly forbidden. The victors of Versailles had meanwhile retained their weapons, infrastructure and any troop levels they desired. How, in the space of only a few years, could Hitler scramble together an armed forces capable of threatening the triumphant powers of World War I?

The answer lay in a new field of weapons design that during the 1930s was reinventing itself on almost a yearly basis. In the fast-evolving world of aviation, the major industrial powers were now competing on a level playing field, military superiority the reward for whichever country correctly assessed how the new generation of warplanes—far larger, stronger and faster than their Great War predecessors—should be employed. As relatively few military leaders had foreseen, the war to come would bear little resemblance to the previous one. Mobile firepower, particularly in the air, would be a crucial factor. And in the quest for a modern air force, all the great powers, even the formerly defeated ones, were starting from scratch.

3

AIR POWER

Model 299 was a beautiful plane. Its airframe was traced by sleek, gradually curving lines that somehow conveyed a sense of elegance. It was huge, weighing in at 35,000 pounds while mounting four protruding 900hp engines on a wingspan that stretched over a hundred feet. Subsequent models would feature a great swooping tail to add even more gravitas, frequently evoking the phrase "art deco." In the summer of 1935, Model 299 flew nonstop over 2,000 miles from Seattle to Dayton, Ohio, to compete with the Martin B-12 and the Douglas B-18 in demonstrations sponsored by the U.S. Army Air Corps. Unfortunately, the prototype suffered an accident near the end of the trials when its test pilot took off with the tail controls locked. The attractive plane dove straight into the ground and disintegrated in a fiery crash. The Army placed its order for 133 twin-engined B-18s. Model 299 was given a small, second chance, however, by airmen at the competition who had gazed approvingly at the experimental craft before its demise. Much to the relief of the Boeing company, these men were able to authorize thirteen more samples. The Army designated the new bomber the B-17, but the Boeing people had already come up with a nickname they thought would fit: they called their invention "The Flying Fortress."

By 1945, there would be over 12,500 B-17s engaged in combat around the world and hundreds of thousands of aircrew and ground-crew employed in wielding this formidable weapon against the Axis Powers. The road to that result, however, was not clearly marked, and the B-17, as well as the entire concept of strategic air war, encountered numerous obstacles.

In the mid-1930s, while enduring the Great Depression and fully inclined to stay at peace, America benefited from great pioneers and innovators in aviation, but had little incentive to field large numbers of aircraft. It was not until the Munich Conference in September 1938 that American military leaders began to seriously contemplate another European war. To those who observed Munich from afar, Germany's intimidation of the French and British resembled not so much a lasting solution to the impending crisis as another victory for Hitler. Another 3.5 million people and 7,000 square miles had been added to the Third Reich. In the wake of public backlash to making major concessions to the Nazis, new, more truculent signals from Paris and London indicated that next time the democracies would show greater resolve. Reacting to the growing storm clouds over Europe, United States Secretary of State Cordell Hull emphatically reaffirmed America's commitment to neutrality. Simultaneously, however, the U.S. chiefs of staff, with the unpublicized support of President Franklin D. Roosevelt, began planning for war. For the United States, as for all the great powers on the eve of World War II, the great unknown was what role air power would play in the approaching conflict.

As early as 1921, Italian General Guilio Douhet had prophesied that air power alone would win wars. A former artilleryman, Douhet viewed long-range bombers as instruments that could liberate military planners from the murderous constraints of trench warfare. In fact, infantry fighting would be obsolete, he thought, because enemy nations could be brought to their knees simply by dispatching explosive-laden bombers to devastate their industry, transportation networks, and/or civilian populations. Fleets of aircraft would replace divisions of infantry, inflicting destruction across hundreds of miles instead of hundreds of yards. In the future, wars would engage entire populations, and the outcome would depend on which nation could wreak the most havoc from the sky.

The American Billy Mitchell seconded Douhet's concept, and in 1921 he performed a series of tests to show that the world's navies, too, were on the verge of obsolescence. Targeting captured German dreadnaughts in a demonstration, he showed that one plane with a well-placed bomb could destroy a 27,000-ton ship and its 2,000-man crew in a few minutes' combat. A few years later, Mitchell was court-martialed for insubordination. The American Army and Navy were not about to be stampeded by his vision of omnipotent aircraft. Nevertheless, by the time of his death in 1936 Mitchell had won many supporters both within the Army and FDR's administration. Two witnesses called on his behalf at his court-martial were Air Corps majors Henry H. ("Hap") Arnold and Carl ("Tooey") Spaatz, and his defense team included a captain named Ira C. Eaker.

By 1939, Arnold was in command of the Air Corps, where he was forced to wage numerous turf battles with his Army superiors. Douglas MacArthur, his successor as Chief of Staff, George C. Marshall, and other officers had little tolerance for the utopian school of thought that armies and navies no longer had a major function in warfare. They recognized the importance of air power, but projected it in a tactical role, supporting the efforts of ground forces and ships. Strategic air power—operations by bombers hundreds of miles from, and miles above, the battlefront—was a chimera, touted only by the flyers themselves, or by those among the public who had no stomach for real war. "Long-range" bombing was, by definition, a strategy that would provide no immediate results for the hard-pressed infantryman in combat with the enemy or for a destroyer crew assailed by enemy ships. In the United States, objections to bombing were also raised by isolationists who saw bombing strategy as inherently aggressive, a recourse that America should foreseeably have no need to resort to.

Still, the problem for the United States in waging war, even a defensive one, was conquering distances as opposed to fighting along its own borders. In the 1930s, the first priority was considered defense against enemy fleets, a purpose for which bombers could be valuable. The Navy, not wishing to see its traditional role usurped by the brash new service, formed its own air arm. The Navy insisted, in fact, that Army bombers not be allowed to range farther than 300 miles from shore. The Army wanted bombers—preferably not long-range, high-altitude ones—for operations that would directly assist ground troops. Outside of the older services, however, visionaries of strategic air war had important allies in President Roosevelt and Secretary of War Henry Stimson, and an even greater asset in that no one, down to the most traditional infantryman or sailor, could be certain whether bombing would indeed live up to its promise.

At the Air Corps training school at Maxwell Field in Alabama, officers were taught that an enemy's war effort could be paralyzed by destroying key nerve centers in his economy. Air Corps theorists focused on industrial "bottlenecks" which, if destroyed, could throttle a nation's ability to arm and supply its troops. Another supposition of air war proponents, viewed cautiously by political leaders, was that civilian morale could be broken far more quickly than that of soldiers. During the Great War, small-scale bombing of London and Paris had horrified civilians, provoking even more fear afterward as aircraft technology progressed. Novelists such as H.G. Wells fueled the general trepidation with apocalyptic books such as *The War in the Air* and *The War of the Worlds* (the latter made notorious when read over the radio by Orson Welles on Halloween, a month after Munich). In the art world, Pablo Picasso's haunting depiction of Guernica, a Spanish town destroyed by German bombers in the Spanish Civil War, came to embody the public's fear of devastation from the sky. If warfare was waged among entire countries rather than just along front lines, how long could popular support for such conflicts endure? For Hap Arnold and his fellow air power enthusiasts, the mere potential of strategic air war in the public mind provided them with the political backing so that their objectives were not completely subordinated to Army and Navy tactical purposes. As a result, the Air Corps was allowed to pursue the development, if not the deployment in force, of heavy long-range bombers.

British military planners, also taking stock of their nation's separation by water from potential antagonists, had been persuaded earlier of the efficacy of bombing. The Royal Air Force had been made a separate service, equivalent to the Army and Navy, in 1918, and had immediately pursued a developmental strategy along Douhetian lines. Prime Minister Stanley Baldwin, fascinated by the concept of warfare at arm's length, stated, "The bomber will always get through." His statement, while inadvertently reflecting British fears, was meant to buttress faith in the RAF's growing Bomber Command. In America, an independent air arm was slower to evolve, even as aircraft designers from a variety of firms were inducing greater optimism with their inventions.

The two- and four-engined bombers coming off the drawing boards were proving larger, faster and more durable than any craft available during the Great War. Their ability to deliver destructive power at a chosen point across hundreds of miles far exceeded the potential of artillery, infantry, or that other child of Mars born during the Great War, the tank. The new bombers were all monoplanes and their speeds more than doubled those of Great War bi-plane fighters. The American C.L. Norden Company was developing a bombsight so precise that it could place "a bomb in a pickle barrel" from 30,000 feet. Historian Geoffrey Perret wrote, "Technological developments in the mid-1930s conjured up a Mitchellian dream world, where heavy bombers flew unimpeded deep into enemy territory, where endless strings of bombs flashed through the sunlight to shatter small, precise targets at will."

By the late 1930s, however, the law of physics that states "every action causes a reaction" had found bomber development no exception. These years witnessed an accelerated development—in Europe if not America—of high-performance fighter aircraft and anti-aircraft artillery, along with a new, previously unforeseen device: radar.

In November 1938, in the wake of Munich, President Roosevelt held a meeting at the White House during which he stated his wish for a vastly increased strength of front-line aircraft. At that time, the total number of military planes in the United States was 1,800, most of them unusable or obsolete. When he addressed Congress the following spring, FDR asked for appropriations to expand the Air Corps to 5,500 modern planes. Along with $180 million for aircraft he requested $120 million for bases and training. In 1938, the Air Corps had trained only 300 pilots; that number had to be increased exponentially. Whether or not aircraft were to be used in a strategic or tactical role, the United States had to have planes. Beginning in 1939, the Consolidated Aircraft Company rushed into development another four-engine bomber, intended to have a longer range and carry a greater bombload than the B-17. It would eventually be known as the B-24, or "Liberator."

In Germany, meanwhile, the air arm had already emerged as a powerful force. During the Weimar Republic, German military leaders had concealed aircraft development within the field of civil aviation; they had also contracted with the Soviet Union to use secret airfields in Russia to test military applications. In 1935, Adolf Hitler ended all subterfuge and announced the existence of the Luftwaffe, headed by World War I ace Hermann Goering. The Germans had considered, and then dismissed, Douhet's concept of war waged by aircraft alone, and had opted instead to create an air force devoted to assisting the operations of their army. In 1937, Hitler decided against the further development of heavy long-range bombers. He wanted the country's resources devoted to a greater quantity of fighters, medium bombers and, especially, dive-bombers. Strategic bombing, even as envisioned by its most ardent supporters, was a long-term endeavor, and Hitler was only interested in quick results.

In March 1939, the beleaguered, abandoned state of Czechoslovakia ceased to exist. Along with the Sudetenland it had lost its most defensible territory; after being subverted by Nazi agents, the eastern half of the country, Slovakia, declared independence and became a German ally. The remainder of the country, formerly called Bohemia and Moravia and today (with the restored Sudetenland) known as the Czech Republic, was forced to accept incorporation into the Third Reich. French and British leaders recognized their folly at Munich. Next time Hitler moved, the democracies would stand firm.

The following month, America's most famous aviator, Charles Lindbergh, returned from Germany, where he had been given a VIP tour of aircraft factories and Luftwaffe bases, and had even been allowed to test-fly German aircraft. Lindbergh saw clearly that a new European war was imminent, but thought that America should not become involved. His view was that the Soviet Union was an even greater menace to future American interests than the Nazi state and that, if Germany were destroyed, there would be little to stop the Russians from overrunning Europe. History proved Lindbergh to be mistaken; however, in the meantime he practiced his principle of "America first." Upon his return from Germany he met with Hap Arnold at West Point and described in detail the Luftwaffe's technical progress, numerical strength and its evident esprit de corps. He stressed that Germany, in contrast to America, was putting enormous resources behind its air arm. After a three-hour conference the men went outside to attend a baseball game between military cadets. While play was under way, few could have guessed that the two men earnestly conversing in the stands were discussing in minute terms the

Luftwaffe and what the American air arm urgently needed to do to equal, and eventually surpass, its prospective opponent.

On September 1, 1939, Germany launched a sudden, overwhelming invasion of Poland, which bravely resisted for about three weeks until realizing that further resistance was futile. Stuka dive-bombers destroyed or demoralized Polish front-line positions. Level bombers hit staging areas and inflicted massive destruction on Warsaw. German fighters roamed the sky in search of Polish fighters, most of which were bi-planes, or simply strafed marching columns when no opposition was to be found. On September 17 the Soviet Union's Red Army attacked Poland from the east to coordinate with the German assault. Many Poles assumed that the Russians had advanced to halt the Germans, not join them. Later, thousands of Polish officers were found buried in mass graves near Smolensk in Russia, thousands more having disappeared. Even before the final end of Polish resistance, on October 6, the German Wehrmacht was rushing its main forces west to confront the French and British. Honoring their commitment to Poland, those nations had declared war on Germany on September 3. World War II had begun.

During the Depression, the American aircraft industry had lived hand-to-mouth. Given the complexity of the new machines and their ever-changing designs, products often cost more to build than they could be sold for. The high rate of accidents had also had a dampening effect on sales. In 1938–39, however, France and Britain came to the rescue of many struggling American firms. The Allies suddenly needed aircraft components, engines and finished planes as quickly as American companies could supply them. When the Air Corps began to place large orders for planes, it was frustrated that much of the industry's production capacity was taken up by foreign orders. Still, specifications from across the Atlantic increased the expertise of U.S. builders, so when the Air Corps finally expanded in earnest, it found that a burgeoning domestic industry had supplanted a skeletal network of quixotic dreamers.

The Americans had some catching up to do. From 1932 to 1939, total military aircraft production in the United States was only 2,195, compared to 7,940 for the British, 8,295 for Germany and 10,382 for the Soviet Union. France, Japan, and even Italy had produced more planes. Nevertheless America, where the worldwide economic slump had lingered longer than in Europe, was in an excellent position to gain ground rapidly. Almost nine million people were officially unemployed, and factories were on single 40-hour-a-week shifts. Not only the fuel and mineral but also the human resources of the country were largely untapped.

On May 16, 1940, during the Battle of France, President Roosevelt asked Congress for the means to produce 50,000 planes a year, a giant step toward making the United States the "arsenal of democracy." The following month, Congress invited Hap Arnold to provide a more detailed request for the Air Corps alone. Senator Henry Cabot Lodge took him aside and explained that he was about to receive a blank check. "All you have to do is ask for it," he said. The initial plan was to create 54 combat groups with corresponding training and auxiliary aircraft and base infrastructure.

Recognizing that manufacturing capacity was lacking for the fulfillment of such orders, Army war planners engineered an alliance between America's "cottage" aviation industry and Detroit: mass production techniques would be applied to aircraft production. Henry Ford was an isolationist with deep-seated animosity toward Roosevelt, and at one point had turned down a contract for aircraft engines when he learned that most of them would be sent to the British. Nevertheless, he feared government action against his company if it did not participate in rearmament. He constructed a gigantic plant in Michigan that would soon be turning out Liberators. Consolidated Aviation had been putting out one a week at their plant near San Diego; Ford's new plant near Detroit would be able to put out one an hour.

In addition to Detroit, the Sunbelt became the magnet for development of huge new factories and airfields, jumpstarting a shift in American demography that has continued since the war. Land was plentiful, costs were low and the weather was nearly always good for flying. Struggling workers who just years earlier might have echoed the tune, "Brother, can you spare a dime?" headed to Texas, Arizona or southern California to become well-paid laborers with all the overtime they could handle.

In June 1941, the Army Air Corps was designated the U.S. Army Air Force. This was in part because in meetings between the Anglo-

American Combined Chiefs of Staff the Americans needed their man to sit with equal authority across from his RAF counterpart. A larger reason was that the war in Europe was answering many of the pre-war questions about the importance of air power. It was vital. For the Germans, the Luftwaffe's strength had proven integral to their string of conquests. The British, meanwhile, had come to owe their very existence not to their army or navy, but to the strength and skill of their Royal Air Force.

After the fall of France, the reputation of the German Luftwaffe, its symbol the evil-looking Stuka dive-bomber, was at a fearsome peak. The Polish air force had been obliterated in days; the French Armee de l'Air completely overmatched. The RAF's Advanced Air Striking Force had been almost destroyed before evacuating its airfields on the Continent. As a tactical force—tied to the German Army's operations while destroying enemy aircraft through fighter sorties—the Luftwaffe was clearly unsurpassed. But in August the Germans launched the Battle of Britain, seeking to effect a strategic decision with air power in a campaign without army or naval participation. It was history's first campaign waged by aircraft alone, and the stakes were enormous. If the Germans won air superiority over southern England, Britain would be rendered impotent to prevent Nazi occupation.

The time parameters of the Battle of Britain can be set anywhere between July and November 1940, but the crucial stage of the battle was fought between August 12, called "Adlertag" by the Germans (Eagle Day), and September 15. It was on the latter that Churchill made his famous tribute, "Never in the field of human conduct was so much owed by so many to so few. All hearts go out to the fighter pilots, whose brilliant actions we see with our own eyes day after day . . ." The crucial event in the battle had occurred on August 24, when a twin-engined Heinkel 111 bomber accidentally dropped its bombs on a residential neighborhood of East London. At that point, Fighter Command had been on the ropes, the Luftwaffe methodically targeting its airfields and radar net, achieving a steady attrition of British pilots. The London attack, however, furnished Churchill the pretext to launch Bomber Command in a raid of 81 planes against Berlin. Hitler, enraged at the attack, ordered the Luftwaffe to hit London with full force in revenge. His decision, though unfortunate for Londoners, gave Fighter Command a respite. The rate of British aircraft production had by then exceeded Germany's, and with cessation of direct attacks on its base network the RAF was no longer in danger of being overwhelmed.

American observers, including Carl "Tooey" Spaatz, the future commander of U.S. Army Air Forces in Europe, were sent to England during the battle where they confirmed reports of the Luftwaffe's Achilles' heel. The renowned Stukas had proven vulnerable to fighter attacks and had had to be withdrawn from the fighting. Heinkel 111 and Dornier 17 medium bombers had been unable to carry sufficient payloads for area targets and suffered from inadequate defensive armament. The Luftwaffe did not possess a high-performance long-range fighter. As events through June 1942 would prove, the German air force was still superb in its primary role as a tactical force. However, the Battle of Britain established that the Luftwaffe needed the German Army to support its operations as much as the reverse. The Germans had no strategic air capability, the very element of air power that Britain and the United States had chosen to develop.

In retrospect, the Battle of Britain can be viewed not as a life-and-death struggle for national survival, but as simply the most visually spectacular of an historic string of colorful battles between European states in which both sides were evenly matched. Churchill, by shifting the focus of the battle from military to civilian targets, ensured that the Luftwaffe would be inadequate to its task, whereas by strictly targeting RAF airfields and infrastructure, the Germans might have succeeded. In the "Blitz" that followed the Battle of Britain during the winter of 1940–41, when German bombers took to hitting British cities at night, the English population suffered heavily, but their travail was minor compared to the devastation Bomber Command would eventually inflict on German cities. It was the British, not the Germans, who had long contemplated strategic bombing as an essential component of their strategy.

In July 1941, the War Plans Division (WPD) of the American General Staff was ordered to create a plan for how the United States could prevail in hypothetical simultaneous wars against Germany, Italy and Japan. Given its small, overworked staff, the WPD agreed to let the USAAF develop a plan of its own to be added later to the Army's proposals. The new Air War Plans Division (AWPD), led by Colonel Hal George, a disciple of Billy Mitchell, thus found an opening to elaborate its concept of strategic air war. The assumption was that the American Army would need at least two years' buildup before it was ready to invade the Continent; the air force could strike much sooner. The RAF, already waging its bombing campaign against Germany, made available literally a ton of target information. The Americans had resources of their own because many of Germany's factories as well as its modern electrical power system had been financed with loans from New York banks. USAAF officers commandeered the files from bank vaults and pored over industrial blueprints—the factories' strengths, their exact locations and what kind of bombloads would be needed to destroy them.

In the United States, even as aircraft designers and industrialists attempted to cope with more orders than they had ever dreamed of, the other challenge was to find men to fly and crew the new aircraft and provide maintenance on the ground. How could they be trained, and who would do the training? By the end of 1941, Hap Arnold had taken over 41 civilian flying schools, placing West Point graduates on the premises in order to instill Army discipline. Bases sprang up throughout the south and west, planes parking alongside bulldozers and dumptrucks that were still leveling out the runways.

Once the system had been established, pilot James Fanelli's training was typical, including the initial "short-arm inspection," its traditional humbling start. Fanelli's odyssey, broken roughly into two-month stints, consisted of, first, basic training in Nashville, Tennessee, followed by classroom training at Maxwell Field, Alabama. Then he received initial flying experience in Stearman bi-planes in Jackson, Mississippi, followed by basic flying school at nearby Greenville in BT-13As (nicknamed the "multi-vibrators"), and advance flying school at Columbus, Mississippi, in AT-9s and AT-10s. He subsequently received his wings, a 2nd lieutenant's commission and a two-week leave. After that brief respite, it was back to Maxwell to learn the B-24, an actual combat plane, followed by a trip to Salt Lake City, Utah, and then Portland, Colorado, for crew training. His next stop was Topeka, Kansas, to wait for assignment overseas. (He had enlisted in June 1942.) He was then ordered to Hoboken, New Jersey, where he boarded the *Queen Elizabeth* ocean liner for a four-day voyage to Glasgow, Scotland. On the trip, airmen were stripped of their insignia and dressed as infantry in order to deceive Nazi spies. From there he was sent to Northern Ireland for theater training and then finally assigned to the 389th Bomb Group based at Hethel in East Anglia, England.

The system that trained thousands of airmen on short notice is all the more remarkable for how quickly it was improvised after mid-1940 and fine-tuned along the way. Still, William Watkins, whose B-17 of the 305th Bomb Group was crippled and crashlanded during one of the first USAAF raids into Germany, stated: "The only thing that saved our skins was that we had a pilot who was a pilot in civilian life. Other ships had guys who couldn't find the door on the airplane. All kids, shoemakers, salesmen. The Germans had been fighting for 4, 5 years and had this well-oiled machine." Of his own training, Watkins recalled, "We were the second class that went through gunnery school at Vero Beach, Florida. The first class that went through was the instructors who were teaching us. They were as dumb as we were!" Given the stringent training required of today's pilots and aircrew, the fact that America suddenly plucked thousands of its brightest young men from civilian life and made them flyers is amazing, not least for the incredible bravery they would need in history's most fiercely contested air war.

The Army Air Corps had a strength of 26,000 men and 800 combat planes when the conflict in Europe began in September 1939. By December 1941, the USAAF possessed almost 3,000 first-line aircraft and 354,000 trained men. On the 7th of that month, the "Day of Infamy," Japan attacked the American naval base at Pearl Harbor, Hawaii, prompting the United States to declare war on Japan. On December 10, 1941, Adolf Hitler, supporting his Japanese ally and assuming that American attention would largely be devoted to the Pacific, declared war on the United States. Hitler didn't realize that Roosevelt and Churchill, anticipating America's belligerency, had already decided on a policy of "Germany first." By May 1945, the USAAF would grow to 2.4 million men with 80,000 frontline combat aircraft. Over 300,000 machines were produced during the course of the war.

Still, the American strategic air campaign against Germany is best described not in production statistics but in terms of flesh and blood, courage and duty. If the United States had produced a million planes, these would still have been no more useful than the citizen soldiers who flew them. Hidden within the War Department's projections were losses—airmen and their craft shot down while attempting to cripple the Nazi state. Beginning in mid-1942, the struggle for air supremacy became a seesaw battle during which U.S. aircrews could take little comfort in the fact that Detroit was continually receiving new orders. As opposed to the safety priority of today's commercial flyers, the priority of American flyers in World War II was, first, accomplishing their mission and, second, survival. The pilots of the Luftwaffe and the hundreds of thousands of Germans manning anti-aircraft weapons were, in the process, trying to kill as many of the newly trained American airmen as possible.

America was the last of the major powers to enter World War II, two years and three months after the invasion of Poland. During that time, a great drama had unfolded for its "Sister Republic," squeezed between the borders of Nazi Germany, Fascist Italy and Vichy France. Switzerland had, in fact, faced the greatest threat in its long history, a crisis that continued throughout the war. But while in 1942 the political map of the Continent showed an otherwise unbroken sea of swastikas—German allies or conquests from the border of Franco's Spain to the gates of Moscow—one "white spot" in Europe remained. American airmen in stricken Flying Fortresses or Liberators would still find a refuge from the alternative fates of fiery death or Nazi capture. Why did this democratic state still exist, and how had it remained independent when every other territory in central Europe, neutral or not, had fallen to German arms or Nazi intimidation?

A subtle change had taken place in Switzerland at the beginning of the war. The state whose very existence over the centuries had been predicated on refusal to live under one man's rule—especially not such as Hitler—had quietly accepted a leader of its own. The Swiss government, a revolving democratic council, was institutionally unable to designate one person to lead the country through the duration of a long war; the military, however, was under no such restriction. Only three generals had been named in Swiss history, in 1847, 1870 and 1914. On August 30, 1939, in the week following the Nazi-Soviet Non-Aggression Pact and two days prior to Germany's invasion of Poland, the Swiss named a fourth.

The nomination of Henri Guisan, commander of the First Corps, as supreme commander of the Swiss Army was approved by the Parliament in Bern by 204 votes to 21. After he had taken his oath to defend Swiss independence, in a ceremony broadcast over the radio, Guisan encountered a scene that would remain a vivid memory for the rest of his life. He emerged onto the square from the Parliament building to find a huge cheering crowd gathered outside. The throng spontaneously began to sing the Swiss national anthem. As events would prove, their faith in their new general would be vindicated.

4

BLITZKRIEG

When Great Britain and France declared war on Germany on September 3, 1939, there was no shortage of small European states proclaiming neutrality. Understandably, countries like Denmark, Norway, the Netherlands, Luxembourg and Belgium had no wish to join the war, instead hoping it would end quickly while not approaching the scale of carnage achieved by the combatants of World War I. The Swiss, more experienced at neutrality than other nations, realized from the start that their centuries-old policy stood for little in the context of a world war instigated and driven by Nazi Germany. Given Switzerland's lingual, cultural and familial ties with Germany, most Swiss were able to recognize from the start that a dark, unpredictable element had burst into European great-power politics.

As a child in 1934, Verena Rothenhäusler visited relatives across the Rhine in Singen and witnessed a parade of Nazi Brownshirts. Her uncle took her aside and said, "It's a pity that things like this must happen." Swiss who owned radios tuned into Hitler's bombastic Reichstag speeches in those years because they generally signaled something momentous was about to take place: reoccupation of the Rhineland, repudiation of Versailles, the Anschluss, threats against Czechoslovakia. Today she says, "I still have his voice in my ears. He cried. He shouted. Such terrible emotion!" Hitler had no respect for political borders, rights or for results of previous history, and had stated openly that he "respected only those rights that were defended" (a remark that paralleled Stalin's famous query, "How many divisions

53

does the Pope have?"). There was never a question of a Swiss Anschluss, following Austria's example of stepping willingly into the Nazi fold. In a radio broadcast in April 1939, as Austria merged with the Reich and Gestapo agents rounded up sullen dissidents in Prague, American correspondent William Shirer reported:

> As for Switzerland, it has taken events this week calmly, though the press has, with considerable bravery considering the German pressure on this country, attacked Germany savagely. Today one of the members of the Swiss Federal Council was quoted as saying the Swiss would fight if attacked. Every Swiss I've talked to takes it for granted. But they're wondering, if they're not exactly next on the list of Germany's intended victims, how far down the list they are. Not very far, they think. One important thing is that Nazism has made no headway at all among the German Swiss, who form a majority of the population of this country. The German Swiss are even more violently anti-Nazi than the French Swiss. Traveling through Switzerland, as I have recently, one notices many more soldiers than usual. Well, it's understandable, isn't it?

The task for General Henri Guisan was to enforce Switzerland's foreign policy with military measures formidable enough to deter the German threat. The Nazis were radical ideologues who would not be dissuaded from their ambitions by mere formal declarations of neutrality; they could, however, be deterred by strong defensive preparations.

A year after Hitler became Chancellor in 1933, the Swiss began fortifying their border with Germany. They found that their Great War earthworks had become useless over time, so the new emphasis was on hard emplacements, blockhouses, concrete dugouts and tank traps. The line stretched from the Fortress of Sargans near Austria to Basel, which sat across the Rhine from the terminus of both the German Siegfried and French Maginot Lines, then through the Jura Mountains in the west to Geneva, which protruded into France. The approach routes into Switzerland from Austria, as many Habsburg nobles had found, consisted of treacherous passes flanked by heights. The Rhine River and Lake Constance were significant natural obstacles on the border with Germany. In each of the French-German wars, the main Swiss problem was considered to be the Gempen Plateau south of Basel, which afforded an invasion route for either side to outflank the other's frontal defenses. The plateau was thought to be as tempting to the French as to the Germans, and Swiss defenses pointed toward both sides. (In 1944, Stalin recommended this route for the American Seventh Army advancing on Germany from southern France.)

On the day the war began, Switzerland implemented a planned troop mobilization of 435,000 men divided into three corps. In part, the mobilization was intended to send a strong signal to the belligerents that Switzerland's neutrality did not depend on the kindness of strangers or on international accords, but rather on Swiss defenses. Another consideration was that the French had massed six divisions along the Swiss border, perhaps to bypass the Siegfried Line through Swiss territory while the bulk of the German Army was preoccupied in Poland. The Swiss General Staff didn't realize at that time that Henri Guisan had made secret arrangements with the French for mutual defense.

As early as summer 1937, when French Marshal Henri Petain visited Guisan's First Corps for a review of troops, talks had been under way between the French General Staff and select officers close to Guisan. In the Swiss government, only the head of the Military Department, Rudolf Minger, was privy to the talks, providing the rest of the government and army with plausible deniability for what could be considered a breach of neutrality. The French, whose Maginot defenses ended at the Swiss border, had every interest in a strong Switzerland and were willing to back it up with their own troops. The Swiss, of course, would have welcomed French assistance in the event of a German attack, although the perception of an alliance with France had to be avoided. According to Swiss historian Willi Gautschi, Guisan's men also held secret discussions with the British Air Attaché about RAF access to landing fields in Switzerland.

The Swiss Federal Council authorized open approaches by the General Staff to both Germany and France during this time, suggesting assistance should Switzerland be attacked by the opposite number of either power. These talks were superficial and not at a high level, but were in keeping with the idea of strict neutrality. Aside from Minger, no one in the government or army, save for a few discreet officers, was aware of the extent of Guisan's arrangements.

After the Polish nation once again, temporarily, sank beneath the waves of great-power avarice, the Germans and Western Allies faced off in the "Phony War," a stand-off on the Western Front during the winter of 1939–40. General Guisan, meanwhile, decided that an additional, stronger, defense line was necessary behind the border to deal with Germany's new blitzkrieg tactics. Additional fortifications were constructed from Sargans to the Gempen Plateau, taking advantage of hilly terrain, the Limmat River and Lake Zurich. It would be known as the Limmat Line, or, in view of its vital importance should an attack occur, the Army Position. It faced northeast toward Germany. William Shirer travelled to Switzerland on October 15 and recorded in his "Berlin Diary": "Swiss train full of soldiers. The country has one tenth of its population under arms; more than any other country in the world. It's not their war. But they're ready to fight to defend their way of life."

In the battle that was anticipated the Swiss had the advantage of their universal militia system, which required every able-bodied man in the country to serve in the Army and to be a marksman. Soldiers kept their rifles and ammunition at home so that the speed of Swiss mobilization, repeatedly demonstrated during the war years, was remarkable. Each time a mobilization was called, the Federal Railways would come under Army control while radio and print media would announce timetables and assignments. By war's end the Swiss could mobilize 800,000 men at a moment's notice. (Proportionally, the American equivalent would have been an ability to place 30 million trained men into pre-assigned positions in two days.) Another advantage was the Alpine nation's topography, a third of the country inclining vertical with much of the rest cut by large, narrow lakes in a more or less east-west orientation.

Switzerland's greatest military problem, aside from the immense size of its neighbors, was a shortage of modern equipment. The Army had no tanks and was sorely deficient in anti-tank guns. Many artillery units were retrained for an anti-tank role, and, to fill in gaps in the order-of-battle, dust was knocked off 84mm pieces, circa 1882. The Swiss also had 120mm guns dating from prior to World War I that were installed at strategic points. Before the war the Swiss had astutely acquired a license to manufacture fighter aircraft, but had unwisely chosen the French Morane 406. The 130 Moranes on hand were suitable for patrolling, reconnaisance or escort but were outclassed by more advanced combat planes. The pride of the Swiss air force was 80 Messerschmitt Bf-109E fighters purchased from Germany and delivered in early 1940, a transaction the Germans would regret.

The mountainous terrain of Switzerland presented a military problem for the defense as well as for an invader, because most of the population and all of the large cities were situated in the lowlands in the north. Places like Schaffhausen, north of the Rhine, and Basel, on the Rhine across from Germany, could not be considered defensible. The largest city, Zurich, astride the Limmat River, was incorporated into the Army Position, though what to do with its 350,000 population should an attack occur remained a dilemma. Zurich, Bern, the capital, and other important cities such as Winterthur and Solothurn did not benefit from the advantage of Alpine terrain. If a blitzkrieg hit Switzerland, the army would be prepared but most of the civilian population would be vulnerable.

On November 30, 1939, the Soviet Union invaded Finland, providing the world with the spectacle of a small, brave nation resisting a giant, aggressive neighbor. In Switzerland, it was assumed by many that the "Winter War" foretold their own future. The Swiss and Finnish military establishments had become familiar prior to the war through international marksmanship and skiing competitions. (In the 1939 rifle contest, Estonia had finished first, Switzerland second and Finland third.) The forested Nordic and the Alpine nation shared an affinity not just in skills and a certain tough individualism but also in their dangerously isolated geopolitical positions.

At first, the Russians impaled themselves on the Finnish Mannerheim Line north of Leningrad, which the Swiss thought comparable to their own Army Position. In the north, entire Soviet armies flailed disastrously in the thick forests, small Finnish ski units penetrating behind them, isolating infantry and tanks. Most of the Red Army casualties came from exposure after mobile Finnish units, sometimes only snipers, cut off their supply lines.

The Red Army would go on to lose 200,000 men killed in the Winter War, perhaps a million casualties overall. Observers of the conflict had different reactions. To the Swiss Army, the Finnish example provided inspiration that they too could perform great feats of arms if attacked by superior forces. In Britain and France, the Finns' courageous stand prompted a public outcry to lend assistance. Allied troops were issued winter clothing and the Royal Navy gathered a transport fleet to ship the expeditionary force to Norway, from where it would march to stand alongside the Finns. This Allied-Soviet war in the making was forestalled on March 12 after the Red Army finally broke the Mannerheim Line, forcing Finland to accept an armistice. In Berlin, the affair was viewed with mixed sentiments. While Hitler and the German General Staff cast a wary eye on preparations for Allied troop movements toward Scandinavia, they also took careful note of what appeared to be breathtaking Soviet military incompetence.

Effective January 1, 1940, General Guisan created a Fourth Corps of the Swiss Army, naming his chief of staff, Jakob Labhart, as commander. This was the culminating move in a struggle for strategic priorities within the army. Labhart and other senior Swiss officers such as Ulrich Wille (son of the 1914 general) and Gustav Däniker had pressed for an even-handed application of neutrality. In their view, the western border, facing France, should be as strongly fortified as the northern one, facing Germany. The preparatory actions of the Swiss Army should not reveal prejudice for one foreign power over another, and, they thought, the appearance of taking sides in the conflict would hasten rather than deter an invasion. These officers' view was rooted in a certain professional appreciation of Germany's Prussian military tradition, as well as a lack of regard for France's vaunted military establishment and its pre-war politics. Patriotic men, their traditional military and political assessments did not, at that early stage, allow for the perception that Hitler's Nazi Party, rapacious in its quest for Continental hegemony, had proven to be a fanatical new element in European politics.

To Guisan, supported by Rudolf Minger, his new chief of staff, Jakob Huber, plus the army's junior officers and nearly the entire Swiss public, the nature of the Third Reich demanded a tacit shift in the interpretation of neutrality. France was clearly not the threat— Germany was. Guisan was fully aware of his duties as commander of a neutral force, but in practical decisions about where to pour the concrete, where to place the artillery and where to set bridge demolitions there could be no ambiguity: on the Rhine front, and in depth. Among senior Swiss officers, Guisan was foremost in grasping the essential challenges that Switzerland faced 1939–45: deterring the Nazis from invasion, or resisting effectively if attacked.

An interesting aspect underlying Swiss-German antipathy in World War II is that Switzerland is primarily ethnic German, and completely so among the cantons along the Rhine. A certain degree of cultural animosity existed on both sides of the border, not unlike, for example, that between Scottish Highlanders and English; but the Swiss and Germans were not traditional, or what one would term "blood," enemies. While Britain could rouse popular support for repelling "the Hun," or France for defeating the "Boche," Switzerland's resolve was founded on abhorrence of the Nazi phenomenon far more than on cultural or ethnic disdain. The primary issue at stake was democracy, which to the Swiss was synonymous with their independence from foreign domination.

Even as Hitler had been welcomed by cheering crowds in Austria after the Anschluss, and had found other German enclaves (in the Rhineland, Czechoslovakia, Poland and other nations) receptive to incorporation into the Third Reich, Switzerland remained separate and apart. The Swiss press, government and people had made it clear from the moment Hitler assumed power that they had no use for the Führer, National Socialism or any suggestion of absorption into the New Order. Every move that advanced the Third Reich only prompted further defensive preparations by Switzerland.

The problem for the German Army's OKW (Oberkommando der Wehrmacht) was that in European history the cantons had not been defeated since the time of Caesar, the only exception being when Napoleon promised more, not less, liberty for individuals. The fact that most Swiss spoke German had the effect of prompting earlier and more extensive efforts to counter the Nazi threat. William Shirer, contemplating the imminent campaign in the west, wrote on March 1, 1940: "From what I saw in the Netherlands, the Dutch will be easy pickings for the Germans. Their army is miserable. Their famous defensive water-line is of doubtful worth. Switzerland will be tougher to crack, and I doubt if the Germans will try."

As events would prove, the German Army's General Staff agreed that flanking the Maginot Line through the Low Countries was the most desirable option. When Germany declined to attempt to flank the Maginot Line from the south, the decision resonated with the conviction, held by German planners from the General Staff to the head of state, that the Wehrmacht was taking the path of least resistance.

The "Phony War" ended on April 18, 1940, with surprise German invasions of Denmark and Norway. The former fell in a day while the latter accepted a counterinvasion by the Allied Expeditionary Force that had earlier been prepared for Finland. The existence of this force had, in fact, largely prompted Germany's attack because it had rendered vulnerable the Reich's pipeline of iron ore from northern Sweden. The German navy had already argued with Hitler that while seizing the Norwegian coast was desirable, preventing Britain from controlling it was essential. After the Royal Navy sailed into Norwegian territorial waters to seize a German supply ship (loaded with British sailors taken prisoner by the pocket battleship *Graf Spee*), Germany launched a combined naval-air assault.

It was history's first example of a strategic air-landing operation. While Norwegian coastal batteries fought well against German ships, the country had no defense against elite airborne troops attacking from within. Norway became part of the Third Reich in May once the last British troops had been pulled off in order to defend their own homeland, the first of a series of British evacuations from foreign countries during the first two years of the war. The retreat was tragically marked by the destruction of the aircraft carrier *Glorious* when it was caught in the open sea and pounded beneath the waves by the battleship *Scharnhorst*.

General Guisan and other Swiss military leaders had by now witnessed massive German tank armies defeating one country, Poland, and air transport fleets bypassing border defenses to defeat another, Norway. Nevertheless, the Swiss could count on infinitely more natural obstacles than the Poles and were far better prepared than the Scandinavian states. As Stephen Halbrook wrote, "While Denmark had only 30,000 men under arms and Norway an even more meager 13,000, Switzerland could muster 650,000 militiamen within a day or two." In addition, the Swiss assumed that when the Germans took on the main armies and air forces of the victors of Versailles—Britain and France—they would finally meet their match.

On May 10, the Germans launched the Battle of France, beginning with strikes against two more neutral countries, the Netherlands and Belgium. The Third Reich appeared to be repeating the Great War strategy of the Second Reich, a northern right hook. The French had spent the prior year discussing mutual defense plans with the Belgians, just as they had with the Swiss, and the elite French First Army, British Expeditionary Force (BEF) and French Ninth and Seventh Armies crossed the border to confront the invaders, the latter assigned to cross Belgian territory along the coast to assist the Dutch. That afternoon, Swiss fighter planes attacked a German Heinkel 111 bomber that strayed over their border. The Luftwaffe craft careened out of Swiss airspace, its fore and aft machine guns knocked out and one engine trailing smoke. On the ground, over half a million Swiss infantry and artillerymen moved into defensive positions.

Scenes throughout the Swiss countryside reflected those taking place farther north. Soldiers kissed their wives, girlfriends, parents or siblings goodbye before heading to the front, unsure whether they would ever see them again. At the same time, urban civilians in the northern parts of Switzerland fled to the interior with a few possessions, leaving their homes behind. The march to the border seemed ominous to some soldiers, as they waded past long convoys of civilians heading the other way, cars with mattresses tied to their roofs as protection against air attack. There was some resentment in Switzerland that those who fled further inland were only the well-to-do, which at that time meant anyone who owned a car. Later, once the country was surrounded, private motor transport was forbidden since all fuel needed to be reserved for military or essential purposes.

General Guisan's famous Order 51 informed Swiss soldiers that once in position they were forbidden to retreat. If they ran out of ammunition they were to use the bayonet. As commander, Guisan anticipated German breakthroughs, but it was essential to inspire the border troops to hold fast as long as they could, delaying the Germans before they reached the Army's main defense lines.

Guisan also issued an order that was unique to the Swiss system of government and defense: no matter how the battle progressed, if the troops heard over the radio or by other means that Switzerland had capitulated they should consider the news enemy propaganda. Switzerland, Guisan stated, would never surrender. In fact, Switzerland's system of revolving national leaders guaranteed that no political figure possessed the authority to order the nation to lay down its arms, as happened in half a dozen other countries. In Switzerland that prerogative, although putative, since it had never been exercised, could only belong to the general. Guisan prepared another order that was to be read to the troops when combat began. It read: "The storm which has engulfed Europe has now reached Switzerland as well. During the coming days the army's and the entire population's resistance will be tested. The army is determined to fiercely defend every inch of our territory. I know that the country will prove itself worthy of its past, of its six centuries of history, honor and loyalty. . . . The only thing that counts today is Switzerland. It must remain ours. . . . At the border the blood of the Confederates has started flowing, the blood of war and of freedom. We shall not be forced to the ground by an invasion."

In retrospect, the question arises whether Guisan, through these orders to his soldiers, was more concerned with German propaganda, a failure of Swiss arms, or with possible weak-kneed reactions in Parliament if the Germans launched an offensive. His own job was to impart to the Swiss Army a simple conviction: fight or die.

In the Netherlands and Belgium, German paratroopers and glider-borne commandos descended on key bridges, forts and airfields to pave the way for panzer assaults. The Dutch fought for four days before capitulating on the fifth. The final straw came when the Luftwaffe obliterated the center of Rotterdam, prompting rumors that 30,000 civilians had been killed. (The number turned out to be 814.) In Belgium, the British arrived at their assigned positions on the Dyle River to find the Belgians had not bothered with fortifications. French Seventh Army had been cut up by air attacks during its advance along the coast, and then found strong German forces waiting for it in the Netherlands. French Ninth Army occupied its positions on the Meuse River, in the quiet sector opposite the Ardennes Forest. As the Belgians fell back on their northern cities, the German 3rd and 4th panzer divisions engaged in the war's first major tank battle, with French First Army at the Gembloux Gap.

By May 12, from the Black Forest just above the Swiss border, French and Swiss intelligence had noted continuous German marching columns heading south. To outpost troops, bridging materials were clearly visible on the other side of the Rhine. As it turned out, these maneuvers by Wilhelm von Leeb's Army Group C were only an elaborate feint. German troops marched by day against Switzerland and then went back at night. The next day they marched south again. The appearance of a massive build-up against Switzerland was intended to impress not the Swiss but the French, who kept forces south of the Maginot Line in anticipation of a German thrust through Swiss territory south of Basel against Belfort and Lyons.

On the night of May 14–15 the Swiss Army braced for an assault. The German advance in the Low Countries was thought to have stalled and both Swiss and French intelligence deduced that the second prong of the great German pincer movement around the Maginot Line was about to be launched. Urs Schwarz, who commanded an artillery unit at the time, recalled in his book *The Eye of the Hurricane*: "As far as I could see when observing the officers and soldiers under my command, beneath their calm exterior there was an excited expectation, coupled with a kind of incredulity. This was easy to understand in an army that had trained and trained yet had never seen a war. Some of the men seemed to look forward to a real fight, some seemed to think that such a thing simply could not happen to us, but nobody looked scared." Everyone assumed that the German offensive would occur on the hour, so at the stroke of 3 A.M., 4 A.M. and so on the Swiss border troops held their breath or squeezed their triggers for the onslaught they expected to face. A reservist on the border, P. Schmid-Ammann, recalled: "I had ammunition for my light machine gun, but I knew that in one or two hours the fighting would start and the ammunition would be sufficient to put up resistance for half an hour at the most, and then I would be done with. Everyone from privates to the colonel was determined to resist. We even said, 'May they come.'"

To the surprise of the Swiss Army, the morning of May 15 did not bring an attack on their country. Instead, it featured a plaintive phone call placed by French Premier Reynaud to British Prime Minister Churchill in London. "We have been defeated," said the French Premier. The initial German attacks against the Low Countries had indeed been a feint, but on May 15th it was seen that the real enemy thrust had been aimed at the Maginot Line's junction with the southern Belgian border, through the Ardennes Forest in Luxembourg.

French Ninth Army in the "quiet" sector had suddenly been over-whelmed. Seven panzer divisions were at that moment pouring over the Meuse River along a front where the French had least expected an attack. By the end of the day the Germans had made a complete break-through, the Allies' elite northern armies in danger of being cut off. The German panzers were dashing for the English Channel.

In the following days the news only grew worse as French and British counterattacks failed against the growing "panzer corridor." The Allies had enough armor and aircraft, but failed to organize them in a fashion to resist blitzkrieg. The Germans massed their tanks into self-sustaining divisions, the divisions into corps and the corps into groups. Assisted by expert tactical air coordination, with Stukas rang-ing ahead of the panzers as flying artillery, the Germans presented a huge, unstoppable wedge. They had furthermore correctly assessed the weakest point in the Allied front. On May 21, General Heinz Guderian, commanding the 1st, 2nd and 10th panzer divisions, reached the English Channel at Abbeville. The Allied northern front was trapped between the panzers and the sea. It only remained for the Germans to move up the coast to capture or destroy the British Expeditionary Force and France's elite armies.

On May 26, the British Army began to evacuate the Continent. It would have been doomed except for Hitler's mysterious "panzer halt" order two days previous, which allowed time for the British to estab-lish a defensive perimeter. The epic evacuation from Dunkirk subse-quently took place during the following week as the RAF's Fighter Command battled the Luftwaffe over the beaches. By June 2, the last British soldier had been put aboard the "small ships," and a London newspaper exulted over the hair-raising escape of the BEF with a head-line that read "Bloody Marvellous!"

On June 5 the German panzers, which had been pulled from the battle at Dunkirk during its last stages, launched the second phase of the Battle of France from the line of the Somme: their direction due south. The French had no means of stopping the Germans, who had obviously arrived at a more effective way to apply the tools of mod-ern warfare than had the complacent victors of the previous conflict. The French Army was so large and heavily equipped with small-arms and artillery that it could still offer serious opposition when the men chose to fight, but a collapse of morale had also taken effect. William

Shirer was allowed to tour the front under German auspices and recorded: "If the French were making a serious defense, why are the main roads never blown up? Why so many strategic bridges left untouched? Here and there along the roads, a tank barrier, that is, a few logs or stones or debris—but nothing really serious for the tanks. No real tank-*traps*, such as the Swiss built by the thousands." The British continued shipping forces to the Continent, including their newly formed 1st Armoured Division, but in the face of continuing German breakthroughs the units had to be pulled off again just as rapidly.

Along the Swiss border, meanwhile, fighting had raged in the air if not yet on the ground. On May 16 a Heinkel bomber returning from a raid south of Paris became disoriented and broke through heavy cloud cover into Swiss airspace. It was immediately attacked by two Me-109s from Swiss Fighter Squadron 21. Two crewmen were wounded and bailed out but the plane continued on, receiving anti-aircraft fire over Zurich. It finally crashed after being riddled with 100 holes. The pilot and a remaining crewman tried to flee but were apprehended by Swiss troops.

On June 1, a German bomber formation crossed into Switzerland over Lake Neuchatel and was bounced by Swiss fighters. One He-111 began burning and went out of control, tearing through some telephone lines before crashing into a woods with the death of its five-man crew. Later that afternoon, Fighter Squadron 6 encountered a flight of 24 German planes cutting across Swiss territory near Basel. The Swiss attacked and severed one bomber from the group. It was observed by Lt. Schenk, who claimed the kill, to crashland just across the French border. The next day another Heinkel, wounded by an encounter with a French fighter, wandered over Switzerland and was immediately shot down. A gunner was killed in the attack and the rest of the crew was interned after crashing in a wheatfield. On June 4 a formation of 29 German planes, Heinkels escorted by Me-110 Destroyers, was met by 12 Swiss fighters over the Frei Mountains. In the swirling dogfight that followed, two Me-110s were downed but a Swiss Me-109 was also lost. Its pilot, Lt. Rickenbacher, was killed after bailing out when his parachute failed to open.

As German losses mounted, the air battles on the Swiss border caught high-level attention. A Luftwaffe memo noted: "Any material received by the Luftwaffe command staff with regard to air fights with Swiss pilots is to be sent to the Führer." At the border, the Germans launched standing patrols of Destroyers to confront the Swiss. On June 8, six Me-110s caught a Swiss observation plane and sent it crashing in flames, killing both crewmen. Later that day two squadrons of 15 Swiss fighters faced 28 German Me-110s over Swiss territory in the west. Three German planes went down, one the victim of Swiss AA fire, against the loss of one Swiss Me-109. The following week, Luftwaffe chief Hermann Goering dispatched a sabotage team into Switzerland to blow up Dubendorf airfield near Zurich and other installations. The nine men, who all wore identical shoes and "civilian" backpacks filled with explosives, were arrested on a train. They were subsequently sentenced to life imprisonment.

By mid-June, the debacle in France was swiftly approaching its climax. Yet while German troops were happy enough simply to receive the surrender of thousands of French soldiers, new orders began to pour from Hitler's headquarters. Their object was to complete the encirclement of Switzerland before an armistice froze the front on a line that would leave the Swiss an opening to what remained of France. On June 10, Mussolini had jumped into the war, intending to crush the French Alpine front and advance along the Swiss border south of Geneva. Italian troops, however, had been stopped cold in the mountains by French fortifications, disrupting the Axis strategy. Guderian's corps on the German left received new orders to attack south, toward the rear of French Alpine positions facing Italy, and east, toward Switzerland.

A reconnaissance toward Switzerland, consisting of three armored cars led by Lt. Dietrich of the 29th Motorized Division, was launched at 1:30 A.M. on June 17. Dietrich wrote: "It is pitch dark, nothing can be seen but we go on and keep cheating our way forward. Suddenly we get onto a real road, everywhere are creepy movements; my gunner calls to me, 'the French!' 'Leave them alone, do not shoot!' We continue along the stopped French columns . . . Heavy French artillery is stopped along the road. Dawn is breaking, it is getting brighter by the minute. Now French vehicles come in the opposite direction. Our armored vehicles rush at full speed toward the border, every village is occupied by Frenchmen. At the front of our vehicle the large swastika flags are flying, the Frenchmen yield in horror. The people look at us thunderstruck. 'The Germans are coming!'"

Dietrich's small column exchanged fire with some of the French troops, forced many more to flee and ran others down on the road. Groping their way forward past the town of Pontarlier, they finally spotted a barbed wire line. Dietrich continued: "The border has to be here! It is almost impossible to turn around on this narrow forest path. . . . Two of us climb over the tree blockade and rush on on foot. I look through the binoculars and we are very happy. 'Swiss customs,' the station is in front of us. We run back. We now can urgently send the message, 'Swiss border reached' to the unit."

French troops closed in behind Dietrich's patrol but the Germans, nearly out of gas, were able to form a defensive position and await reinforcements. Later that morning General Guderian was delighted to receive news of 29th Motorized's success and set off for the border himself. In his memoirs he stated, "We sent a message to supreme headquarters informing them that we had reached the Swiss border at Pontarlier, to which Hitler signalled back, 'Your signal based on an error. Assume you mean Pontailler-sur-Saone.' My reply, 'No error. Am myself in Pontarlier on Swiss border,' finally satisfied the distrustful OKW."

Hitler's problem was that Mussolini had made no headway against the French from the south, so sealing off the Swiss border would have to be done by German troops, most of which were not in position or were fully occupied with other tasks. Chief of the General Staff Franz Halder wrote disdainfully in his diary: "The political command [Hitler] wants the direct connection between Switzerland and France severed, and would like to have this political expediency dressed up as a military necessity. This is sure to have some unpleasant consequences." The French inquired about an armistice on June 20, but the German High Command took its time drawing up terms. After the war, Field Marshal Wilhelm Keitel wrote, "We were at no pains to hurry ourselves, because the Führer wanted to see certain strategic objectives, like the reaching of the Swiss frontier, attained first of all."

In the end, time ran out for the Germans to improvise maneuvers in the difficult terrain along the French-Swiss border. France signed an armistice on June 22 with terms to take effect after midnight on the 25th. Barely an hour after the armistice came into force, General

Halder noted in his journal: "Morning. Disagreement with Army High Command: the political leadership wanted to have railroad connection severed between Switzerland and France. To this end [General] List had been given orders to do a thorough wrecking job on the railroad line La Roche–Annecy. Owing to the course of events, this order was not executed. Now [the High Command] wants that, with armistice in force, destruction of the line should be carried out by patrol action. I object. Once a truce has been declared, any such military undertaking is ruled out. If at all, this could be done only by Canaris."

Wilhelm Canaris, head of German military intelligence, the Abwehr, indeed tried to sabotage the rail line, in September, but failed to cause serious damage. Switzerland retained, through a combination of luck and Italian military ineptitude, a small window to the outside world. Until it was closed two years later, the opening would prove invaluable for the Swiss and the Allies, and remain a festering sore for the Germans. Nevertheless, to the Swiss, a minor rail line through Vichy France was small consolation for the total collapse of Allied power on the Continent.

5

THE CRISIS

The sudden fall of France and the expulsion of Britain's army from Europe came as a shock to the rest of the world, but may have been felt most in Switzerland, the only remaining democracy on the Continent. Indeed, the question had to be asked: Was the war over? Could Nazi boasts about the inevitability of a Thousand-Year Reich be correct? At midday on June 25, the day of the French armistice, Swiss Federal President Marcel Pilet-Golaz went on radio to deliver a disturbing speech. After announcing a partial troop demobilization he spoke of "adapting to the new circumstances." Henceforth important decisions needed to be made quickly by the government's authorities, he said, "without being able to consult on, discuss and deliberate them." He stated that "Events change at a rapid pace, so one has to adjust to this rhythm."

Pilet-Golaz sounded fatalistically resigned to accept the new, German-dominated Europe, and furthermore appeared to imply that the Federal Council should assume new, unprecedented powers. His words were carefully chosen and in retrospect seem vague, but the one element clearly missing from his speech—the one the majority of Swiss instinctively felt—was defiance. The words emanating from Bern caused many to doubt whether the Federal government retained the will to fight.

Pilet-Golaz immediately came under fierce attack in the press and throughout Switzerland, in cafés, meeting rooms or simple gatherings of farmers or workers in the Alpine cantons. Reaction also came from the army, where junior officers formed a secret alliance dedicated to the principle of "no surrender." Another group called Aktion was formed, composed of officers, businessmen, journalists and other prominent citizens dedicated to keeping the spirit of resistance alive. Nevertheless, to many Swiss the situation verged on hopeless. The German presence that had always loomed from the north now shadowed the country on all sides. Swiss independence, if not crushed by military force, could be slowly strangled by economic means, particularly deprivation of fuel and food. How could Switzerland survive? In fact, the following month would be the period of Switzerland's greatest peril, not just in terms of morale, which clearly had been shaken by the fall of France, but due to even more serious developments of which the Swiss were unaware.

On the day Pilet-Golaz gave his speech, a German staff officer named Otto von Menges was ordered to draw up an attack plan against Switzerland, the first of a series over the next few months that would collectively come to be known as Operation Tannenbaum. On June 23, Hitler ordered two mountain divisions to join von Leeb's Army Group C, positioned along the Swiss border. The motorized SS units Leibstandarte (Bodyguard) Adolf Hitler and Totenkopf (Death's Head) were also assigned to Leeb's force.

Strategically, Guisan had made an enormous miscalculation. He had poured almost all of Switzerland's defensive resources into fortifying the Army Position facing Germany, only to find the victorious Wehrmacht facing him along the French border. It was like the classic bit where someone piles up all their furniture against the front door, only to be tapped on the shoulder by the intruder from behind. (Of course, Guisan was not alone in failing to predict the French catastrophe.) The Germans had never intended to include Switzerland in the Battle of France, but now the Alpine nation, along with Britain, was the only remaining target in western Europe. If the Germans had attacked then, traversing the Juras, they would have found Bern defenseless, its strategic location in a loop of the Aare (so formidable in medieval times) useless against modern artillery. The entire Swiss plateau, containing most of the country's industry, would have been exposed, Swiss infantry helpless to stop the panzers.

The nature of von Menges' pragmatic approach can be seen from the following example, which refers to the assault of his projected 2nd Attack Group on the Swiss capital:

29th Motorized attacks with strong sections from the area east of Gex towards Nyon, as the mountain ridge there has already been passed before the border and there are apparently no enemy fortifications. Use here one motorized division in order to rapidly block the retreat road near Thun.

4th Panzer as central group to Berne. Use only after parts of the 5th [Inf.] Division have breached the border fortifications.

Later use of the 5th Division for the occupation of Berne, of its local industrial area and of the area seized by the XVth Corps appears necessary. Use of a small secondary section through Neuchatel towards Berne may ease the break through the mountains near La Chaux-de-Fonds for the adjoining division. Putting latter under the command of the XVIIIth Corps may be planned.

Of the Swiss Army, von Menges commented:

Fighting strength: A suitably organized, rapidly available war army. The state of training appears to be high due to the long mobilization. Only theoretically trained command. Methodical command. Deficiency in weaponry. The individual soldier is a tough fighter and good shot. The mountain troops are said to be better than their neighbors to the south [Italians]. The fighting strength of the Swiss living in the west [French-speaking] is moderate, while those who live south of Constance [German-speaking] would be bitter enemies. Conclusion: army just suitable for defense, which is totally inferior to the German Army.

Given the depression that had settled over Switzerland in July 1940, combined with vacillation in the Federal Council and a rare sense of national helplessness, von Menges may have been justified in speculating, "With the current political situation in Switzerland, it is possible that it would accede peacefully to ultimatum demands, so that after a warlike border crossing, there would be a rapid transition to a peaceful invasion." More damning words could not have been heard by the small nation which for centuries had fiercely defended its independence against foreign aggressors, and whose entire male population was trained in arms. Still, even in a nation that disdained "rule," someone needed to step forward.

On July 25, General Henri Guisan called upon 600 ranking officers of the Swiss Army to take leave of their posts and assemble for a meeting. It was a dangerous move—gathering the entire Swiss officer corps in one place—but Guisan considered it a risk worth taking. The spot he had chosen was the Rütli Meadow, in the Alps by the Lake of Lucerne. It was there that in 1291 the herdsmen "Companions of the Oath" had founded the Swiss Confederacy. With his officers assembled in a semi-circle before him, Guisan began, "I decided to reunite you in this historic place, on this ground which is a symbol of our independence, to explain the urgency of the situation, and to speak to you as a soldier to soldiers. We are at a turning point in our history. It is a question of the very survival of Switzerland."

At the Rütli, Guisan revealed to the officer corps the new strategy he had decided upon: redeploying the bulk of Swiss strength into the Alps. He said:

Come what may, the fortifications you have built preserve all their value. Our efforts have not been in vain, since we still hold our destiny in our own hands. Don't listen to those who, out of ignorance or evil intention, spread negative news and doubt. Let us trust not only in our right but also in our strength, which enables us, if everyone is possessed of an iron will, to defend ourselves successfully. . . .

On August 1 you will fully realize that the new positions that I have ordered you to occupy are those in which your arms and your courage in the new situation will be most effective for the defense and the good of the country. . . .

Currently there are, beyond our borders, more troops—and excellent troops—than ever before. We can be attacked on all fronts at the same time, which a few weeks ago was inconceivable. The army must adjust to this new situation and take a position that allows it to hold on to all the fronts. It will thus fill its inviolable, historic mission.

Guisan's speech was not taken down verbatim, but over the following days officers recalled it to others and parts were broadcast on the radio. As word got out, the effect on the country was electric. The sense of deep gloom that had followed France's defeat had been lifted, replaced by a stirring reminder of what Switzerland had always represented: a country that would fight for its independence and freedom. On August 1, Swiss National Day, bonfires blazed on heights throughout the country; patriotic songs were sung and people at countless celebrations quoted the general's words. Historian Willi Gautschi wrote: "It is no exaggeration to say that at the Rütli some kind of miracle happened. The briefing by the General changed the basic attitude among the majority of the armed forces and the population; despair and resignation gave way to the determination to brave any aggressor, no matter how powerful he was nor what happened, and if necessary to sell oneself as dearly as possible. . . . His words lit a torch and gave direction to Switzerland's domestic and foreign policy during World War II."

Its inspirational qualities aside, Guisan's strategic decision to move the main strength of the army to a National Redoubt in the Alps entailed a massive movement of troops and resources. In military terms, the decision was considered controversial then, as it remains to this day. Among firebrands in the army, the shift of defensive lines was unwelcome, and had all the appearance of a retreat. One young soldier, marching away from his border position, grumbled that he was joining "a Swiss Dunkirk." Others questioned the value of a strategy that ensured defense of barren mountain peaks while the country's major cities and most of its population could fall easily into German hands. Guisan's plan called for a screen of troops on the border, an intermediate line and mobile forces to slow the enemy in the middle lands, and then the final, impregnable position in the Alps. A cold look at Switzerland's strategic situation, however, reveals the wisdom of Guisan's move, which in the final analysis echoed Clausewitz's view that in warfare the opposing army is the only vital objective.

With no other allies within reach, Guisan called on Switzerland's most ancient one, the Alps. Despite the bravery of his officers and soldiers, he determined that they really did not stand a chance if Germany chose to focus its blitzkrieg tactics against Swiss soil in the north. The Swiss might have gone down harder than the other countries that had previously succumbed, but they would not ultimately have been able to withstand a massive combined-arms assault. By placing the Swiss Army in the Alps, Guisan erased blitzkrieg as a tactical factor in a Swiss–German war. The German panzers and motorized formations would have been useless against the Redoubt, the Luftwaffe reduced to hitting impregnable rock formations. The battle would have evolved as German infantry climbers against Swiss marksmen deployed in depth. The Germans would have faced hidden fortifications with heavy weapons, and defenders far more familiar with the ground.

In German operational plans during 1940, the recurring imperative had been to cut off the Swiss Army's retreat before it could reach the Alps. Guisan pre-empted that strategy by making the mountains Switzerland's primary line of resistance. Switzerland's historic value to European conquerors, since the time of Rome, had been for its transit routes, connecting Italy and Germany, or, to a lesser degree France and Austria. The small nation had few natural resources and, to the Germans, its industry was not a great prize compared to the wealth of industrial output they had already conquered. What Guisan presented to German military planners was a dilemma: the Wehrmacht could violate Swiss neutrality, but by doing so would activate a Swiss Army in impregnable positions that could not be overwhelmed by force. German divisions would have been tied down indefinitely in, at best, a gigantic, lengthy siege; at worst, an unwinnable war. By attacking Switzerland the Wehrmacht would only have opened a bleeding sore that it would not be able to close.

Another element of Guisan's strategy was to blow the Alpine transit routes immediately upon an Axis attack. Swiss neutrality allowed for non-military traffic on the rail lines (the huge St. Gotthard tunnel had been built in the 1870s with German and Italian funds), but if the Germans wished to seize the routes they would find the tunnels blocked, the rails destroyed.

In August 1940, the mountain divisions Hitler had ominously dispatched to the Swiss border were moved to the Channel coast where they were to take part in Operation Sea Lion, the planned invasion of Britain. By mid-September, after the Luftwaffe's failure to establish air superiority over the English coast, Sea Lion was cancelled. Most historians agree that Hitler had little enthusiasm for that amphibious undertaking from the beginning. Once the summer ended, the unpredictability of the Channel rendered an invasion attempt impractical.

On October 4, von Menges submitted a revised attack plan against Switzerland, and on the same day an additional plan, drawn up separately, was submitted by a Major Bodo Zimmerman to XIIth Army Group.

The economic squeeze on Switzerland had already begun. William Shirer wrote on October 15: "This winter the Germans, to show their power to discipline the sturdy, democratic Swiss, are refusing to send Switzerland even the small amount of coal necessary for the Swiss people to heat their homes. The Germans are also allowing very little food into Switzerland, for the same shabby reason. Life in Switzerland this winter will be hard." Despite their disadvantageous position, however, the Swiss would concede nothing to the Germans except what was expected of a neutral state under international law. As opposed to Sweden, which allowed an entire German division to cross its territory the following spring, prior to the invasion of Russia, as well as numerous Luftwaffe overflights, the Swiss would not allow foreign troops on their territory. German soldiers en route to the Mediterranean theater would have to bypass Switzerland, through France or Austria. The Germans had already learned how Swiss fighter pilots reacted to encroachments in the air.

Swiss intelligence had meanwhile come across unsettling news. During the French collapse in mid-June, German troops had discovered a load of documents on an abandoned train at the town of La Charité-sur-Loire, near Dijon. Included were records of the secret arrangements made between Guisan and French military leaders for mutual defense. Hitler was said to have discussed the documents with Mussolini at a meeting on July 1, and then furiously read parts of them aloud to Joseph Goebbels at a conference in the Black Forest on July 2. If Hitler needed a pretext to order an invasion of Switzerland— whether to justify the action to his General Staff or to the German people—he now had it in his hands. The famously neutral state, he could claim, had secretly been conspiring to ally itself with France.

The fact that the Germans did not publicly announce the documents, and only through intelligence did the Swiss learn what they knew, increased Guisan's anxiety. Given Hitler's methods, the powder keg of La Charité would only be set off in conjunction with a military action, simultaneously used to justify the attack. Once the Nazis released the documents, too, most of the Swiss government and army staff would be learning of Guisan's arrangements with the French for the first time.

Throughout the fall, Swiss troops and artillery took position in the Alps. Guns were sighted on approach routes through defiles, and emplacements were located to command fields of fire from above. As small units maneuvered among the mountains to gain knowledge of the terrain, vast caverns were blasted into the rocks to hold ammunition and stores, and to provide quarters for the men. The question, however, remains: if the Germans had attacked Switzerland, occupying the cities in the nothern part of the country, how long could the Swiss Army in the Alps have held out? Stockpiles of supplies, once the Redoubt concept was fulfilled, were only designed to last for six months. How, beyond that time, was the National Redoubt to sustain itself?

General Guisan had had one unfortunate experience reaching out for an ally. Almost comically, in fact, the French corps that had been intended to support Switzerland in the event of an attack had indeed crossed the border during the Battle of France—45,000 men had laid down their arms and become internees. Nevertheless, by enacting his Redoubt strategy in 1940 in the face of overwhelming German military might, Guisan evidently looked beyond the catastrophe of France toward other nations that would eventually rise to contest the existence of Hitler's Thousand-Year Reich.

During the period when only two democratic nations—Britain and Switzerland—held out against what appeared to be overwhelming Nazi military might, Winston Churchill, from London, and Guisan, from his field headquarters, can be seen as leaders integral to their respective countries' independent existence. Both nations could have succumbed to Hitler's threats—in Britain's case simply by accepting an armistice; in Switzerland's by foregoing its national identity, handing over its Jewish population and accepting the "New Order" in Europe—but were determined not to do so. This is not to underestimate the courage of the populations of both nations, who were resolved to resist Nazism in confrontational combat, and to whom leaders may have reflected, rather than have created, the national will.

Still, if Britain had fallen, or worked out an accommodation with the Third Reich, Switzerland's stance in 1940–41 would have been untenable. A New Order would indeed have settled on Europe and the Swiss would sooner or later have had to join. Instead, Britain held a trump card, an English-speaking people from the New World who were already supporting the Allied war effort against German hegemony in Europe with material, and who were preparing to commit their young men to battle in total war. As Swiss historian Jürg Stüssi-Lauterburg wrote: "Morally Switzerland held out because of its belief in democracy, freedom and God. Politically, Switzerland held out because Great Britain did, and because behind Britain there would eventually be the great power of the United States."

6

DAYLIGHT BOMBING

At seven o'clock in the morning on August 13, 1943, 114 B-24 Liberators assembled in the air over Benghazi, Libya. Their mission was to cross the Mediterranean, Balkans and Alps to destroy the Messerschmitt fighter works at Wiener-Neustadt near Vienna, 1,200 miles away. The bombers were equipped with extra gas tanks in their bomb bays, but still had only enough fuel there and in their wing tanks to reach the target and then, barely, return to North Africa.

Pilot Alva ("Jake") Geron's B-24, *Death Dealer*, was an oddity because it had survived the Ploesti raid two weeks earlier in condition to fly again. On August 1, a fleet of Liberators had made a daring attack from Benghazi on the Romanian city of Ploesti, the largest oil center of the Axis. Coming in on the target at treetop level, the B-24s had suddenly been devastated by a wall of AA fire bursting from guns hidden in haystacks, barns, rooftops and even church steeples. The boxcars of a German freight train had dropped their walls to reveal flak batteries as the train raced along the bombers' path, firing away. The B-24s were flying so low they were convulsed by their own bomb blasts over the target; some were destroyed while flying through debris thrown up by bombs of the ship in front of them. Inevitably, German fighters came racing in from above to find the American formations broken up, no longer able to protect each other with defensive fire. Like wolves on a herd of deer, the fighters tore at the Liberators as the survivors turned and tried to make it for home. Out of 177 B-24s, 53 were destroyed on the raid, 55 others so badly damaged they were scrapped. *Death Dealer* was one of only 33 planes that escaped intact enough to return to the air on short notice, though it needed to replace one crewman, Sgt. Paul Daugherty, who had been killed during the mission.

On August 13, an air raid alert sounded over eastern Switzerland near the Austrian border. Beginning in May 1940, many Swiss border towns had been bombed, presumably by accident, by German or British planes. The approach of any combat aircraft across the border was thus cause for alarm. On that day the alert was prompted by the American plane *Death Dealer,* which had lost its number three engine en route to Wiener-Neustadt and then its number two when it was hit by flak over the Messerschmitt works. The craft had fallen out of its formation and was trailing smoke. Pilot Geron said, "We were no longer able to maintain altitude. We then took up a heading that we thought would take us to Switzerland. We flew through mountains, avoiding those peaks that were higher than we were."

Geron passed over a body of water he thought was Lake Constance. The sinking plane circled above Swiss territory looking for a place to land. Sgt. Donald Grimes, the radioman, recalled, "We were in the back of the aircraft and were prepared to bail out on a signal from the pilot—but we never got the signal and suddenly we found we were too low to jump. There was nothing to do but ride it in." The crew assumed crash positions. Geron found a field near the town of Thurau and was able to make a landing with the wheels down. After landing, the U.S. airmen still weren't sure what country they were in, and began setting off charges to destroy the plane. The crew moved off a couple of hundred yards and were watching the B-24 burn when an old man walked up. Grimes said, "He was smoking a long curved pipe and looked like my vague idea of what a Swiss was supposed to look like. I said, 'Switzerland?' and he said 'Ja.' This was the first time I knew where we were!"

Unfortunately *Death Dealer*'s crew would suffer an additional loss before the war was over. While housed at the U.S. airmen's internment camp at Adelboden, gunner Sgt. Richard Ryan tried to escape but was caught and sent to the Swiss punishment camp at Wauwilermoos. His determination to escape only having increased, he tried again and succeeded in getting across the border to France. There, however, he was caught in civilian clothes by the Germans and transferred to a prison camp in the Reich.

Death Dealer was the first U.S. combat aircraft to arrive in Switzerland during the war, its crew the first of the American internees. Swiss specialists from Dubendorf air base near Zurich arrived to examine the wreckage of the B-24. This was their first look at one of the big American bombers they had heard of. In the weeks and months to come they would encounter scores of others as well as hundreds more airmen. It would be only days, in fact, before the Swiss would have their first close-up look at a Flying Fortress.

August 17, 1943 marked the first anniversary of the start of the U.S. strategic air war against Germany. The campaign had gotten off to a slow start, the Americans having not fully assessed the magnitude of the challenge that lay ahead.

In 1942 the American effort began with a raid by twelve B-17s against railyards at Rouen, France. All the planes returned without serious damage. The newly formed Eighth Air Force in England mounted similar small raids in the following months against targets in France and the Low Countries, losing only two planes in 13 missions. The Luftwaffe fighter pilots, though already seasoned in destroying British craft, seemed to be holding back, sizing up the huge, heavily armed American bombers. Then, on October 9, the Luftwaffe contested a U.S. raid on steelworks in the French city of Lille, knocking down three Forts and a Liberator while suffering the loss of two fighters. For a few weeks bad weather grounded the U.S. fleet, but on November 23, Americans in 56 B-17s met a nasty surprise in a raid on St. Nazaire. Instead of coming in from behind, the traditional fighter approach to a bomber, German fighters from JG (Jagdgeschwader, or fighter group) 2 began attacking them head-on at closing speeds of up to 600 mph. The nose of the B-17 was the most vulnerable part of the U.S. aircraft and the least heavily armed. Six bombers went down and two others had to ditch in the Channel. The days of Luftwaffe hesitation had ended.

The slow start of the U.S. air campaign brought to a head the ongoing argument between the leaders of the USAAF and Britain's Bomber Command. The British had been fighting for three years and had already wreaked massive destruction on Germany. On May 30–31, 1942, when nothing else was going right for British arms, Bomber Command had all but destroyed the German city of Cologne with its first "thousand bomber raid." The raid was as much a propaganda effort as a military one and had required every aircraft the British could muster from their training schools and reserve, mostly twin-engined Wellingtons. They were able to launch two more raids of comparable size the next month before settling back to their normal level, about 300 planes per mission. Nevertheless, the British had already established a means to hit hard at Germany and desired the Americans to reinforce their air strategy: area bombing of cities at night.

The neophytes from the New World had their own ideas about how to conduct air war and refused to join the British program. The Americans believed in daylight precision bombing of industrial targets. U.S. air doctrine held that Germany could be rendered impotent by destroying certain key sectors of its economy and armaments industry far more quickly than by lavishing bombs blindly in the dark on civilian "housing." And the USAAF believed that its Flying Fortresses and Liberators—fast, sturdy craft defended by ten or more guns aiming in all directions, could do the job, even in daylight.

Unfortunately, in late 1942 Eighth Air Force had difficulty building up strength in planes due to America's late start in the war. Many raids were launched against German U-boat pens on the Atlantic, targets that called for daylight precision; however, the steel and concrete structures had been built specifically to withstand bombing and suffered only superficial damage. That fall, too, several B-24 groups had to be transferred from England to North Africa, where the only land fighting between the Western Allies and Axis was taking place. By then British leaders had soured on the Americans' independent strategic air effort and were preparing to insist that the USAAF's remaining strength in England be incorporated into their nighttime program. The showdown came at the Casablanca Conference, where on January 20 Eighth Air Force commander Ira C. Eaker met privately with Winston Churchill. The Prime Minister stated his case:

> Here we were at the beginning of 1943. The Americans had been in the war for more than a year. They had all the time been building up their air power in England, but so far they had never thrown a single bomb on Germany by their daylight methods. . . . We had been led to believe at Washington the year before that in four or five months very heavy deliveries of

bombs would be taking place by American aircraft, but nothing had happened, though an immense expenditure of resources had been made.

Eaker, however, tenaciously made his argument that within a few months the American preparations would pay off. He also included a catchphrase, "round the clock bombing," which appealed to Churchill's sense of theater. The world would learn that the Germans were to be given no respite from the power of the Western Allies, day or night. Churchill, savoring his new slogan, withdrew his objections to the American strategy. One week later, Eaker delivered early on his vow by launching nearly 100 U.S. bombers against the German naval base at Wilhelmshaven, forty miles into Germany from the Dutch border. Due to bad weather and fighters (three Forts were lost) the target emerged from the smoke largely unscathed, but the U.S. air campaign against Germany had at long last begun.

As spring of 1943 arrived, Eighth Air Force continued to mount as many attacks on the Third Reich as it could, refining its tactics while struggling to maintain frontline strength. The worst raid came in April against a Focke-Wulf factory at Bremen. The approaching fleet of 115 B-17s was torn apart by a frontal attack by the Luftwaffe's elite JG-1 with the loss of 16 aircraft (48 others damaged). At Bremen, as elsewhere, American gunners thought they had shot down dozens of fighters, but German claims, proven by postwar records, were otherwise. Aside from the common circumstance of gunners on different planes claiming the same kill, bomber crewmen were often misled by the German fighters' evasive tactics: a sudden twisting dive to gain airspeed and to avoid defensive fire, while exhaust smoke would pour from the fighter's engine. During this period, the 305th Bomb Group's Colonel Curtis LeMay developed the "combat box" formation, which provided fields of fire for an optimum number of guns to bear on interceptors. The box consisted of three staggered squadrons separated by 1,000 feet: a lead and then two squadrons following, one above and to the left, the other below and to the right.

By April 1943, Eighth Air Force had lost, along with 100 aircraft, two-thirds of its original crew strength. General Eaker, backed by Hap Arnold, not only had to fight the Germans but his superiors in Washington who themselves were beset with requests for more planes from the Navy, Pacific Theater, and the Ninth Air Force in North Africa. Thus far Eaker was making do with four B-17 bomb groups—the 91st, 303rd, 305th and 306th—and two B-24 groups—the 44th and 93rd. An additional, albeit minor, front in the war opened up between crewmen of the two American bomber types when they were off duty, a conflict in which the B-24 men did not hold the advantage. The Liberator was not only a strikingly homely aircraft—in canine terms next to the B-17 like a big basset hound next to a collie—it also had various mechanical problems due to its accelerated manufacturing development. Most disturbing was a sentiment discovered by test pilot Crocker Snow, who interviewed bomber crews in England on behalf of the USAAF command. He reported: "When discussing tactics with experienced B-17 crews, many of them observed that they would just as soon be accompanied by a squadron of B-24s on a raid as have fighter cover. Their reason: the German fighters would concentrate on the B-24s and leave the B-17s pretty much alone; why, they weren't sure."

On further investigation, Snow found that on the Liberator, which unlike the Flying Fortress had all manually sighted machine guns, the gunners were aiming wrong. Enemy fighters approaching a bomber from the flank would employ a "pursuit curve," first aiming their nose ahead of the target and then angling back to rake the entire plane with fire. B-24 gunners were apparently "leading" the attacking fighters, firing ahead of them, when they should have been firing behind them, anticipating the curve. The shortcomings in gunnery tactics and mechanical teething pains of the B-24 were, however, soon ironed out. The Liberator, superior in range and more versatile than the Fort in some respects, went on to become the most numerous American bomber of the war, with more than 18,000 employed in all theaters.

In May 1943, Eighth Air Force benefited from the fact that Allied leaders had finally begun to contemplate an invasion of France, which could only be preceded by a vast increase in the USAAF's efforts against Germany from England. Eaker was promised an additional 1,000 aircraft by mid-summer and nearly 2,000 more by the end of the year. The Anglo-American Combined Chiefs of Staff termed the new offensive that was about to take place "Pointblank." Its main target was the Luftwaffe—in the air and at its industrial source. The Americans still lacked a long-range escort fighter, but were confident that their "heavies" could range deep into Germany by themselves to deliver lethal blows.

On August 17, exactly a year after its first raid and less than three weeks after Ninth Air Force's maelstrom over Ploesti, Eighth Air Force launched its largest raid yet, a two-pronged assault on Messerschmitt works at the city of Regensburg and on ball bearing factories at Schweinfurt. That morning, German radar stations throughout France and the Low Countries locked on to the approaching armada, radioing course and direction to fighter airfields throughout Germany and its occupied territories. The 140 B-17s of the Regensburg contingent went in first and began losing planes over Belgium, then more over Germany as some 300 Luftwaffe fighters attacked. The trick invented by Eighth Air Force was that while the enemy fighters were refueling, awaiting the bombers' return journey from Regensburg, the B-17s were really continuing south to U.S. bases in North Africa—the war's first "shuttle" mission. In the confusion it was hoped that the 220 Fortresses assigned to Schweinfurt could slip in and destroy the Germans' vital ball bearing works.

It turned out to be the worst day yet for Eighth Air Force. Thirty-six of the Fortresses assigned to Schweinfurt went down in flames on their way to, over, or on their long return trip from the target. At ten men per ship that meant a loss of 360 trained pilots and aircrew. In the Regensburg wing another 24 planes were shot down although the Germans were indeed surprised that those shattered bomb groups kept heading south, not re-running the gauntlet back across Germany and France to England. In North Africa, the B-17 crewmen were dismayed to find poor maintenance facilities and supplies. Gunners had to refill their own planes with gas. Dozens of machines had to be left behind in the desert because they couldn't be repaired. Later, on the return flight to England, three more were lost to German fighters over France. Once all tallies were in, of the 360 planes involved in the dual raid, a total of 147 were lost or written off. The Germans lost 36 fighters and another 12 badly damaged.

A B-17 named *High Life*, piloted by Donald Oates, flew in the 100th Bomb Group of the Regensburg wing. Radioman Jim Scott recalled: "The enemy fighters swarmed on us about the time we crossed into Germany. The fighters came at us like jackals. I felt like an old man whose nerves had become petrified." In a bomber stream there was no option to retreat and nowhere to hide. If a plane was forced to drop out of formation its danger only increased because it lost the relative protection of other gunners in its formation. From the Luftwaffe perspective, single crippled bombers were the best targets; groups that had lost their cohesion were also attractive. The greatest challenge for the enemy were groups that stayed tightly in their box, protecting each other with defensive fire.

But *High Life* had no choice. Its number two and three engines were hit by fighters and another was windmilling, dragging the aircraft down. In order to lighten the craft Oakes ordered the bombs released, and they fell somewhere near Heilbronn, but the B-17 had fallen behind its group and was falling from the sky. Scott said, "The pilot ordered the crew to prepare to bail out. But before he made the final decision and rang the bailout alarm, our navigator, Hiram Harris, advised Oakes that Switzerland was only about thirty to forty minutes away." Deciding that he should make a run for Switzerland, Oakes swung *High Life* on the course that Harris had plotted.

"Our crippled Fortress was now down to about ten thousand feet as we sighted Lake Constance in the distance. We continued to lose altitude as we neared the lake. Suddenly a barrage of flak erupted around us. Luckily our Fortress was not hit and no one in the crew was hurt. We made it safely across the lake without further incident. The pilots looked for a flat piece of land and spotted an open field, empty, except for a farmer. The landing gear would not go down so we cranked the wheels down manually only to discover that a tire had been ruined by flak. Hastily we cranked the wheels up again and assumed our crashlanding positions. I prayed and silently cursed the Germans as our Fortress was making the approach for a crashlanding. When the pilots brought *High Life* in for a wheels-up landing, there was a terrifying shock from the initial impact, together with the sound of tearing metal. As soon as the aircraft came to a halt, we scrambled out of the various exits."

Scott continued: "Swiss soldiers, in full battle dress and armed with rifles, appeared and surrounded us. The Swiss officer in charge told us in flawless English, 'For you the war is over. You are in Switzerland.'"

One more B-17 came into Switzerland that day, *Battle Queen/Peg Of My Heart* from the 390th Bomb Group assigned to Regensburg.

Piloted by Stephen Rapport, the Fortress had lost two engines to fighters and, unable to stay in the air, crashlanded in a meadow east of Bern. A young Swiss girl was the first person to greet the airmen as they scrambled out of their plane, and she graciously informed them they had made it to Switzerland. The tail gunner, Ricardo Robledo, had been hit by an enemy fighter pass, so he was rushed to a hospital. The rest of the crew, in violation of standing orders, didn't try to destroy their plane. Perhaps an aircraft nicknamed "Peg Of My Heart" resists demolition once it has delivered a crew to the only safety within reach. *Peg,* as well as *High Life,* were considered for repair by Swiss airmen who soon arrived on the scene, but instead the machines were only examined, dismantled and put into storage. Many more American bombers would soon be arriving.

That night British Bomber Command made a contribution to the Allied war effort far greater than its usual nocturnal assaults on German population centers. Almost 600 British four-engine heavies— Lancasters, Stirlings and Halifaxes—crossed the North Sea and the neck of Denmark to hit a small island off the German coast named Peenemünde. Only toward the end of the raid did the German night fighter groups around Berlin realize what was happening, and they raced north to down 40 British bombers at the tail end of the raid. But the net result of the attack was positive. Along with a number of facilities and workshops destroyed, the British had killed one of Germany's leading rocket scientists, Walther Thiel, as well as a large number of laborers. They had hit the developmental staging ground for the V-1 flying bomb and V-2 rocket which would eventually soar against England. Wernher von Braun and his fellow scientists were forced to disperse their testing and production to more secure locations. The secret German rocket program had been set back to a significant degree.

Three weeks after Schweinfurt-Regensburg, which in the American mind may be viewed, perhaps with a trace of bitterness, as most successful only as a diversion for that evening's Peenemünde, the Eighth Air Force launched another big daylight raid into southern Germany, this time aimed at factories around Stuttgart. The elements took a hand as 338 B-17s arrived over the city on September 6 to find it completely clouded over. The leads couldn't identify the target; some groups flew past the city while others circled around. In clouds, the tight formations tended to loosen up because of fear of collision, and

Luftwaffe fighters jabbed in and among the bomb groups, downing 33 planes. It was mass confusion over the target, with bombers eating fuel while disoriented and under fire. Twelve additional Fortresses were lost in the English Channel when they ran dry attempting to return to base. Others tried to make it to Switzerland through the cordon of fighters over southern Germany, four of them succeeding.

Vance Boswell was navigator of a Fortress called *Raunchy*, piloted by Sam Turner, which lost three engines over Stuttgart. In the ball turret underneath the aircraft, gunner Sgt. Joe Moloney had been killed by enemy fire though the rest of the crew weren't initially aware he had been shot. Boswell recalled, "The fighters came on us like a bunch of bees. . . . We were on one engine as we flew over Friedrichshaven at 300 feet, then out over the lake [Constance]. Sam did some great flying. He had no flaps, no air speed, indicator, nothing but guess and by golly. The landing on the water was perfect—the B-17 broke apart in the middle but we all got out. The Swiss came out by boat and took us to land. The Germans also came out, but the Swiss would not give us up. Thank God for that!"

Boswell was permanently blinded in his left eye and lost the use of his left arm on the mission; pilot Turner had been wounded by shrapnel in the chest. It took over a month before the Swiss could raise *Raunchy* from 230 feet beneath the surface of Lake Constance and recover the body of the ball turret gunner. In the interim, the interned American crew's accommodations at the Swiss town of Adelboden were dubbed "Camp Moloney," after their fallen friend and shipmate. It was a name that endured.

Pilot Edward F. Woodward, Jr. arrived in Switzerland that day without a crew or an airplane. His B-17, called *Poon Tang II*, had been hit in the nose over Stuttgart and set on fire. Unbeknownst to Woodward, his entire crew had bailed out after the Fortress appeared doomed. He set the controls on auto-pilot and went back through the plane looking for men. Upon finding himself alone he bailed out from the tail and landed in Switzerland, while the other nine members of his crew came down in Germany. *Poon Tang II* meanwhile veered out of Swiss airspace and crashed on German soil. To the Swiss soldiers who soon arrived at the terminus of his parachute jump, Woodward had to explain that just minutes earlier he had been the pilot of a fully-manned Flying Fortress.

Three other B-17s from the ill-fated Stuttgart mission landed in Switzerland that day: *So What?*, a plane of the 305th Bomb Group on its first mission, short of fuel and with two damaged engines; *Impatient Virgin II* of the 388th Bomb Group; and the incredibly named *Est Nulla Via Invia Virtuti*, flown by a young graduate of St. John's College of Maryland, Martin Andrews. Andrews, in addition to his achievement of convincing his crew to adopt an obscure Latin phrase as their plane's nose art, instead of a scantily clad female or cartoon character, went on to further notable deeds in Switzerland after landing his crippled craft.

Colonel G.F. Ruegg's anti-aircraft unit, stationed three miles from the Austrian border, was the first in the Swiss Army to be equipped with heavy Vickers 75mm guns. The batteries had blasted away on several occasions at foreign aircraft trespassing over the border, but on October 1 they would claim a kill: a B-17 named *Sugarfoot*.

It was the first raid against Germany launched by the Twelfth Air Force in North Africa, aimed at Messerschmitt plants in the city of Augsburg. Unfortunately, the Fortresses that had taken off in the bright, sunny skies of Tunisia found a grim, cloud-covered continent once they had crossed the Alps. Groups back in the bomber stream would encounter other formations returning, having aborted the mission. The Luftwaffe, however, was lurking above the clouds. U.S. Colonel Upthegrove recalled, "We decided to abort and had turned back when thirty or so yellow-nosed Me-109s appeared and began frontal attacks in groups of four to six abreast. I thought I had an idea of how to combat this and as they wheeled around to start their next firing run, I would dive down about 200 feet. They flew right through our formation and after they passed I would climb back 200 feet. We repeated this over and over until the fighters used up their ammunition and withdrew. We continued and the navigator tried to get a position report, but the overcast prevailed until we reached the Alps."

Other ships had a more difficult time. According to *Sugarfoot*'s waist gunner, Marion ("Dale") Pratt: "We were flying on the extreme left of the formation and enemy fighters singled out our plane for concentrated attacks. On the first attack, our ship was hit by cannon and machine gun fire that caused a lot of damage to the front of the plane. A minute or so later, the fighters attacked again, with one diving at us from above. This time we were hit by everything they had. The front, waist and tail were filled with bullets and exploding cannon shells.

"Suddenly, the plane gave a buck and I was thrown to the floor. This may have saved my life for just as I went down a burst of fire went through the waist and back towards the tail. During this attack, I believe that most, if not all, of the five men in the front of the aircraft were killed. I am also convinced that this burst killed Elmer Wheadon, our tail gunner. The B-17 was on fire but I did not know it at the time. We had also crossed the Swiss border and the Swiss were shooting at us as well. I found this out later from a Swiss officer."

Throughout eastern Switzerland, air raid sirens wailed as the U.S. bombers salvoed their bombs through the undercast before turning for their 900-mile journey back to Africa. The German town of Feldkirch near the Swiss border suffered 168 dead; other bombs landed in Switzerland but missed population centers. Swiss AA gunners had been ordered not to fire at three or fewer planes but could fire at larger formations. Colonel Ruegg described the action of his Flak Detachment 21 as *Sugarfoot*'s 99th Bomb Group approached the Swiss border. "The group was flying in three moderately open wedges in line over the Sargans basin. There, the group was once again attacked by German fighters and the battle was observed by Flak Detachment 92. The group did not change formation during the aerial fighting and flew, with some loss of altitude, directly towards our anti-aircraft position." Ruegg's fire control officers directed their sights on the lead B-17 of the left squadron and its wingmate farther to the left. Thirty seconds after the group passed into Switzerland the battery opened fire. Ruegg said, "The second aircraft of the left unit was shot down by our AA fire and plunged towards the earth with long flames trailing from the engines. After a few seconds, the Flying Fortress exploded. Two men bailed out of the plane, their parachutes opening immediately."

One of those parachutes (there were actually three) belonged to Dale Pratt, who, after the vicious fighter attacks, had no recollection of a hit by AA fire. "Just as I was trying to get on my feet again, our plane exploded. I cannot say for sure whether it was the gasoline or the oxygen supply that exploded. When the Fort exploded, it nosed forward and started toward the ground at a tremendous rate of speed. The plane was going down so fast that [the other waist gunner] Norris King and I were floating against the top of the plane.

"Suddenly what was left of the plane, or at least the part that King and I were in, leveled off a little and we fell back on the floor. Everything was a turning and twisting dream. My mind began to clear a little and I began to wonder if I could get out. Through the haze, I saw the waist window with the gun torn off. I gathered all my strength and rolled myself toward the window. I reached it and placed my foot on the edge of the window and shoved myself out into space."

Pratt, King and radio operator Joseph Carroll were *Sugarfoot's* only survivors, the plane crashing into the Swiss countryside. An eyewitness reported: "From the direction of Sargans I could easily see at an altitude of about 2,000 meters an orderly formation of 15 Flying Fortresses. As the formation flew over Bad Ragaz, the AA station there opened fire. Suddenly on one of the planes a stream of fire could be seen. Then an enormous pillar of flame shot skywards. With a powerful explosion the machine burst into pieces and fell flaming east of Bad Ragaz in a wide area left and right of the State Road." The Swiss AA battery had done its job, and may well have caused the final explosion that destroyed the plane. Nevertheless the fruit of its labor was bitter and would be deeply regretted by many Swiss.

Equally tragic was the fate of another B-17 that had run the same gauntlet of fighters over southern Germany. Pilot William Cantwell remembered, "My aircraft was hit repeatedly by machine gun and perhaps cannon fire from the attacking fighters. Engines number one, two and three were out and I had no control of the power setting on number four. It could only be controlled with the ignition switch. All intercom and radio communications equipment was shot out and I could not talk to anyone on board except the co-pilot. The bomb bay doors would not function, so I pulled the manual release for the doors and the bombs. If any were released I did not know it. My altitude at this time was about 18,500 feet and we were going down rapidly. I signaled the men in the nose area to jump. I had previously flipped the bailout alarm switch, and since I could not control the aircraft any longer I abandoned it via the nose hatch behind the others." The pilots, the bombadier and navigator (both wounded) and the top turret gunner escaped the falling Fortress.

Often after being raked by enemy fire a bomber's alarm and intercom were shot up and the men in the back of the plane couldn't hear an order to bail out. Cantwell wrote in his after-action report, "The ship came apart in the air and exploded on contact with the ground. The plane was completely destroyed. Other members of the crew were either wounded or dead at the time of bail-out. No contact with them was possible." The radioman, ball turret gunner, tail and waist gunners all went down with the ship, as did a photographer, Herbert McArdell, who had asked to come along on the mission.

On October 5, a funeral was held at Bad Ragaz for the 13 Americans killed over Swiss soil during the Augsburg raid, and for Joe Moloney whose body had been retrieved from Lake Constance. Attending, along with Swiss officers and civilians, were surviving aircrew, the British and Polish military attachés, and the American attaché, Brigadier General Bernard Legge. James Scott, who had arrived in Switzerland after Schweinfurt-Regensburg, was one of the pallbearers. He wrote: "Each coffin was draped with the Stars and Stripes. After a moving ceremony reflecting on the realities of savage warfare, we lifted the fourteen coffins and began the slow procession.

"As we moved along the few blocks to the cemetery, my hands felt wet. I looked down. What I felt was blood, blood that had seeped out of the coffin and run along the American flag to my hands. I looked around. The hands of other pall bearers were glistening red. We looked at each other. We knew we could not let what was happening detract from the honor and dignity of the occasion. We kept quiet, marched along, and finally reached the cemetery. There, with gentleness and poise, we laid our comrades to rest."

Est Nulla Via Invia Virtuti, the unusual name for Martin Andrews' Flying Fortress, resonated both for the Swiss, who against enormous odds held fast to their independence in the midst of history's most terrible war, and for American airmen, who displayed awe-inspiring bravery simply by following orders. The phrase meant, "No way is impassable to courage." A truly inspirational sentiment, its truth would continue to be tested by the USAAF command.

7

"BLACK THURSDAY"

Beginning with "Blitz Week" at the end of July 1943, Eighth Air Force had made its power felt in Germany. Despite suffering heavy casualties the Americans were now putting 250 to 400 heavies in the air per raid. On October 2, port facilities at Emden on the North Sea were flattened; on the fourth, industrial complexes around Frankfurt. On October 8, Bremen and Vegesack were hit, and the next day factories at Marienbad, the latter with stunning accuracy.

German Armaments Minister Albert Speer recognized, by the fall of 1943, what the Americans were up to. British nighttime raids against German cities, the only targets RAF Bomber Command was capable of hitting in the dark, were more the problem for Joseph Goebbels and his Propaganda Ministry, their task being to buttress civilian morale. In daylight raids, however, the USAAF was evidently alternating attacks against shipyards and aircraft factories with raids on Germany's industrial nerve centers, Speer's domain. The August assault on Schweinfurt, a small city of 65,000 whose primary product was a nondescript industrial component, ball bearings, had revealed the enemy's acumen. The Americans were clearly familiar with the mechanics of industrial mobilization and willing to commit their bomber force to strangle Germany's war economy at its most vulnerable chokepoints. Over 40 percent of German ball bearings—items essential for almost every war machine from guns to tanks to aircraft—had come from Schweinfurt prior to the August raid. Speer hurriedly arranged to disperse the manufacturing; he also allocated greater resources to the Luftwaffe's fighter arm and to its ground anti-aircraft capacity. He only wondered why, having deduced German vulnerabilities, the Americans were not hitting them more repeatedly until they were destroyed.

On the foggy morning of October 14, 1943, at the 305th Bomb Group's base near Chelveston, Northamptonshire, waist gunner Christy Zullo wasn't scheduled for a mission. The preceding week, Eighth Air Force bombers had flown over 1,000 sorties, losing 88 planes with a greater number damaged, so crew and aircraft assignments were being shuffled. But even on his day off, in the early morning hours Zullo walked over to the operations room to see the rest of the boys off. While he was standing around a sergeant called over, "Hey, Christy, do you want to fly?" A ship called *Lazy Baby* was short a waist gunner. To Zullo, there was always the possibility that that day's mission would be a milk run over France, a quick way to get one step closer to the magic number 25, so he decided to step inside the briefing room. Unfortunately, as he later recalled, "Once you go in, they won't let you out." A glance at the map informed him that the day's target was Schweinfurt, a name already notorious to Eighth Air Force flyers. The raid was intended to pit 383 planes against the "killer city" in northern Bavaria, east of Frankfurt, cutting deep into Germany to paralyze enemy industrial capacity with a large unexpected attack. A message from Brigadier General Frederick Anderson was read at each bomb group's briefing:

> This air operation today is the most important air operation yet conducted in this war. The target must be destroyed. It is of vital importance to the enemy. Your friends and comrades that have been lost and that will be lost today are depending on you. Their sacrifice must not be in vain. Good luck, good shooting, and good bombing.

Zullo's 305th Bomb Group had been lucky so far, losing only one ship at Bremen and two on the first Schweinfurt raid, while accomplishing many other missions without loss. This day would be different, and by evening groundcrews at Chelveston would be waiting in vain for ships that would not return. The 305th's luck had run out. Today, the operation known to history as Second Schweinfurt is considered to be the most savagely fought air battle of the war. To the men of Eighth Air Force it has always been known as "Black Thursday."

The timing was off from the outset due to rain-laden fog over England. Taking off on full instruments at one-minute instead of the usual 30-second intervals, it took two hours for the B-17s of the First and Third Air Divisions to assemble above the clouds. The 60 Liberators of the Second Division took so long they were pulled from the mission, some of them returning to base while 24 were diverted to a secondary target off the Dutch coast. The B-17s of the First and Third Divisions were assigned to form into three wings of three groups each. *Lazy Baby*'s 305th Bomb Group, however, had difficulty finding its position in the First Division and ended up crossing the Channel by itself. It finally caught up to the 1st Combat Wing and took up a low, rear position as the fourth group in the wing. Within the group's "coffin corner," so-called because it was most vulnerable to fighter attacks, *Lazy Baby* was in the lowest squadron. The 40th Combat Wing, to which the 305th had originally been assigned, flew on in the center of the division with only two groups.

After a number of ships aborted due to mechanical problems, 291 Flying Fortresses crossed the Continent's coast to rendezvous with their fighter escorts, P-47 Thunderbolts. The big, flat-snouted P-47 was more than twice the weight of a Spitfire or Me-109, and as a consequence could outdive opposing fighters but not outclimb them. Only at high altitude, thin air, could the pug-nosed fighter perform like a greyhound. The Thunderbolts weaved above the bomber formations, eagerly looking for German interceptors to bounce. Dogfights took place over Belgium, with one P-47 and two B-17s shot down, but most of the German fighters, alerted that morning by radar and ground controllers from Calais to Leipzig, held back. The Thunderbolts would soon run out of fuel and then the Forts would be on their own. When the escorts turned back, the Germans began arriving in force. Christy Zullo recalled: "The P-47s left us about five minutes from Frankfort, and there they were, Focke-Wulfs by the dozens. They began with their first pass at our formation, and they were painted exactly like our escort ships. I couldn't tell they were German aircraft until I saw the flashes from their cannon. I began firing and they just kept coming in, one right after another. I hardly knew which one to fire at, but I kept my gun going all the time.

"One Wulf made an attack at the nose of our ship coming in at about eleven o'clock. He hit the bottom of our waist, putting a rip in the floor right between my legs. It went through my boot and cut a nice slice in my heated flying suit, but it did not reach my leg. It frightened me for a while, but when I saw that I was not bleeding, I went back to shooting my gun. On their next pass at us, my oxygen system was shot out, my mask drew close to my face every time I took a breath. Everything began to get black for me, and falling to the floor I managed to reach the walk around bottle. I plugged my mask in and taking a few heavy breaths I began to feel alright again. Another 20mm shell hit in the waist, bursting right over our heads. It put a few big dints in the right waist gunner's helmet and a few scattered holes all over the back of my flak suit. At that instant a piece of flak hit the nose of our ship, breaking the plexiglass and hitting our bombardier and navigator."

Beneath the plane, ball turret gunner Ray Baus was firing away in all directions at nimble fighters that raced with guns blazing through the formation. But then a German shot out the glass of his turret and burst the hydraulic system, drenching Baus with oil. The turret was stuck and Baus, who didn't wear a parachute because of the cramped space, couldn't move it manually. Every time he twisted the crank, the turret shifted the other way.

The nose of the plane had been shattered by a direct hit and subzero wind was pounding the broken bodies of navigator Don Rowley and bombardier Carl Johnson. Both of Rowley's arms were shattered and Johnson was bleeding in torrents, his buttocks shot away. Seconds later, another 20mm shell exploded in the radio room, breaking Hurley Smith's arm and lacing him with dozens of bits of shrapnel. In the waist, a big hole was shot through the floor next to Zullo; he didn't know where it came from. The view from the cockpit was just as bad. One after another, the ships of the 305th Bomb Group were falling in flames from the sky. Quick strings of parachutes would billow beneath some of the doomed bombers, not nearly enough to represent each ten-man crew. Many airmen were either already dead, badly wounded or unable to get to their escape hatches in time. The big fear for flyers in the stricken bombers still in the sky was that gas from the wing tanks would ignite, reaching the bombs and destroying the aircraft in one sudden flash.

The Germans were not only committing all their day fighters—Me

109s and FW 190s—to the battle, they were also sending up Me-110 Destroyers and He-111 and Ju-88 bombers against the American formations. The larger enemy planes would fly outside the 1,000-yard range of the Forts' machine guns, lobbing rockets into the combat boxes. Exploding with four times the impact of flak, the 250-pound rockets could instantly destroy a bomber. Even misses could shake up a formation, forcing it to disperse, making individual aircraft easier prey for single-engine fighters. The 305th was not the only group being slaughtered that day; in the middle wing of First Air Division, where the 305th had originally been assigned to fly, the 306th Bomb Group was losing ten of its fourteen planes. The path of the bomber stream was marked across Germany by spiraling smoke from the pyres of crashed machines and hundreds of aircrew floating down to the certainty of German POW camps.

In addition to the fighter attacks, by the time *Lazy Baby* crossed into Germany it was being rocked by flak from AA emplacements along the Rhine. The port engines were knocked out, and pilot Lt. Edward Dienhart had lost throttle control for numbers three and four. Staying with the formation was no longer imperative because the bomb group had been destroyed, only two of its 16 planes surviving the day. At one point an FW-190 raced in against *Lazy Baby's* shattered nose and Dienhart steered the plane directly at the fighter, forcing it to veer off. The German fighters had begun with slashing attacks from unexpected angles but had grown more confident as the massacre continued. A Focke-Wulf 190 bore in on the B-17 from dead astern, unaware that aboard the smoking sieve of a bomber tailgunner Bernie Segal had been waiting for just that opportunity. The German fighter was ripped by Segal's dual .50 machine guns and disintegrated less than 100 yards away.

In order to save his crew, pilot Dienhart rang the bail-out alarm, but the plane's electrical system had been destroyed, so no one past the cockpit could hear it. He was able to verbally order co-pilot Brunson Bolin and engineer/gunner George Blalock to bail out; Dienhart himself planned to stay with the plane no matter what happened. Ray Baus, still trapped in the ball turret under the plane, saw the two parachutes billow from his craft while the ground was coming ever closer. Dienhart was in a steep dive. Gunners Christy Zullo and Robert Cinibulk came over from the waist and began heaving at the emergency cranks above the turret until finally the three men turned the ball so that Baus could crawl out. By then the bomber was skimming the treetops of southern Germany. Baus recalled, "We were very lucky to only be followed by one Focke Wulf who, having seen the two chutes and dead engines, figured we were goners and left us alone."

Tailgunner Segal emerged from his isolated compartment, traversed the gaping holes in the waist, and came upon the blood-splattered scene of carnage in the front of the plane. Somehow, the badly wounded bombardier Johnson had been able to drag Rowley from his navigator's position in the shattered nose up to the cockpit where he strapped him into the abandoned co-pilot's seat. (Co-pilot Bolin, who spent the rest of the war in a German stalag, later resented being ordered to bail out.) Johnson himself was now lying face down in agony in the nose, almost unconscious from his wounds, being blasted by icy winds generated by the 150 mph airspeed. Segal ripped off the bombardier's equipment and poured sulfa on his wounds. Waist gunner Cinibulk came up and hoisted Johnson on his shoulders. The bomb bay doors were hanging open, so Cinibulk had to do a high-wire act across a 9-inch catwalk to deposit Johnson in the relative protection of the radio room. There, Zullo had dressed Smith's wounds, and the crew, except for Dienhart and Rowley in the cockpit, gathered to wait for what would happen next. They were now far too low to bail out.

For almost an hour, Edward Dienhart piloted the plane alone, heading south. Next to him, blood dripped from Rowley's nearly severed left arm. Then came the good news with the bad. Down on the ground he saw a Swiss flag, meaning there would be no more threats from German fighters or AA fire. But at the same time the terrain was becoming more difficult, hills and ridges cutting the landscape. How to put the plane down, and where?

The navigator sitting next to Dienhart in the co-pilot's seat had been a muscular fellow, always doing push-ups off duty. It was ironic that his arms had been shot off by German fire, and that as the only one of the crew to die, he was the only married man on the plane. It was a further irony that navigator Rowley, barely conscious, was in the cockpit at that moment yet unable to help Dienhart know where to go. Dienhart did not quite trust the Swiss flag he had seen, since the Germans were capable of any sort of treachery. Nevertheless, he had to set the plane down before they lost hydraulics or the engines quit and they helplessly crashed.

Every foot of altitude lost would now be gone for good, even as the terrain was getting higher. Ahead, Dienhart could see a gigantic wall of cloudy peaks. He dodged through a gap between tree-covered heights and then circled, desperately looking for a place to land. After squeezing between two more hills, there it was—a series of fields to his left with what looked like a city beyond. Heading north, he circled back over a small village. He lined up the aircraft on the center of the valley and began to set it down. But at the last minute he saw farm people working in the fields, gaping up at his approach. Using nearly his last ounce of strength, Dienhart pulled up again, not wishing to purchase his crew's safety at the price of innocents on the ground. By now he had run out of choices; no question of an airfield but simply any flat stretch where he could crashland.

Finally he saw a short plateau. He couldn't put the wheels down so the B-17 would go in on its belly; there was no other option this time. Thank God Baus had gotten out of his ball turret. The mortally wounded Rowley called out airspeeds as the plane made its last-chance approach. As *Lazy Baby* came down, Dienhart realized the plateau was not as flat as he had thought, actually broken by rocks and ditches and verging downhill. The ball turret and bomb bay doors were cleanly ripped off the aircraft as it skidded across the ground. A line of trees rose like a wall on the far side of the field and the B-17 appeared to be racing for a collision. Then, fortunately, the field turned into a potato patch of soft ground, dirt flowing in through the open bomb bay, slowing the plane's speed. It twisted sideways but came to a halt just short of the woods. The dying navigator, strapped into the co-pilot's seat, commented through his pain that it was the best landing Dienhart had ever made.

Lazy Baby had landed south of Basel, just a few miles into Switzerland from the German border, about five miles from France. Swiss from three small villages rushed to the scene, along with doctors and Swiss Army troops. The latter were there "more for crowd control than for us," Ray Baus observed. Aside from the three crewmen rushed to a hospital in Basel, the American flyers were put up at a hotel in the village of Aesch. Dienhart checked on Johnson and Smith the next morning and was pleased to find they were doing well.

Rowley didn't make it, however, and was buried in a local cemetery on October 18.

His funeral was attended by hundreds of Swiss, including dignitaries and soldiers in dress uniform. *Lazy Baby*'s surviving crew carried the coffin draped with the stars and stripes. At the end of the service, a score of Swiss troops fired a ceremonial volley, and then, to everyone's surprise, Germans on the other side of the border fired a three-gun salute.

Lazy Baby was the only plane to make it to Switzerland from the fleet that embarked on the second raid against Schweinfurt. Fifty-nine others had been destroyed in the air or gone down over enemy territory; 17 more were termed damaged beyond repair after limping back to their bases or crashlanding in England. By the end of the month several additional airmen from the raid had made it to Switzerland after parachuting into France. 2nd Lt. John Chandler of the 94th Bomb Group landed in Alsace, wounded in the hip and having broken his toes when he hit the ground. He spent a week without food before making contact with the French Resistance. On October 28, he and another airman, Brooklynite James Festa, whose shoes had been blown off during his jump and who suffered from badly blistered feet, were passed across the Swiss border. Another flyer, Mississippian Douglas McClendon, had been shot in the leg before bailing out but was found and cared for by the French, and smuggled across France into Switzerland on the 26th.

As for the attempt to deprive German industry of ball bearings, 221 bombers had reached Schweinfurt and delivered heavy damage. But it turned out that the Luftwaffe had hoarded its own reserve supplies, plus more were made available to the Reich from Sweden. The factories themselves, though temporarily disrupted, had not been put out of commission. Albert Speer doubled his efforts to make sure that essential components of German industry would not again be concentrated in one place, vulnerable to a sudden massive American strike.

From the Luftwaffe's point of view, Second Schweinfurt had been a success. The commander of Germany's air defense forces, Adolf Galland, wrote: "On this memorable day we managed to send up almost all the fighters and destroyers which were available for the defense of the Reich and in addition part of the 3rd Air Fleet, France.

All together, 300 day fighters, 40 destroyers and some night fighters took part in this air battle which for us was the most successful one of the year 1943. We were able to break up several bomber formations and to destroy them almost completely."

There were no more raids into Germany by the Eighth Air Force during the remainder of 1943. Weather was an inhibiting factor as winter closed in, but more important was the fact that daytime deep-penetration raids had proven suicidal against German fighter defenses. It had become statistically nearly impossible for a given bomber crewman in Eighth Air Force to complete 25 missions. (The first plane that beat the odds, *Memphis Belle,* was immediately sent back to the States for a barnstorming tour.) As matters stood by the end of the year, the Germans were trading fighters for bombers, a manpower ratio of 1–2 Germans for 8–10 Allied airmen. The Douhet/Mitchellian concept of war waged from the air had fallen short over Germany, just as it had over Britain when attempted by the Germans. Only British Bomber Command was coming close to implementing the concept, and then only by wreaking mass havoc at night on civilian rather than military targets. Still, the USAAF command remained determined to prove that daylight bombing, as envisioned by its prewar enthusiasts, could eventually be a decisive instrument of modern warfare.

During the production rush just prior to the war, the U.S. had concentrated on bombers rather than emphasizing fighters, as Britain and Germany had done. During the disastrous attacks of 1943, however, it had become clear that American fighters were necessary to protect the bomber streams from enemy interceptors. The United States' twin-engined P-38, the P-39 (given mostly to Russia) and P-40, not to mention the variety of carrier-based aircraft the U.S. employed against the Japanese, had not made the grade over central Europe. The P-47 was a formidable fighter, but its great weight prohibited adding the extra fuel required for long-range missions. Nevertheless, by late 1943 the U.S. had come up with a new invention. Designers melded a sleek fighter airframe with a British Rolls Royce engine and the capacity, through extra fuel tanks, to range alongside the bombers deep into the Third Reich. The new American fighter was the P-51 Mustang.

By January 1944 the Mustang, destined to change the entire nature of the U.S. air campaign, had begun to arrive in strength at airfields throughout England. German fighters would no longer have a free approach at the daylight bomber fleets but instead would have to fight their way through high-performance American fighters every step of the way. Thousands of new aircraft—both fighters and bombers— were pouring from factories in the U.S., tens of thousands of newly trained personnel moving into barracks in England. The Luftwaffe had wrested control of the daylight skies over Germany in the bloody battles of 1943. But as the dismal winter weeks ticked away, the USAAF prepared for the rematch.

8

ARMED NEUTRALITY

Wartime Switzerland, described in the American press at the time as an "oasis of democracy," had by the end of 1943 come to resemble a nation under siege. The government, following the National Redoubt strategy laid down by General Guisan, had poured enormous resources into making the Alps—along the fortress linchpins Sargans–St. Gotthard–St. Maurice—into an impregnable bastion. Tens of thousands of Swiss soldiers manned gun emplacements while 50,000 select ski troops trained among the peaks. The Swiss Army set up two "avalanche schools" to teach officers techniques of creating and aiming snowslides in winter and mud and rock slides in summer. Using a revolving system, citizen soldiers alternated between serving in the Redoubt and returning to their homes to gather crops or work at their jobs. Every man was on call to join his unit should attack appear imminent. Caves, blasted deep within the mountains, had been filled with enormous quantities of food and munitions.

The Swiss population meanwhile had to make do with whatever they could grow, or buy in barren shops. Oil was a precious commodity, coal almost as rare, and both dependent upon German trade shipments. Food (including all edible fats), fodder and heat were rationed, as were certain textiles such as wool. Motor transport was strictly reserved to the army and for essential civilian uses. Refugees had poured into the country, despite efforts by the Federal government and police officials to diminish the flow. At customs houses the Swiss could post regulations, but in the countryside, opposite the long borders with France and Germany, Swiss found themselves sharing their tables with and housing an endless stream of fugitives from Hitler's conquered territories.

The war around Switzerland had developed with one shock after another. In early 1941, the divisions of German Army Group C, which had lain just beyond the Swiss border for over a year, began slipping to new positions in southeastern Europe. On April 6, the Germans launched a dual blitzkrieg against Yugoslavia and Greece. The Yugoslavs, as today, were internally divided, and the country fell in less than two weeks. Some elements of the Yugoslav confederation actually joined the Axis in order to fight the Serbs, who offered the only serious resistance. Greece fell by the end of the month despite the efforts of a 30,000-man British expeditionary force, which evacuated to Crete. On May 20, the Germans invaded Crete by air, forcing the Empire troops to evacuate again, to Egypt.

This new surge of Nazi military aggression sent tremors through Switzerland, which had become the only state on the Continent not conquered by or aligned with the Axis. Even though it had made far more extensive defensive preparations for its size than any of Germany's victims, surely Switzerland's turn would come next. During this period, the Swiss had little to count on other than faith in their own courage, their prepared defensive works, and the determination not to succumb to the expected German attack. Days before the German blitzkrieg in the Balkans, the American Military Attaché in Switzerland sent an appraisal to the Military Intelligence Division of the U.S. General Staff:

> Senior and junior officers recently questioned believe that Swiss morale is high. The nation as well as the Army has confidence in the ability of the latter to defend the National Redoubt. . . . With a determined Army holding this position, its defense appears assured for as long as food and ammunition last. As pointed out previously, the redoubt is not self-sufficient. The valley of the Rhone between Martigny and Brig is the only area which produces foodstuffs in quantity. The Swiss industrial area is north of the position. After a brief delaying action it would necessarily fall into the hands of the enemy.
>
> The Federal Council is weak. Mr. Pilet-Golaz, former President and now Minister of Foreign Affairs, lacks the confi-

dence of the Swiss people. The present President, Mr. Wetter, lacks force. These structural weaknesses, however, are not believed to be of importance from the viewpoint of national defense. In case of a threat of invasion, the Army and the people will follow General Guisan, and the Swiss Army can be depended upon to fight. It is always ready and can be mobilized to full strength in 48 hours.

The analysis accurately portrayed the Swiss paradox. They could not save their entire country in the event of an attack, but on the other hand they, unlike the other small nations of Europe, would not be easily conquered. The Swiss were willing to sacrifice their economy and population centers so that the Army would be able to continue to fight.

Swiss apprehensions of battle, however, were allayed on June 22, 1941, when Hitler implemented his most important decision of the war. The bulk of the Wehrmacht—144 divisions, backed by Romanian, Hungarian, Finnish and Italian troops—invaded the Soviet Union. Stalin, as was the rest of the world outside of British foreign intelligence, was taken completely by surprise. The Swiss breathed a sigh of relief. Few who did not live through the war can appreciate today how the immense power of the Soviet Union, when it stood behind Germany, providing vast amounts of raw material for the German war machine, appeared to put a seal of permanence on the Third Reich. Now the two totalitarian behemoths of Europe were fighting each other, the front moving east toward Asia.

By December the Germans had finally been halted 600 miles deep into Russia on a line Leningrad–Moscow–Rostov on the Black Sea. Contrary to German and most other expectations, the Soviet Union had not collapsed; in fact, during the winter of 1941–42 the Red Army counterattacked. Hitler and Stalin had seemingly become engaged in a prolonged duel to the death.

On December 7, 1941, came Pearl Harbor, through which the Japanese Empire inadvertently provided a means of salvation for democracy in Europe. America immediately became a combatant in the world war. Hitler, not quite realizing the enormity of his problem in Russia, cooperated—fulfilling the hopes of both Churchill and Guisan—by declaring war on the United States. America reciprocated without hesitation, putting into practice the "Germany first" strategy decided upon earlier in talks between Roosevelt and Churchill.

For the next year, Switzerland was out of the crosshairs. As the Germans battled in North Africa against the British, at sea against the Anglo-Americans, and in the Eurasian steppes against the Russians, the small democracy in the center of Europe, in military terms, was relatively unthreatened. This was, nevertheless, a dark time for the Swiss as they stood alone in the Third Reich's shadow receiving the dismal news of continuing Axis victories.

After retreating before Japanese thrusts in the Philippines in early 1942, an entire American army was cornered and forced to surrender. Its commander, Douglas MacArthur, departed Bataan with the vow "I shall return." At Singapore an even larger British Empire force was captured by Japanese troops. In a "naval" battle that would have provoked a grim nod from Billy Mitchell, Japanese aircraft caught two British battleships, the *Repulse* and *Prince of Wales,* off Malaysia and sent them to the bottom. In the Atlantic during the spring of 1942, German U-boats racked up huge totals of sunken Allied shipping, captains dubbing their rich hunting off the well-lit American coast the "happy time." In Africa, General Erwin Rommel shattered the British Gazala Line in Libya, captured 30,000 Empire troops at the port fortress of Tobruk, and by June was advancing on Alexandria and the Nile. On the most important front of the war, deep within the Soviet Union, the Germans had evaded their most dangerous opponent yet, "General Winter," and by mid-summer were advancing on Russia's main oil fields. In May they destroyed a huge Soviet Army near Kharkov and on July 4 successfully concluded their conquest of the Crimea.

It was in this context that Britain's first "Thousand-Bomber Raid" flattened the German city of Cologne (Köln). The only structure left standing in the center of that city after the late-May attack was the ancient Gothic cathedral, which survived only (it was said) because RAF crews were instructed to use it as an aiming point. Bomber Command also unleashed devastating nighttime incendiary attacks on Lubeck and Rostock, two medieval German cities built largely of wood. In response, Hitler ordered Luftwaffe attacks on England that came to be known as the "Baedeker Raids," after the travel guides. Canterbury, Exeter, Bath and Oxford were hit in retaliation for the RAF's attacks on German cultural centers.

In November 1942 an American army landed in French North Africa, in response to which the Germans suddenly occupied Vichy France in order to protect the French Mediterranean coast. Switzerland's last lifeline to the world outside the Third Reich was cut. For two years Vichy, a tenuous enough state, had at least allowed Switzerland to trade with nations outside of Nazi-occupied Europe. A steady flow of chronometers, diamond dies and small machine parts had traversed Vichy from Switzerland since the 1940 armistice. For a while, the Germans had not thought to oversee the postal system, and thousands of small components had been exported from Switzerland in letter packets through the mail. In addition, Swiss craftsmen had disguised tiny components essential for aircraft uses into normal-looking watches, shipping them out by rail past hostile customs officials. Vichy's occupation meant the end of those shipments. Henceforth, all materials coming into or out of Switzerland would be carefully overseen by Gestapo officials.

As for direct trade with Germany, traditionally, as since the war, Switzerland's largest trading partner, the Third Reich demanded ever larger credits for goods. Underlying the tough trade negotiations that Swiss officials were constantly engaged in were two sets of opposing realities: Germany could, at any time, finally launch the military invasion that the Swiss had expected since the beginning of the war; it could furthermore reduce the Swiss population to abject misery simply by cutting off shipments of food and coal.

On the other side, the Swiss had by now gained confidence in the strength of Guisan's Alpine redoubt strategy. Painful as an invasion would be for Switzerland's northern population, the Swiss Army presented the Wehrmacht a challenge that could almost literally be termed insurmountable. In summer 1942 the Germans had ordered their elite 1st and 6th Mountain Divisions to break through the Caucasus range by the Black Sea—a barrier comparable to the Alps—near modern-day Chechnya. Russian forces had blocked key passes and pinned the mountain troops down with small units counterattacking their flanks and rear. The Germans encountered immense difficulties supplying their soldiers among the heights, and finally the entire offensive had to be abandoned. The mountain troops had fought well, but against determined opposition in such terrain could not force a strategic decision. Within the German General Staff the prospect of a war against the Swiss Army fortified in the Alps had become more undesirable than ever.

In credits and trade, Swiss representatives were indeed forced to make concessions to negotiators from the Reich's Economic Ministry, a fact that brought criticism upon Switzerland long after the war (more from the United States than from fellow Europeans). Still, during the entire course of World War II, Swiss military-related trade amounted to only half of one percent of Germany's total output. Given that Albert Speer could have acquired most of that material from other sources, Swiss negotiators in effect permitted only a nominal amount of trade with the Third Reich in return for the means to keep the nation of Switzerland and its people alive. The continued existence of a democratic oasis in central Europe subsequently proved beneficial not just to tens of thousands of refugees, but for millions of other people assisted by the Geneva-based International Committee of the Red Cross, as well as by Switzerland's decision to act officially as protecting power for Allied prisoners of war. Switzerland also played a vital role as a "window on the Reich" for Allied intelligence services. In postwar and even more so in post-Cold War years, the great value of the small democracy that survived in Nazi-held Europe through its own military resources and through a careful economic balancing act to sustain its population has often been underestimated.

Of all the factors that influenced Germany's decision whether or not to invade Switzerland immediately after the fall of France, perhaps foremost was the fact that Switzerland had no coastline or other geographic advantage that would assist Germany against its larger enemies. Economic factors had little or no influence on German military planners during the heady days of 1940. At that time, the German General Staff had assumed that the Alps would be a dividing line between their responsibility and Mussolini's, not anticipating that their inept ally would soon need massive German support. Once the Germans were forced to come to Mussolini's aid, for two years the fighting in the south took place on the Mediterranean Sea and in North Africa. Switzerland, for centuries regarded as a vital crossroads in European wars, had not been considered essential by the General Staff for operations in the first years of World War II. Its free press, defiant independence, and the existence of its territory as a haven for refugees—irritating as these factors were to Nazi leaders—did not by themselves amount to a significant enough rationale to justify invasion when there was a larger war to be fought elsewhere.

The pending Allied invasion of southern Europe in 1943, to be met by the German counterinvasion of Italy, changed the equation. The armed neutral now stood as a formidable barrier separating German reinforcements and supplies from its armies confronting the Allied onslaught in the south. Swiss transit routes through the Alps, now wired with tons of demolitions ready to be set off at first news of a German attack, had regained their vital importance.

On March 3, 1943, General Guisan met with the head of SS Foreign Intelligence, Walter Schellenberg, at an inn near Bern. Sitting down with such a high-ranking Nazi was a risky move, but Guisan chose a public place and even signed his name in the inn's guestbook. At the meeting, Schellenberg posed an important question: Would Switzerland defend itself against *any* foreign invader? Guisan thought the question superfluous and simply referred the SS general to a detailed interview he had recently given to a Swedish journalist. Three days later, Schellenberg met with Guisan again, having sent a request for Guisan to provide a direct reply. Guisan handed him a newly composed declaration that spoke of Switzerland's historic role as guardian of the Alpine passes. It concluded:

Whoever invades our country is self-evidently our enemy. He will be confronted by a united army of the greatest strength and a nation imbued with a single accord. At such a time there exists only one militant Switzerland inspired by one will. Because of the topography of our country we are able to defend above all our Alpine front.

Whatever may come to pass this assurance is immovable and unalterable. No doubt can arise about that either now or in the future.

On March 19, Swiss intelligence reported a series of discussions at Hitler's headquarters about an invasion of Switzerland. A specialist in mountain warfare, General Edouard Dietl, had supposedly been transferred from Finland to Munich, where he had been given the pick of Germany's airborne and mountain troops. This information set off a flurry of reactions, collectively known as the "March Alarm," during which the Swiss braced themselves for an attack. It soon became evident, however, that the Germans had not massed their forces on the border, and after the war it was learned that concrete plans for an invasion in March had not been formed. One theory is that the Germans prompted the alarm to reinforce a particularly tough round of trade negotiations that were then under way; another is that the Germans wanted to test Swiss preparedness. In any event, Schellenberg took credit for Germany's decision not to invade, claiming to his contacts in Swiss intelligence that he had talked the Nazi leadership out of the idea.

The Germans' primary anxiety about the Swiss at this time, focusing particularly on General Guisan, was that the country might open its borders to the Anglo-Americans once the Allies invaded southern Europe. The Germans themselves were debating whether to hold Italy in its Alpine north, as Rommel counseled, or south of Rome, as advocated by Field Marshal Albert Kesselring. At this time they were also wary of Allied invasions of Sardinia, Greece or southern France. The possibility, strongly suspected by the Nazis, that Switzerland might abandon its neutrality and join the Allied cause once the Anglo-Americans arrived on the Continent played an important role in German strategic planning. By this point the Germans had discovered Guisan's secret arrangements with the French in 1939–40. What if he had made similar plans with the Anglo-Americans? Swiss territory, if opened to the Allies, would be a springboard into southern Germany.

Of course, Guisan's mutual defense plans with the French had been contingent on a German attack against Switzerland. He had not betrayed the centuries-old policy of Swiss neutrality but only planned ahead should it be violated by Germany. If the Germans attacked in 1943, it could be anticipated that the Swiss would request Allied assistance, already potentially available in the form of air power. Schellenberg's mission, which may or may not, as he claimed, have been prompted by admiration for the Swiss, was to determine if Swiss neutrality was still in force. If the Germans respected Swiss territory, it was vital that the country not become a staging ground for Allied offensive operations. Schellenberg, after the meetings, thus calmed his superiors in Berlin by receiving from Guisan what amounted to a firm vow that Switzerland would resist *any* invader. For his part, Guisan, who had no fear of invasion by fellow democracies, took the opportunity to impart his country's utter determination to resist attack, which in his estimation could only come from Germany.

Guisan received a reprimand from the Swiss Federal Council on April 6 which, amid expressions of flattery, criticized him for meeting with a German officer so close to the Reich's center of power. Such discussions, he was told, should be left to the political, not military, authorities. In retrospect, however, any meetings between Walter Schellenberg and Federal Councillors, except for stalwarts in the mold of Rudolf Minger, would have raised more eyebrows than General Guisan had by simply taking the opportunity to convey to the Germans his clear conviction: Switzerland, as always, was ready to fight.

By the summer of 1943 the Third Reich was contracting from its far-flung battlefields on Europe's periphery. In the Atlantic, B-24 Liberators flying from Newfoundland, Greenland, Iceland and Northern Ireland had proven to be a scourge to U-boat wolfpacks in the Atlantic. In Russia, the Germans had gone in too deep and lost an entire army on the Volga at Stalingrad. One of the casualties there was Otto von Menges, who had drafted the initial 1940 assault plans against Switzerland and had subsequently been promoted to chief of staff of the 24th Panzer Division. He died on February 2, 1943, the day the last German pocket in Stalingrad surrendered. In July, the Germans attempted one last strategic offensive in Russia, on either side of the city of Kursk. It resulted in history's largest tank battle, but more importantly in conclusive proof that the Red Army had at last—even without the help of the weather—grown as strong as the Wehrmacht. The Russians promptly launched a series of counteroffensives, with the Germans falling back, at first barely able to maintain a cohesive front.

In the Mediterranean, after liquidating Axis forces in North Africa in spring 1943, the combined Anglo-American armies invaded Sicily in July. Their next stop was mainland Italy, which was invaded on both sides of its boot by British and American armies in September. Mussolini was overthrown in a royalist coup, backed by the army, and Italy attempted to switch to the Allied side. Germany, however, invaded the country and set up defensive lines across the peninsula as far south as possible. The "soft underbelly of Europe," as Churchill termed it, was in fact crisscrossed by formidable mountain ranges and east-west rivers. The Allies' initial second front would entail an arduous climb against a succession of jagged, German-held heights.

To the Swiss, a sense that the war had once expanded beyond Europe was replaced by a sense that it was falling back on them. In particular, Allied advances in the Mediterranean meant that the Swiss transport routes through the Alps would become essential, not only for German support of Italy with coal and other goods, but with munitions and supplies for entire German frontline armies. The Swiss, as neutrals, were committed to the principle that no aggressive military transport could take place on their territory. Meanwhile, the Brenner Pass, which connected Italy and Austria through the Alps, was the primary conduit for German war matériel to the south. U.S. bomber crews viewed the pass as a death trap, with flak batteries emplaced so high on the flanking mountains it seemed as though the AA guns were actually firing down at them. To German soldiers traversing the pass, however, the constant Allied air attacks seemed equally lethal. Possession of the Swiss Alpine routes, miles of which consisted of tunnels impervious to bombing, would have solved the Germans' dilemma.

In December 1943, while the American 5th Army hammered against dug-in German divisions around Monte Cassino, an SS colonel named Hermann Böhme was ordered to draft another plan for the invasion of Switzerland. Included in his analysis was the unpromising observation: "The fighting spirit of Swiss soldiers is very high, and we will have to equate it approximately to that of the Finns." Nevertheless, Böhme estimated that 15 Wehrmacht divisions attacking from four directions, assisted by airborne landings in the mountains, could overwhelm the Swiss. He evidently anticipated Allied progress in Italy that would make seizure of the Alps necessary. He recommended that his plan be executed in late summer 1944, a timing that indicates he did not anticipate the more important front that would open up in northern France on June 6, D-Day.

Part of the problem the Swiss faced as the Germans continued to contemplate invasion was that the nature of the Wehrmacht had changed dramatically since the sunny spring of 1940. While in the intervening years the encircled Swiss had been able to upgrade their army incrementally in infantry weapons and considerably in its training and Alpine fortifications, the Germans had made a larger leap into the latter half of the 20th century with larger, more powerful weapon designs. Whereas most German tanks in the war's first year had been Mark III's, mounted with small cannon, or Mark II's with machine-guns, now the German Army was equipped with huge Tigers and Panthers, sporting, respectively, high-velocity 88mm and 75mm guns. German infantry had been rearmed, carrying rapid-firing Schmeissers, and had a higher proportion of mortars and machine guns per unit than any army in the world.

The Wehrmacht, due to its experiences in Russia, had also taken on a darker political hue. Waffen SS divisions, Nazi-indoctrinated military units, had proliferated. Independent units like the Dirlewanger and Kaminski Brigades had been formed to ruthlessly suppress civilian resistance. The motorized regiment Leibstandarte Adolf Hitler, once earmarked for Operation Tannenbaum, had evolved into the 1st SS Panzer Division. The Totenkopf (Death's Head) Division was now 3rd SS Panzer, its reputation blotted by atrocities. Due to Himmler's influence in the highest councils of the Third Reich, Waffen SS units had been given first priority in weapons and—mostly volunteer—manpower. They had become the cutting edge of the Wehrmacht in offensive operations.

Adding immeasurably to the horrific depth of history's greatest war, in January 1942, after a secret conference at Wannsee near Berlin, the Nazi leadership had embarked upon a program of mass murder of Jewish civilians. The Third Reich thus departed from the lineage of Europe's previous conquering powers—Napoleonic France, Charles XII's Sweden, Phillip II's Spain and others back to Charlemagne and ancient Rome—and instead revealed itself as a criminal aberration in world and European history. Adolf Hitler did not behave along rational lines or according to accepted rules of warfare, a fact the Swiss had begun to perceive as early as 1933. As the war went on, the German Army, once made up of draftees or enlistees not unlike the Swiss themselves, increasingly consisted of hardened veterans accustomed to killing in the service of a government that seemed to revel in it. An invasion of Switzerland, undertaken by soldiers withdrawn from the crucible of the Eastern Front, would make up in viciousness, in addition to modern equipment, what it lacked in buoyant enthusiasm or national pride.

To Henri Guisan, confidence had to be placed in the Swiss citizen-soldier, who, once bloodied, would be able to confront the Wehrmacht man to man. After the first clashes, he hoped, the Swiss soldiers would have vindicated their hard training with valuable combat experience. He continually invoked the proud battles across centuries of Swiss history—from Morgarten to Marignano—as a means of inspiring his soldiers not to fail.

On April 28, 1944, searchlights at Dubendorf airfield near Zurich caught a nocturnal intruder in their beams. The aircraft fired distress signals, so the Swiss held their fire and lit up a runway. But the foreign plane refused to land, and the Swiss responded by illuminating the sky with more beams, sighting their AA guns. Unable to dodge the searchlights, the craft finally came down, oil pouring from one engine. Flown by Oberleutnant (1st Lt.) Wilhelm Johnen, the plane was a Luftwaffe nightfighter. It had just shot down a heavy British Lancaster bomber over southern Germany, and, after suffering a failure in one of its engines, had become disoriented and wandered over Switzerland. The Me-110's landing immediately provoked a crisis.

As soon as Luftwaffe intelligence learned of the incident, a series of demands poured over the border at the highest levels. The Swiss were requested to either give back the plane or blow it up. If the Swiss failed to comply, a commando force would be dispatched to do the job, or Dubendorf would be visited by countless other Luftwaffe craft, delivering bombs. The Germans were deadly serious. Johnen's Me-110 had been equipped with the Luftwaffe's very latest advances in airborne radar, including a secret device that allowed nightfighters to hone in on British navigational beams. It was also equipped with "Jazz Music" ("Schrage Musik"), obliquely aimed 20mm cannon behind the cockpit that fired upward. The Germans had discovered a blind spot in British defensive armament. The British had been slow to realize that many bombers that appeared to be hit by flak had really fallen prey to nightfighters stalking them from directly below.

The urgency of the German demands stemmed from a trauma that had shaken the country after a series of raids on Hamburg in late July 1943. The British termed the attacks Operation Gomorrah, but the result was known in Germany simply as "Die Katastrophe." The chief of the RAF's Bomber Command, Arthur "Bomber" Harris, was a true

believer in strategic air power, differing only from his American counterparts in his utter conviction that, as opposed to industrial targets,
civilian lives (or, as he put it, their "housing") comprised the most vulnerable part of the enemy war effort. With Operation Gomorrah he
set out to wipe Germany's second largest city off the map, and,
through an unusual convergence of circumstances, was nearly able to
do so.

Both British and German scientists had been aware that radar
could be fooled simply by deploying thin strips of metal in the sky; yet
the trick was so simple that neither side had tried it, since use of the
ploy by one side would only prompt countermeasures from the other.
On the night of July 24–25, nearly 800 RAF bombers suddenly
crossed the Channel pouring out tons of metal foil—or, as Churchill
called it, "Opening the Window." German radar stations were surprised and overwhelmed. The bombers got through to Hamburg and
devastated the city, knocking out its water mains and civil defense. On
the following days smaller numbers of USAAF craft followed, dropping their bombs into the smoke. Then, on the night of the 27th, the
British came again, armed with incendiaries. Hamburg had suffered a
drought that summer, and thousands of fires still blazed around the
city. The new attack created a phenomenon that exponentially exceeded the effects of bombing: firestorm. The entire city exploded in a bon-
fire with hurricane force winds, sucking oxygen into the pyre, inciner-
ating every flammable object beneath its blast, including humans hiding in basements or gathered in shelters. At least forty thousand people died in the conflagration.

After Hamburg, the war waged in the dark skies between Bomber
Command and the Luftwaffe nightfighter arm rose to a new intensity.
German scientists were reassigned to the electronic warfare on which
their fighters relied for navigation. Both sides developed means to
hone in on the other's signals. Radar was fine-tuned to weed out "window." The British sent fluent German-speakers aloft to misdirect
nightfighter squadrons on the radio; the Germans responded by enlist-
ing female ground controllers. German pilots were allowed to test new
tactics, in addition to the Kammhuber Line of sector defense in France
on which they had previously relied. Formations called "Tame
Boars"—twin-engined gun platforms like the Me-110—were sent in
pursuit of British bomber streams by radar guidance and ground con-

trol. Their single-engine counterparts, the "Wild Boars," simply raced among the British formations once they had arrived at their target, risking their own flak to attack bombers illuminated in the glare of searchlights over German cities.

While the Eighth Air Force stood down during the winter of 1943–44, Bomber Command had only grown more confident with its growing fleet of four-engined Halifaxes and Lancasters (the latter perhaps the best bomb delivery aircraft of the war prior to the B-29). On November 19, 1943, Arthur Harris launched the Battle of Berlin, his intent being to raze the Third Reich's capital. Harris believed that, by waging strategic air war in its purest form, his bomber crews could fight the culminating battle of the war without ground forces having to be involved. The Berlin metropolis, however, having expanded later than many of Germany's other cities, had wide streets and brick structures that resisted firestorm. Joseph Goebbels evacuated a million civilians from the city prior to the attacks, and the remaining three-and-a-half million were schooled in air defense procedures. Throughout the winter months, Bomber Command launched 35 raids against Berlin and nearby targets in a head-to-head duel unmatched since the Battle of Britain. This time the Luftwaffe came out on top. British aircrew morale plummeted while German nightfighter squadrons gained new aces with each raid and 88mm flak batteries claimed scores of aircraft. Six thousand civilians were killed, but that total was exceeded by British aircrews in the 1,047 bombers shot down during the battle. The city of Berlin, despite its growing piles of rubble, remained as defiant as London had during the Blitz of 1940–41.

In a coda to Bomber Command's winter efforts, it launched an 800-plane raid against Nuremburg at the end of March. In the worst disaster yet, 95 bombers were lost in the moonlit skies, mostly to nightfighters, and 14 more crashed or collided on their return to cloud-covered England. Just as the Luftwaffe had wrested control of the daylight skies over Germany from the USAAF in the fall of 1943, it had regained control from the British during the following winter.

Such was the situation when one of the latest German nightfighters accidentally landed near Zurich in 1944. The Germans assumed that Switzerland was a direct conduit to Allied intelligence and demanded that the gadget-enhanced, specially-armed Me-110 be returned or destroyed. The Swiss, meanwhile, had dismantled the advanced radar gear and examined it in an underground bunker. Finally, Swiss negotiators arrived at a settlement with the Germans. The Swiss would blow up the aircraft, but in exchange required delivery of 12 of Germany's latest model Messerschmitt fighters. On May 19, after the Swiss had reattached the radar equipment, the Me-110 was destroyed before the watchful eyes of Nightfighter Squadron 5's executive officer. The next day the Swiss received a new squadron of Me-Bf109G fighters, although, according to one account, they turned out to be of poor quality—real "lemons."

The nightfighter affair was the second time in the war that the Swiss acceded to demands from the Luftwaffe. The first was in late 1940 when the Germans requested that Switzerland observe blackout rules at night. Swiss cities, they claimed, were standing as a beacon for British bombers, in effect directing them to southern German targets such as Augsburg and Munich or targets in northern Italy. The Swiss, though realizing that observing a blackout would render their cities more vulnerable to accidental bombings, reluctantly agreed to the German demand, much to the annoyance of Bomber Command.

The truth is that many Europeans, including some British, lacked great enthusiasm for "Bomber" Harris's program of area bombing of civilian population centers at night. His pursuit of Douhet's concept of using noncombatant deaths as stepping stones to victory from the sky stepped out of bounds in two respects: first, his almost fanatic conviction that air power alone could win the war, rendering land invasion unnecessary, failed to take into account the Red Army which was then advancing on Europe. If the Soviets were not met by ground forces in central Europe at a line such as the Elbe they would eventually have to be greeted at the Channel. Air forces cannot hold ground, and Harris's strategic view was, at best, too narrowly focused. Second, the British public, though cheering Bomber Command on during the early years, began to recoil at Harris's method of waging war. "Following the devil's example" was a well-circulated phrase, and it was only the postwar revelations of far greater German ruthlessness toward civilians that provided Harris's efforts some moral justification. For their part, Nazi leaders used the British policy of waging war against civilians to good advantage in justifying their own programs. Who could object to the most extreme measures of total war when one after another German city was going up in flames after attacks in the dark by anonymous intruders? In retrospect, the question of Bomber Command's civilian targeting policy, in the context of a war against Nazism, is not easily answered. Still, in the glow of victory in 1945, Harris, alone among the major service chiefs, was passed over for elevation to the British peerage. On the first anniversary of one of his subsequent triumphs, the firebombing of Dresden, he relocated to Rhodesia.

For American proponents of strategic air war, 1943 had proven that unescorted daylight raids deep into Germany had simply become too costly. With average eight percent loss rates, the chances of survival for crews across 25 missions had theoretically become less than zero. (In practice, casualties were heavier among novice crews; as in the ground war, survival rates increased once men had passed their first baptisms of fire.) Hap Arnold, convinced that the American air arm could not possibly be bested by the Luftwaffe, was beside himself with frustration and decided to shake up the USAAF command. As 1944 began, Carl Spaatz was assigned to a newly created post as chief of U.S. Strategic Army Air Forces Europe to oversee all operations in England and the Mediterranean. Ira Eaker was reassigned to the Mediterranean, a demotion from his command of the Eighth Air Force. The Eighth's new leader became Jimmy Doolittle, of "Thirty Seconds Over Tokyo" fame.

After his surprise raid on the Japanese capital from a carrier in the mid-Pacific, Doolittle had led the first American raid on Rome, Italy. He was determined to cap his trio of Axis capitals by leading the first U.S. raid on Berlin, but was refused permission because by 1944 he knew too many secrets, including plans for the coming invasion. By any measure, though, the force that would soon, quite justifiably, be known as the Mighty Eighth had gained a leader of exceptional dynamism. The Americans continued to disdain terror bombing and remained convinced that the German war economy could be crippled through intelligent daylight raids on the crucial centers of its industrial power.

Doolittle had the advantage that U.S. air strength in England had grown by leaps (literally, from Newfoundland) during the winter of 1943–44. Hundreds of new bombers had arrived, replacing losses and forming additional groups on dozens of newly created airfields. The latest, "G" model B-17s sported a chin turret with twin .50 guns to help ward off frontal attacks. The P-47 fighter had been upgraded with a new propellor to help it climb and a water injection mechanism to increase its speed. And the best news of all was that the Mustangs had arrived and had already worked through some teething pains in combats over France. By the hundreds they were poised to accompany the bombers, like cavalry screening the wagon train, on deep-penetration raids. In the south, American bomber groups, redesignated the Fifteenth Air Force, had abandoned North Africa and were now based in southern Italy, far closer to targets in the Reich. The Ninth Air Force had moved to England. Composed largely of B-26 Marauders, it was given a tactical role, freeing up the heavies for strategic targets.

Doolittle began launching the Eighth Air Force at Germany immediately upon assuming command on January 6, 1944. The next day, 420 bombers hit an I.G. Farben chemical factory at Ludwigshaven near the Swiss border. Twelve aircraft were lost, one of which, a B-24 of the 93rd Bomb Group, experienced engine trouble and diverted to Swiss airspace. While circling over Bern, it was joined by 14 Morane fighters that guided it to Dubendorf airfield. One can easily surmise that the Swiss were glad to see the American aircraft, the only one to arrive in Switzerland during a period of over four months following October's Black Thursday. During that time three German and two Italian aircraft had landed, but the Americans appeared to have backed off. In the months to come that impression would clearly prove mistaken.

9

RETURN TO POINTBLANK

As 1944 began, Doolittle was eager to pit his burgeoning host against the Luftwaffe, but he encountered two obstacles. First, weather conditions in what turned out to be an exceptionally severe winter frequently grounded his fleet or forced missions to be aborted. Hundreds of planes swirling at 150 mph in the murky skies over England created their own challenge. Airman James Goings recalled, "The weather was bad but we'd take off in the fog. If we could get above the overcast the mission was on—if not, it would be scrubbed. All these planes in the air trying to land in the fog. There'd be crashes and collisions." During one five-day stretch in early March, six bombers were lost in collisions. Less lethal crashes on landings or takeoffs were almost daily occurrences.

Doolittle's second problem was Operation Crossbow, devised to destroy the launch pads being set up by Germans across the Channel for their mysterious rocket bombs. British intelligence had tracked the secret German rocket program for two years yet was still unsure how great a threat it would present. To pre-empt the menace, over half of the Eighth and Ninth Air Force's sorties in early 1944 were aimed at obliterating the furtive, camouflaged enemy preparations in and around the Pas de Calais.

The dominant American imperative remained, however, to resume Operation Pointblank, attacking the German Luftwaffe head-on, in the air and at its manufacturing base. On January 11, Doolittle finally found clear skies and all three air divisions of the Eighth ranged over central Germany against aircraft factories. German fighters and flak knocked down 60 bombers, and a dozen more were scrapped after crashlanding. These were serious losses but, unlike in the previous year, ones the United States could now sustain. Doolittle launched his crews whenever the weather allowed in often murderous battles over German soil. Then came "Big Week" at the end of February, during which the Eighth Air Force together with Fifteenth Air Force in Italy touched down at every target on the Pointblank list, including, on February 24, Schweinfurt. Almost 50 of 500 bombers were lost on the return to that death trap on the Main.

The next day, two American heavies came smoking into Switzerland out of 70 lost in a dual attack from the south and north against Luftwaffe plants. *Liberal Lady*, a B-24 of the Italian-based 450th Bomb Group, had been assailed by fighters over Regensburg and lost two engines. Upon veering into Switzerland it was intercepted by five Swiss Moranes, but the bomber could no longer stay in the air. The crew bailed out as the *Lady* went on to crash near the town of Wil. The second plane came in minutes later, a B-17 named *Dottie G* from the 92nd Bomb Group in England. Having run afoul of a rocket-firing Me-110 over Stuttgart, pilot Clifford Beach put her down at Dubendorf, his number three engine afire.

By the time "Big Week" ended on February 25, the Eighth Air Force had flown 3,300 and Fifteenth Air Force 500 daylight sorties against German military industrial targets, delivering more bombs than had been dropped by the USAAF in all of 1943. The cost—over 300 bombers downed or written off with 2,600 airmen killed, missing or wounded—was considered acceptable. The Luftwaffe had suffered worse, both in fighter pilots killed in aerial combat and in terms of ground losses—often in the form of rows of mint, freshly manufactured aircraft at its production plants. German fighter pilots who had savored the prospect of more unescorted bomber trains now had to struggle through swarms of American P-51s flying above and alongside the bomber streams, and cocky U.S. pilots anxious for combat. The Luftwaffe rearmed and armored the Focke-Wulf 190 as a "B-17 killer," capable of wading through 50-caliber fire for attacks on bombers with four 20–30mm cannon and two 13mm machine guns. More nimble Me-109s—G models, upgraded with a new Daimler-Benz engine—went aloft to fend off the Mustangs.

A week later, Doolittle launched the Mighty Eighth against the

"Big B," Berlin. As much a rite of passage for the USAAF as a practical target, the heavily defended city had been the obsession of Britain's Bomber Command since fall but had never seen an American daylight raid. On March 6, almost 800 U.S. bombers escorted by an equal number of fighters bore in on the capital of the Reich. Luftwaffe interceptors grappled with the escort of the First Air Division, which was in the lead; the remaining U.S. fighters guarded the Second Division in the rear. But a German ground controller realized the Third Division in the center of the bomber stream was undefended by escorts. Enemy fighters closed in. Sixty-nine heavies went down with over 100 badly damaged. Two days later the American fleet attacked again, losing 37 bombers. The next day a smaller force lost 9 before bad weather—gratefully welcomed by exhausted pilots on both sides—called a halt to the operation.

The American effort then switched to southern Germany. On March 16, over 700 bombers attacked Augsburg and the city of Friedrichshaven on Lake Constance along the Swiss border. The Germans tried to hide Friedrichshaven by sending smoke into the air from barges on the lake. By the end of the day, 23 bombers had been lost, seven of which came down in Switzerland.

From Augsburg limped a B-17 called *Lonesome Polecat* that had been damaged by fighters. Tail gunner Jarrell Legg said, "At the Swiss border we were picked up by an escort of Swiss fighters. They were very similar to the German 109s, so they lowered their wheels and flaps and began to fire flares. We acknowledged with a flare and they came in and tried to lead us to a landing field, but we were unable to stay in the air. At about 500 feet, the pilot gave the order for us to bail out." One man's chute failed to open; some overzealous Swiss marksmen near Lake Zug took shots at the parachutists, evidently suspecting an airborne invasion. The pilot, Lt. Robert Meyer, landed the plane in the lake and in the five minutes before it sank was rescued by Swiss in boats.

Other bombers that arrived in Switzerland that day were *Mount'n Ride,* which featured one of the best nose art paintings in Eighth Air Force but had lost its number two and three engines; *Galloping Katie,* which had lost its numbers three and four; and two B-17s that emerged crippled from the fog over Friedrichshaven. Both crews bailed out. In one case, two men landed in Austria and eight in

Switzerland; in the other, eight came down in Austria and only the navigator and left waist gunner made it to safety.

Another B-17, from the 95th Bomb Group, carried the Command Pilot for the Augsburg raid, Major Noel Strader. Navigator Murray Ball said, "We received a direct hit on the number three engine, which immediately caught fire, and all attempts to feather the propellor failed. The vibration was so severe that the plane had to be slowed to about 115 miles per hour. We were prepared to bail out over Germany but were reluctant to do so with Switzerland so close, so we immediately headed for Switzerland with one or two German fighters making passes at us.

"Our gunners had considerable experience and were quite good. I don't know what happened, but after a while we were alone. Soon the vibration in the engine stopped, we guessed the crankshaft broke. What a sight—Lake Constance." Ball told the pilot they were in Switzerland and pointed out a field on which to land. The pilot circled for his approach and temporarily recrossed into Austrian territory. By that time the crew was in the radio room braced for a crashlanding, when suddenly the pilot ran back and yelled to Ball he had just seen a swastika on a roof. Ball told him to just land in the field he had pointed to. "He said I had better be right," Ball recalled. "That faithful old B-17 landed like a pair of skis, wheels up."

On a curious note, another plane, called *Big Noise*, landed at Dubendorf that day and was listed by examining Swiss airmen as undamaged, with over 1,000 gallons of remaining fuel. Cursory Swiss inspections would often overlook such problems as electrical and hydraulic failure, or even engine trouble if there were no telltale signs of smoke or pouring oil, but in the case of *Big Noise* their report was difficult to fathom. The Missing Air Crew Report filed by other planes on the mission stated that the B-24 had suffered a seriously damaged right wing and rear turret. Repair crews at Dubendorf, headed by American Lt. Colonel Peter De Paolo (an Indianapolis 500 racecar Hall of Famer) logged almost 500 hours of work on the plane. In fact, *Big Noise* did not join the fleet of bombers repatriated to U.S. control after the war and instead was scrapped. Reports or rumors of unscarred aircraft landing in Switzerland, erroneous as they would turn out to be, would soon become a major concern to USAAF commanders.

Two days later, on March 18, Doolittle launched the entire Eighth Air Force of over 700 serviceable bombers once again at southern Germany. The B-24s revisited Friedrichshaven while the B-17 groups hit Munich and other cities. Sixteen of the 43 bombers lost on the raids landed in Switzerland, the highest total for any day of the war. The story of *Superball*, a B-17 assigned to hit a Luftwaffe airfield at Landsberg, was typical. As recounted by crewman Richard Hobt:

"Almost immediately after the bomb run, FW 190s attacked us from the six o'clock position level, passing through our formation. They turned and made a head-on pass from 12 o'clock. . . . We were struck in the nose, a 20mm shell exploding in the navigator's compartment, and another shell exploded at the base of the pilot's control column. A large hole was blown in the left side of the fuselage just below the top turret. Numbers one and two engines were shot out and an oil fire started in number three. The pilot was stunned by the exploding shell and lost control of the aircraft."

Hobt had already seen the three lead planes of his squadron riddled by fighters. He continued, "We went into a steep dive, passing under our left wingman just as he exploded. We fell from 18,000 feet to about 5,000 feet before the co-pilot and pilot regained control." *Superball* managed to limp across the Swiss border where it was joined by four Moranes who led it to Dubendorf. The plane landed immediately on sighting the airfield, its landing gear collapsing on impact with the ground.

Jack McKinney was on his first mission when his 384th Bomb Group B-17 lost two engines to flak south of Augsburg. The plane was on fire as it fell out of formation, heading south. He said, "Two P-51s came over to escort us but after ten minutes we told them to go on ahead, we had the Alps in sight." The crew followed procedure by destroying the IFF, radar and bombsight, and ate the mission documents, printed on rice paper. They had to circle into Austria in order to land against the wind, and another barrage of flak burst around the aircraft. The plane landed in a field, burning at both ends. McKinney recalled, "I could see soldiers waiting for us to get out of the airplane. 'That's it,' I thought. 'They're Germans. They sure look like it.' But then a little boy about 10 or 11 runs up and says, 'Die Schweiz. Ist gut.' I gave the little fellow my helmet and goggles."

Throughout the afternoon, Swiss fighters dashed back and forth along the border, making contact with damaged U.S. aircraft, guiding them to the nearest airfields. The remaining crew of one B-24 had suffered a harrowing experience. Before reaching the target, the plane from the 392nd Bomb Group had been hit by enemy fire, not seriously, but the pilot panicked and rang the bail-out alarm. He jumped first, followed by three gunners. Meanwhile the co-pilot, Lt. Donald MacMullen, stuck with the aircraft in order to complete the bomb run. Over the target the plane was struck by flak in the nose, which exploded ammunition, causing a fire, and it lost one engine. MacMullen put the plane into a dive to extinguish the flames in the engine while navigator Ken Parks put out the fire in the nose. The two men set a course for Switzerland where they finally crashlanded at a small airfield called Diessenhofen.

Radioman Edward Winkle flew aboard *Pistol Packin' Mama*, a 445th Bomb Group B-24. Winkle had originally been assigned to the Pacific Theater, but on taking off from an airfield in California his plane had crashed, killing or wounding the pilots and half the crew. Reassigned to the European Theater, he was on his 15th mission, over Friedrichshaven, when the plane lost two engines. "Immediately we lost both altitude and air speed, and were left alone out there, as every plane in the Eighth Air Force seemed to pass us. We hid in the B-17 contrails for awhile, but they passed us too. At this time we lost our electrical system and superchargers. There went the heat, the instruments and the radio." *Pistol Packin' Mama* dropped from 15,000 to 5,000 feet as it neared the Swiss border. Past Lake Constance it was met by four Swiss Me-109s, one of which fired a green flare. Winkle fired his own flares in response while a crewman hand-cranked the landing gear into position.

Pilot Jan Sefton told the crew to prepare for a crashlanding. Winkle said, "He made a very long approach, with little or no instruments, no flaps, no brakes and only two engines. A large crowd was watching, and as we neared the ground our landing gear went through high tension wires which fell on two small boys on bicycles, killing them. We will never forget them. We were surrounded by Swiss soldiers who immediately took everything we had except for a few personal things, and led us away from the plane. We remained in Zurich for two days with several other crews who had landed there with badly crippled planes." *Pistol Packin' Mama* had torn through electrical wires over a railroad track. The two boys were buried after a ceremony attended by U.S. diplomats.

One after another, the big American aircraft came limping into Switzerland that afternoon, at low altitude, trailing smoke or fuel. Every plane was damaged; however, at least two might have still made it to base had they not run low of fuel. The greatest problem that day was that the 44th Bomb Group had had to make two passes over Friedrichshaven in order to be sure of hitting the target. It was a gutsy call made by the group's Command Pilot, Robert Cardenas—similar to a decision made over Stuttgart on September 6, 1943 with equally disastrous results—and one, incidentally, which RAF Bomber Command leaders didn't need to consider during their area bombing missions at night. On their second run-in to the target, the American Liberators were pulverized by German flak batteries able to concentrate on them alone. Of eight planes lost by the 44th, either damaged or low on fuel, six staggered out of the black clouds of flak across Lake Constance to Switzerland. The B-24 in which Cardenas flew, named *Sack Artists,* was hit by flak on the first bomb run, then lost three engines and its electrical power on the second. Cardenas, who later became one of America's foremost test pilots, and the crew bailed out as the Liberator went on to crash in the Swiss countryside.

On April 1, the Swiss city of Schaffhausen was devastated by Liberators of the 44th and 392nd Bomb Groups. Forty civilians were killed, over 100 wounded and nearly 450 made homeless by the rain of 598 incendiary bombs and 180 100-pound explosives. The B-24s, whose original target was Ludwigshaven, 120 miles to the north, had wandered over southern Germany for an hour, buffeted by high winds over a dense undercast. The air-to-ground radar (H2X) of their lead planes had malfunctioned. When they finally encountered clear skies and spotted a city below, they evidently didn't realize how far off course they had flown. The first wave, 23 planes of the 392nd Bomb Group, unloaded its ordnance in a woods outside Schaffhausen, perhaps accidentally missing the city. The next wave was 9 Liberators of the 44th Group, who evidently realized the navigational error and held their fire. They went on to bomb (and miss) the town of Grafenhausen in Germany. The third wave, consisting of 15 44th Bomb Group B-24s, inflicted all the damage on the center of Schaffhausen, hitting the railway station (where 16 died), the city's courthouse (where 10 died), a museum, which lost precious artworks, and other buildings.

Schaffhausen, as a result of an unusual twist in Swiss history, lay north of the Rhine River, which roughly forms the border between Switzerland and Germany. It's understandable that American aircrews, having recently emerged from zero visibility, might have assumed it was German. Nevertheless, an enduring mystery about the attack is why the lead navigators of the second wave of American bombers—the only ones who realized their location—didn't radio warnings to the other two waves, an omission that historian James H. Hutson describes as "criminally negligent." This may be too harsh a judgment for flyers who undertook extremely dangerous missions over Germany with fragile early-generation navigation devices. The fact is that precision bombing, for the USAAF, was as much a goal as a reality. Hutson commented further that "The unhappiness of many Swiss extended beyond the devastation at Schaffhausen to the Allied policies which, they believed, had sown the seeds of the disaster: the violation of Swiss neutrality by the unrelenting Allied penetration of Swiss airspace."

American military and civil officials, led by Army Chief of Staff George C. Marshall and Secretary of State Cordell Hull, apologized profusely for the accident. The citizens of Schaffhausen stoically cleaned up the mess and held a mass funeral. Observers noted a lack of bitterness on the part of Schaffhausen's residents, a restraint not matched by the majority of the Swiss press. Today, young Swiss seem to remember this incident as well as any other in World War II, and one explained in detail to this author how clear the skies were over the city that day and that Schaffhausen was miles away from any legitimate German targets. "If they were not aiming at Schaffhausen, what were they attacking?" he asked. However, most contemporary Swiss, even though moved by the loss of life at Schaffhausen, were thankful that young American airmen risked their own lives in such large numbers to remove the scourge of Nazism from Europe.

On that same April 1, 1944, both Carl Spaatz's USAAF and Trafford Leigh-Mallory's RAF command came under the control of Dwight Eisenhower, the supreme commander of Allied forces for the upcoming invasion of France. The bomber chiefs nevertheless persuaded

Eisenhower to extend Pointblank—deep incursions into Germany—for two more weeks. The Eighth Air Force had finally begun to demonstrate the value of strategic air power: crippling the enemy by ranging far behind his front lines. The Luftwaffe was clearly on the ropes. American raids had been somewhat successful in demolishing German aircraft factories, even though German production increased throughout the year. Factories that were knocked out were made to appear functional so that the Allies would waste more bombs on them; working factories were disguised as bombed-out wrecks. Meanwhile, manufacturing was dispersed as much as possible into tunnels, caves and dugouts where slave laborers lived a troglodyte existence.

The greater effect of Pointblank was that the Luftwaffe, by being forced into the air to defend well-chosen American targets, was running short of experienced pilots. German airmen flew until they were killed, wounded or captured, and with each raid more aces were going down in flames. While Allied airmen could perfect their skills in the peaceful skies over Texas or Canada with unlimited fuel at their disposal, Germany had no means of providing extensive training for new pilots. There was hardly any fuel for training, no bases immune from bombardment, and precious little airspace over Germany where a novice trainee could earn his wings without being jumped by a squadron of Mustangs. American combat airmen began to notice the difference. Some German pilots seemed to possess great skill and guile; but an increasing number of others flew like sitting ducks. Japan, which suffered a similar problem, began to train its new pilots for suicide missions. In Germany, tactics were adjusted to minimize contact with the American fighter escorts. Luftwaffe squadrons picked their spots and then raced through a bomber stream in one sudden rush rather than staying to harass the formations. Bomber crews encountered fighters less frequently, but often in large, deadly waves of 30 to 50 planes. The bottom line for Pointblank, however, was that while German manufacturing somehow continued apace, the Luftwaffe had been crippled at its most vulnerable point: its supply of trained pilots.

In the second week of April, the Eighth Air Force lost 200 more bombers in attacks on north and central Germany, northern France, and Poznan, Poland. On the 13th, the armada flew against southern Germany again, with over 400 bombers assigned to Schweinfurt and

Augsburg, and about 200 more arrayed against German airfields. Of 38 aircraft lost, 13 made it to Switzerland, all with various degrees of battle damage caused mainly by flak. Some of the flak came from Swiss AA gunners along the border who may still have had Schaffhausen on their minds.

One B-17 crew from the 390th Bomb Group tried a ruse after it had crashlanded in a Swiss field. Familiar with the rules governing evadees versus internees (unarmed "visitors" as opposed to armed combatants subject to POW regulations) the crew set their damaged Fortress down and then rushed to a nearby woods to hide. A few hours later, after being found by Swiss soldiers, they claimed that they had just escaped from a German POW camp. Interrogated by Swiss Captain Geoffrey von Meiss, the ten men, still dressed in their flying suits, steadfastly maintained that they had nothing to do with the B-17 that was lying in the field next to their hiding place. Von Meiss, a gracious officer who fortunately did not lack a sense of humor, called in an officer from the American Legation, who ordered the crew to confess.

On April 14, Pointblank officially came to a close, as the Allied air forces in England gathered to pave the way in northern France for D-Day. The Italian-based Fifteenth Air Force, in addition to interdiction missions against German forces on the peninsula and attacks on southern Germany, opened an all-out campaign against Ploesti in Romania, a target more vital to the German war effort than Berlin. But it was still vital to keep pressure on the Luftwaffe, not giving it time to recover. Ten days later, over 750 Eighth Air Force bombers accompanied by an even greater number of fighters flew against aircraft plants and bases in southern Germany. The Swiss fighter force took off to receive 13 of the 40 U.S. bombers lost that day. Tragically, one B-17 of the 92nd Group made it to Dubendorf trailing smoke and fuel from its starboard engines, but then suddenly dove nose-first into the ground while on its final approach. All ten crewmen died in the crash.

Another Fortress crashlanded at Altenrhein, on a small grass strip near the Austrian border. Pilot Lt. William Parramore recalled, "My decision to head for Switzerland was not premeditated, but was made just after 'bombs away' near Munich. A propellor ran away when I added power, and with another propellor feathered the group flew off and left us. We had been under heavy fighter attacks since about twenty minutes before reaching the Initial Point. In addition to the condition of the aircraft, my flight engineer, Sgt. Roy Hommer, was lying on the floor slowly bleeding to death. The crewmember who attended him had been unable to stop the bleeding from wounds he had received in one of the first fighter passes. It was at this point that I asked the navigator for a heading to the emergency landing field in Switzerland that we had been briefed on that morning."

A B-17 named *Frostie* was well protected by fighters when it left England but was nevertheless hit by flak, wounding the tail gunner, as it crossed the French coast. Staying with its group, the Fort braved more flak across France and then "a thick black wall" of AA bursts over the target. According to crewmen Joseph Piemonte and Frank Pizzi, "By this time we had commenced our bombing run. Just how long it lasted is a question, for at that moment we were attacked by enemy Messerschmitts. We had three attacks of thirty ships each." Two engines had gone out and the remaining two were overheating. Number three was pouring oil. The ship headed for Switzerland, only 70 miles away, but just as it reached Lake Constance the Germans around Friedrichshaven threw up still another barrage of flak. This offended Piemonte and Pizzi because *Frostie* had by then lowered its landing gear and fired off distress flares. Across the lake the B-17 was met by Swiss Me-109s who guided it down.

The intrepidness of American aircrews was further demonstrated by a Flying Fortress of the 95th Bomb Group piloted by Max Wilson of Nebraska. Its number four engine failed on the way to the target, yet Wilson stayed his course. Over Germany, a Focke-Wulf raced in and scored a direct hit on number two, almost knocking it loose from the wing. It was at that point Wilson was informed that two parachutes had been damaged, so the entire crew decided to ride the plane down. Crossing the Swiss border they were met by an Me-109 marked with a white cross, which came up alongside. The bomber almost made it to Dubendorf, crashlanding in a nearby field. It skidded across the ground dragging its left wing, made a right-angle turn and then demolished a Swiss radio shack. The big steel tower next to the radio station finally stopped the B-17.

The next day, April 25, the First and Third Air Divisions of the Eighth Air Force attacked railway targets in France while the Second

Division's Liberators flew against aircraft plants in Mannheim. Of five bombers lost on the raid, three landed in Switzerland. An additional B-24 from the Fifteenth Air Force came in on one engine after attacking a target in northern Italy. One of the Mighty Eighth's planes, *Rum Runner*, was unusual because it landed at Dubendorf with a full bomb load. (It had flown that day without a bombardier.) The craft had about 600 gallons of fuel remaining. Another, *Borsuk's Bitch*, had experienced engine problems due to electrical failure and determined it did not have enough fuel to return to England. The story of the third, *Commando*, was related by co-pilot Lewis Sarkovich, who included in his tale a slice of life in the Eighth Air Force:

"It was my 24th mission and the same monotonous briefing. Same four o'clock breakfast and the usual trudge through the mud to the dressing room and then out to the planes in the still dark hours of the morning. One thing that really helped morale in England was the eternal mud which never dried up and was always getting on everything you owned. As usual, once over the French coast up came the flak—the boys on the invasion coast were a little sharper than usual today for many close misses shook our ship from stem to stern.

"On into France we flew with an occasional shot from scattered flak batteries. Over to our right I noticed a group headed over Paris. Our flight plan called for us to skirt Paris to the left-northwest by about 10 miles. This group flew dead over the town and was really catching hell from the flak defenses of the town. One ship was already hit and the men were bailing out. I counted six chutes while the ship, which was undoubtedly on automatic pilot, flew in big graceful circles. One of the men parachuted into the heart of Paris. I could see his chute disappear among the buildings of the town. The Eiffel tower was clearly visible and also the flashes of the anti-aircraft guns that were putting up the barrage. They succeeded in disabling about four ships in the group. Two went on and the others turned back toward England.

"Everything was quiet for about an hour and then suddenly and without warning number two engine virtually exploded. Lt. Schroeder looked out at the engine and watched parts of the engine cowling being ripped off piece by piece. Fire broke out and the engine started smoking badly. We immediately feathered the engine. I called back to the waist to ask one of the gunners if it was burning.

The gunner told me that the fire had gone out but that the engine was still smoking badly. I told him to keep an eye on the thing and if it started to burn again that we would have to bail out. It was better to be a POW than a mangled mess scattered all over France.

"The B-24 had a funny habit of blowing up when that happened and we didn't want to be around. It was then that I noticed that number three engine was also acting up. By now we had lost our group and could not possibly keep up with the 90 mph head wind on the way back. The trip would probably take up all our gas before we ever reached England. And then, with the possibility of losing another engine there was just one alternative. It was either crash-landing in France, trying to get back to England, or else make it to Switzerland. We chose the better deal of all and decided to go to Switzerland."

Commando was losing 500 feet of altitude a minute when it finally encountered an Me-109 marked with the Swiss flag. Sarkovich continued: "It was then that I became suspicious of a ruse. Was this a phony German fighter dolled up as a Swiss? It was the first time I felt worried. The fighter wiggled his wings from side to side and we wiggled ours. He then fired a flare and we did the same. He then dropped his landing gear and we dropped ours, indicating to him that we wanted to land. He finally pulled up in front of us and we followed him around in a huge circle as he led us into the field.

"This is where we made our bad mistake. We tried to land even though it was plain to see we would overshoot the field. 'Better go around!' I hollered. The reply from the pilot was simply, 'To hell with it! We're going in!' and so down went the flaps. By now we had badly overshot the field and were about two-thirds of the way down the runway. Lt. Schroeder eased it over on the grass, which we hit and then bounced into the air and continued to float. We were now headed for the secondary fence that was surrounding the field parallel to the road. And as fate would have it on the road dead in front of us was a man on a horse and buggy slowly trotting along. When I saw this I let out a big cry and yelled, 'Watch the damn fool with the horse and wagon!' I could see the man whip the horse into a gallop as he saw us bearing down on him. Lt. Schroeder and I grabbed the wheel and pulled back; the ship rose into the air once more and we leaped over the man and horse, wagon and all.

"On the other side of the road now we continued to float across corn fields and fences. Our nose wheel was ripped off as we plowed through the cement poles. Out through the corner of my eye I could see the fences being dragged along with us as we continued to plow up the countryside. Next came more fences, and as we plowed through more I finally decided to feather the props. This I did and also cut the ignition switches at the same time. We were still floating wildly down the countryside when suddenly up ahead I noticed a row of tall heavy poplar trees. I thought to myself, 'If we don't stop flying before we get to those trees we'll all be killed.'

"I started to pull up the flaps so as to get the ship on the ground. Lt. Schroeder was now trying to guide the ship so we would hit between two of the trees and not head-on into one of them. Smitty, who was standing behind our two seats, suddenly yelled, 'Look out for those trees!' He had no sooner finished his sentence when there was a terrific crash as we smashed into the row of trees. I flew out of my seat and hit the windshield with my head and then everything went black.

"About ten or 15 seconds later I came to, still dazed, and realized that the ship was on fire. 'Let's get the hell out of here,' I said, and Lt. Schroeder unhooked his safety belt and started to climb out of his seat but got caught between the two armor plate backs of the seats. 'Take your goddam chute off!' I yelled. He said, 'Yeah,' still in a daze. I had already taken mine off so I climbed out of my seat and out the top escape hatch where I jumped to the ground. I ran like mad from the ship and climbed over the first fence I came to. A woman, who was working in the garden nearby and who had seen the whole thing, was making the sign of the cross as we all came scampering out of the ship. I quickly took a count of the men. I could only see nine—'Good God!' I thought to myself, I hope there is no one in the ship. The Swiss fighter now buzzed us and I took one glance at him and then went back to my counting. I finally spotted the tenth man on the other side of the ship. I breathed a slow sigh of relief and then turned around to hear the siren of the Swiss ambulance that was streaking across the field toward us. I turned around and looked at the ship once more. It was burning fiercely; the right wing was hanging up in the top branches of the poplar trees. The wing tanks were split open and the gasoline we had left was pouring out in gallons and liquid fire covered the entire ship. Number three engine was completely torn off and was buried about 3 feet in the ground 200 yards from the airplane. The tail was torn off and was scattered all over the countryside. The fuselage with two engines attached was all we had left in one piece when we finally quit rolling.

"By now the Swiss ambulance had reached us and Swiss soldiers and officers with pistols drawn were running out toward us and hollering 'Switzerland!' The soldiers had steel helmets that looked like German design and for a moment I thought that we were in Germany. We finally surrendered our .45 automatics to the Swiss officer in charge. He asked us if anybody was hurt. We finally collected everybody together and found out that no one was injured. They all finally gathered around us and began gazing.

"The officer then asked us to get into the ambulance. As we all climbed in we heard the ship explode. One of the petrol tanks evidently went up in flames and showered gasoline over the whole area. Then the ammunition started to go off. We warned the men not to go near the aircraft as there were 11,000 rounds of ammunition aboard. We all finally settled down in the ambulance and started congratulating each other on the fact that nobody was hurt. One soldier in the ambulance with us said in German, 'Und für Sie, der Krieg ist fertig.' 'For you, the war is over.'"

In March and April 1944, 55 American Flying Fortresses and Liberators landed in Switzerland, and the U.S. brass had become worried. In that Axis-encircled country, who could be sure that American heavies weren't just gliding into Dubendorf without a scratch on their paintwork? The German propagandist Lord Haw Haw claimed on the radio that airmen were arriving with golf clubs. The Swiss themselves confirmed they were putting the flyers up in hotels. Who could tell what kind of "life of Riley" was going on in Switzerland? In addition to what they suspected or heard, Spaatz and Doolittle may have also had their own, private, reasons for suspecting bomb crews of avoiding the air war.

Operation Pointblank, when it resumed in 1944, resulted in a decisive and, as it turned out, lasting defeat of the Luftwaffe. But it had been purchased with the lives of the bomber crews. When Doolittle had assumed command of the Eighth Air Force, he noticed a sign over the desk of General William Kepner, head of VIII Fighter Command. It read: "The first duty of the Eighth Air Force fighters is to bring the bombers back alive." Doolittle ordered the sign removed. The real task of the fighters, in his view, was to destroy German fighters. To the dismay of the bomber crews, the rapidly growing U.S. fighter arm was ordered to cease flying close support of the bombers and instead to range at will along the general route of the bomber stream, hunting their Luftwaffe counterparts. In effect, the bombers were to be used as bait to lure the Germans into the air, whereupon they could be ambushed by American fighters hanging far above or away from the formations.

One result was that Hubert Zemke's "Wolfpack" of P-47s wracked up impressive numbers of kills, matched and eventually exceeded by Don Blakelee's 4th Fighter Group of Mustangs. The American fighters not only sought dogfights with the enemy anywhere in the sky, but followed them to their bases, shooting up airfields when the Germans tried to land. Short-range Thunderbolts and Lightnings, once the Mustangs had taken over the majority of air combat, took to attacking ground targets in France. The fighters had thrillingly engaged in what Blakelee, for one, would call "a grand sport."

The other result was that in countless instances the freewheeling fighters left bomb groups alone, exposed to enemy attacks. In addition to the flak the bomber crews were forced to endure over their targets, they had to accept that their lives had become a secondary consideration to the USAAF command. The first big raid on Berlin was an example where U.S. losses amounted to 69 ten-man bombers and only 11 single-engine fighters. As the Fortress and Liberator crews well knew, the German fighters were only interested in them. And they were being placed like meat on the table.

In March, Doolittle raised the number of missions to be flown by bomber crews from 25 to 30. The only consolation to the airmen was that now, if they got shot down on their 25th mission (a great fear), "at least we won't have to fly the other five."

Of all the aspects of the air war, the single most impressive is the awe-inspiring bravery of the bomber crews. Nine out of the ten men in the heavies had little or no choice in their fate. The tenth, the pilot, had to have nerves of steel simply to guide the plane on its mission in the face of enemy fire. He couldn't evade fighters or dodge flak. There was little to count on but courage and luck, and, when a plane was going down, split-second decisions that would result in life or death. Throughout World War II, combat airmen suffered a higher casualty rate than their counterparts in the U.S. Army, Navy or Marines. Within the USAAF, strategic bomber crewmen suffered a higher rate of loss than flyers in other types of aircraft, and those who fought in the European Theater suffered proportionately far worse than their counterparts in the Pacific. The men who waged the strategic air campaign against Germany, in short, faced the greatest risks of all U.S. servicemen in performing their duty.

At the end of April 1944, Carl Spaatz, head of the United States Strategic Air Forces in Europe, ordered an investigation into rumors of American planes landing in Switzerland with insufficient reason. He found the rumors unjustified. Nearly every Fortress and Liberator, with a very few possible exceptions, had gone down fighting as a result of damage inflicted by the enemy. And, though the topic of saving lives may not have been a primary concern to Spaatz and Doolittle, it was fortunate for the safety of hundreds of American bomber crews that the small nation of Switzerland still existed in the center of Axis-held Europe.

10

LIFE IN INTERNMENT

If nations have characters, the national character of Switzerland is an aggregate of its citizens' habits of diligence and prudence. The stability of Switzerland's government, which has survived countless political storms in Europe, is a reflection of its citizenry: efficient yet modest; confident yet politely reserved; and heavily armed yet neutral. During World War II the military was omnipresent, at the border, in the Alps and on the railways. The striking difference between the military presence in Switzerland and that which one might observe in an autocratic state, however, is that in the Alpine nation the soldiers are Swiss citizens themselves. Every young man in the country is required to serve. Switzerland's independence from its larger neighbors, an independence which safeguards its 700-year-old tradition of democracy, has never been taken for granted in the midst of Europe's many great-power struggles. Rather, it is an independence earned by calm determination. During World War II the Swiss Army, in addition to its primary job of defense, inherited the task of shepherding a veritable horde of foreign nationals.

When soldiers and civilians by the thousands began pouring into Switzerland at the start of the war, steps were taken to assure that Switzerland's status as a neutral would be strictly honored according to international law. Though Switzerland might be drawn into the conflagration—General Guisan's area of responsibility with the front-line fighting troops—the country would meanwhile perform humanitarian duties and functions attendant to its neutral status to the degree its limited resources would allow. By the end of the war Switzerland had taken in 300,000 refugees and foreign military internees, the latter representing every combatant nation in the European Theater.

By January 1, 1944, there were 86 American airmen in Switzerland, with the distinct possibility, despite the lull forced upon Eighth Air Force that winter, that the number would grow. Thus, just three months after the first American airman landed in Switzerland, the camps at the Hotels Bellevue at Macolin and Trois Sapins at Evilard were abandoned and U.S. flyers were moved to an isolated village in the Alps south of Bern called Adelboden. A summer resort whose tourist trade had disappeared during the war, Adelboden had 23 hotels, ranging from a tiny 10-room bed-and-breakfast to establishments with up to 175 beds. Nestled at the head of a valley and over 4,000 feet in elevation, Adelboden was overlooked by giant Alpine peaks. There was no way in or out save through the valley, which eventually led to a small town called Frutigen. It was a good spot to keep the American internees—prisoners of war in a neutral country—and required minimal security. The airmen were initially put up at a large hotel, curiously named The Nevada Palace. The flyers themselves, in tribute to the ball turret gunner who had been the first U.S. airman to die on Swiss soil, called their new home Camp Moloney.

As bombardier James Misuraca put it, "We were assigned rooms in a stripped down hotel and were supervised by a Swiss army detachment that ran the mess hall and performed the guard duties." The main job of the guards was to perform bedchecks at night. With Switzerland surrounded by the Axis and Adelboden nearly surrounded by the Alps, there were few other challenges.

Sergeant Clinton Norby recounted his first impressions upon entering the internment camp: "When we reached the top, the bus took us right through town (one street about four blocks long) to the other end where The Nevada Palace was located. There was a 30 foot picture window about 15 feet high which looked out over a valley about 2,000 to 3,000 feet below us. You could see clouds move up the valley and then they would just stop below the hotel. In fact, one day when I was looking out the window, the sun was shining on us, but looking down the slope, you could see it snowing." Airman Lt. Martin Andrews commented after the war, "Ever since that experience in Switzerland, I've been of two minds about mountains. I find them beautiful, but also a little bit oppressive."

U.S. flyers were given a small stipend from the American Legation in Bern, which amounted to about $7 (30 Swiss francs) every ten days. Airmen reported that this was eventually taken away, which affected not only their meals but also their ability to buy other essentials while in Switzerland. Sergeant Edward Pribek explained, "At first we were able to supplement our meager diet with food purchased in restaurants, but most of us had to forego this when the per diem and exchange rate was cut by our legation. Prices were extremely high and nearly all our clothes were bought at our own expense."

The Americans received the same amount of food as soldiers in the Swiss Army—the bad news was that due to rationing Swiss soldiers were alloted only 1,500 calories a day. Reports from American airmen about their spare diet prompted the U.S. government to supply the Swiss with a supplemental compensation of 1.4 Swiss francs (35 cents) for each airman to increase their daily food intake. Major Jack E. Torin recommended in a memo, "The 1,500 calories per man per day as allowed by the Internment Committee to the American Internees is barely a subsistence diet even by Continental standards. The American standards have always been higher and there should be some attempt made to approach the American standard of nutrition for active internees." American Army standards were approximately 2,100 to 2,300 calories per day, with allotments for more if the soldiers were particularly active.

Charles Cassidy of the 303rd Bomb Group magnanimously pointed out, "The meals were probably as good as any that the Swiss people were eating when war-time scarcities were taken into consideration." His was a rare neutral voice when it came to the internees' meals. "The food was rotten in Switzerland," said airman John Fanelli. In Adelboden, on Fridays, mushrooms were the main course. One time I ate a toadstool and got sick. They made soup out of everything—I swear they made soup out of wallpaper paste. I had one meat meal while I was there—that was on Christmas Day. They must have killed a bunch of mountain goats. You couldn't chew it."

George Patrick of the 44th Bomb Group recalled lots of cheese. "We had cheese for breakfast, lunch and dinner. One time they gave us a beef stew but there was no meat in it." Another airman recalled a meal of cheese appetizers, cheese for a main course, and cheesecake for dessert.

At the height of World War II, nearly 20 percent of the Swiss population was on call for Army mobilization. Meanwhile, the civilian public helped to raise food to make the country self-sufficient. Soccer fields, yards, parks, and in one case the front lawn of a library were torn up to be used for growing potatoes. One Swiss said, "I remember how sad it was when my father decided to transform his rose garden into a potato field—we all nearly cried when he threw out those roses." French fries were outlawed because they needed oil to be cooked; whipped cream was forbidden. Energy had to be conserved and daily life was defined by a standard of basic need. Excess consumption meant possible starvation in the future if the war should take a turn for the worse. The distinction between "soldier" and "citizen" all but disappeared, and the rations supplied to airmen were the same as those endured by the Swiss.

The 1907 Hague Convention statutes forbade obligatory labor for military internees. Some other types of refugees did have work requirements in exchange for their food and housing, which did not exceed the obligations the Swiss themselves faced during the war. But the Americans did not have to work and relied on the Swiss for their care, the American Legation for official support, and on themselves for activities. Pilot Jack McKinney recalled days of "endless bridge games, skiing and photography" as the basis of existence at Adelboden. Lt. James D. Mahaffey remembered: "In Adelboden, about the only thing we had to do was drink, read a few books, and eventually they had movies twice a week." He adds, "I did manage to get in about a month of skiing, which I enjoyed quite a bit. Such was my life during the months of April, May and June of 1944."

The town was open to the internees as long as they stayed within its boundaries and followed a proper code of conduct with Swiss citizens. Outside travel was restricted but occasionally permitted to individual airmen. According to Captain Oliver Keller, "Through the aid of a Swiss sergeant I was able to get one pass to Geneva, the only pass I had during my internment." James Mahaffey recalled that the best experience he had during internment was the occasion he got to travel: "About the only time I thoroughly enjoyed myself during the stay in Adelboden was when I received a pass to go to Zurich. In my opinion, if the men interned in Switzerland were permitted to travel around the country and were not always confined to one camp there would be far less trouble and fewer cases needing disciplinary action."

In an official Army Air Force report, the "notable restlessness among the men" is attributed to the fact that "well planned recreation is practically negligible." It went on to say that "Quite a few of the internees are drinking excessively. Some are beginning to manifest nervous and mental irregularities peculiar to alcoholism." The effects of this drinking on the town are reflected in some of the accounts from officers interned during the period. Many describe rude behavior from airmen directed toward women and other citizens when the drinking got out of control. The report recommended closer supervision of the camp, which according to most airmen was never carried out by the American Legation.

Time and again, the ineffectiveness of the American Legation is echoed in the airmen's reports. Captain Keller observed, "The Legation did very little to aid in recreation; in fact they did very little except to continually warn us against escaping." Sgt. Milton Epstein reflected upon his experience with mixed emotions because of what he viewed as lack of support: "We had virtually the run of the town. At first we had ample money, but soon both per diem and rate of exchange were cut, and this left us very pressed financially. Prices were exorbitant, and we had to buy our own clothes. It was hard to make ends meet. We were not fed nearly enough and there was nothing we could do about it, though I don't want to imply that we starved." He placed the majority of blame for this not on the Swiss people but on his own government: "The American Legation either had its eyes closed or hands tied, for they did nothing for us. It was very difficult to get to a doctor and many boys were treated unnecessarily and with improper or insufficient medical attention."

Edward Winkle describes a slightly easier time while interned, even though he would have wished for additional activities. He recounted: "We were allowed to go up into the mountains, but we were not allowed in the towns except on special pass to see a doctor, dentist, etc. As the summer went by and we were getting more bored, four softball teams were organized, one from each of the living quarters. We played a schedule, then had playoffs. Our team was beaten in the championship."

Inevitably, the isolation affected him as well. "Then the boredom set in again. I listened to news of the invasion and the attempt to assassinate Hitler. I also watched the Seventh Army clear the border between France and Switzerland with interest, and I wanted out. News began to get around that a few of the fellows had gotten out; but the Swiss were getting wise, and if they caught you, you went to the concentration camp at Wauwilermoos. But it was worth a try."

The curfews and other restrictions often displaced any appreciation of the small comforts the airmen enjoyed while in Switzerland, as Sgt. Alfred Fairall recalls from March 1944: "[At Adelboden] we received fifteen francs every ten days. We had nice hotel rooms and a movie theater, set up by the Americans, showing two pictures a week. We had a curfew, which we had to be in our hotels by 10:00 on weekdays and 10:30 on Saturday nights. Failure to comply with this meant five to fifteen days in the Frutigen jail. Among all the crews, there was just one deck of playing cards, and for lack of anything to do, the cards were in use most of the time. By the time we left, this deck of cards was really worn out."

In a telling memory from his internment, Fairall touched on the spartan nature of life as shared with the Swiss during World War II: "Every ten days, the hot water was turned on in the rooms at about 2 P.M. On that day, everyone headed for their rooms to get ready for a bath. The rooms were not heated so the plan was that the tub would be filled with hot water, then a flip of a coin would determine who was first. We turned on the water and got ready; however no hot water ever came out. Getting dressed, we went to the hall and were joined by all the others on the third floor. We went downstairs and discovered that the hot water was only on for two hours and since everybody had the water on at once, those above the first floor didn't get any." Switzerland was dependent on Germany for coal during the war, which meant that the Swiss public—and U.S. internees—made do with the bare minimum of heat and hot water. After the war, some Swiss claimed that the cold was actually good for their health.

Not surprisingly, American internees captured the attention of local children, some of whom had learned their English from watching Westerns. Jürg Allig, who later became a mayor of Adelboden, remembered the holiday season of 1944 when he was 13: "At Christmas time they had the biggest room available in the village in the Regina Hotel so every night they had a cinema. We had no cinema for the Swiss in Adelboden. In the week before Christmas they invited all the school children to the cinema and showed Mickey Mouse, and they gave paper bags full of nuts and fruit and of course chewing gum to every child. Everybody loved them, they were friendly young men."

Fritz Lavener, about 12 during the war, son of a concierge at one of the hotels, remembered, "The Americans were entertaining—wild boys! We always had great battles with them with snowballs. The Americans made such big ones! They always had money and lots of chewing gum. Most important for us boys, they had Jello—a powder and you just had to add water!" According to several airmen, snowball fights were not just waged with the Swiss kids, but between rival crews and hotels.

While many American airmen tried their hand, with varying degrees of success, at skiing, additional sport at Adelboden was provided by the local hockey league. The small village had a team that played against neighboring communities. Eventually the internees were allowed to put together their own team, which introduced the Swiss to "Hockey, American style." According to William Watkins of the 305th Bomb Group, "We couldn't skate but we tripped 'em, kicked 'em, knocked 'em over the mountainside. The Swiss made maybe one hit all year. The Americans gave 'em 32 every game. The Swiss just looked at us. The rink was on a tennis court on a hill. Our guys would trip them and there would go the Swiss guy, over the boards and down the hill. They'd have to hold up the game waiting for him to come back. And we'd be screaming! The Americans thought it was a pro football game, jumping in the stands, going 'Kill 'em! Kill 'em!'" When asked if the Americans won any games, Watkins replied, "Hell no. The Swiss beat the hell out of us!"

The situation would be reversed after the fall of Mussolini, when thousands of British Empire troops made their way to Switzerland from Italian POW camps. Among these troops, captured during Rommel's early victories in North Africa, were Canadians. When time for a hockey rematch came around, the Americans used ringers to make sure it was the Swiss who fell by a lopsided score.

One U.S. flyer who had an interesting time in Switzerland was Martin Andrews, the scholarly pilot who had named his B-17 *Est Nulla Via Invia Virtuti*. When Andrews had come limping out of the foggy maelstrom over Stuttgart on September 6, 1943, he actually overflew Switzerland into northern Italy. Upon spotting German airfields on the ground below, he turned back over the Alps, one engine smoking and the plane rapidly losing fuel. Fortunately, Captain Geoffrey von Meiss of the Swiss Air Force had just set down his Morane at an airfield near Magadino. A mechanic clambored on the wing, knocked on the cockpit and told him an American Flying Fortress was circling aimlessly around the Alps. Von Meiss immediately took off and guided Andrews' plane to safety.

While being escorted on a train two days later, a distinguished but somewhat rumpled gentleman introduced himself to Andrews as Allen Dulles, the head of the Swiss branch of the U.S. Office of Strategic Services (the predecessor of the CIA). Dulles had made it into Switzerland on the very last train to enter the country before the Germans invaded Vichy France. Since then, he had combined the roles of master spy and talent scout, because the only human assets available were people already in the surrounded country. The exception was intelligent, young American airmen who had come parachuting or crashlanding into the country on wounded bombers. On the train ride, Andrews cautiously refused to discuss military matters but had a pleasant conversation with Dulles about childhood and college. Dulles appreciated circumspection and remembered the young man.

In February 1944, Andrews was summoned to meet Dulles at 23 Herrengasse in Bern, the master spy's legendary residence and headquarters (today a completely nondescript, though charming, building in the heart of the medieval city). Dulles, like a salesman able to hit all of his quotas with one fabulous account, had found a source privy to the most secret communications between the Wehrmacht and Joachim von Ribbentrop's Foreign Ministry. He had more information than he could send from Switzerland by encrypted wireless. He needed couriers. According to historian Douglas Anderson, "Andrews was astonished by what Dulles had been able to learn: the placement of every German division in France, details of fortifications on the French coast, German production figures and much more." Andrews was asked to memorize "code names of Germans who were spying for the Allies, reports on which British diplomats Dulles didn't trust, and a lot of things I just didn't understand."

Dulles arranged for an exchange of seven American flyers for seven interned German ones. The group, aside from Andrews and another American officer similarly briefed by Dulles, included Jake Geron, whose *Death Dealer* had been the first U.S. bomber to arrive in Switzerland. Andrews, once he had gotten out of Switzerland, was to head straight for Washington to convey the important intelligence he had learned.

On March 3, the seven airmen were escorted to Basel on the German border. The contrast with Switzerland was striking. At the German end of the train station, gigantic, blood-red swastika flags hung from the walls. A contingent of SS men dressed in black walked up to the Americans, and its commander, who sported a dagger on his belt, raised his arm and shouted, "Heil Hitler!" Fortunately, the Germans kept their side of the bargain, and the U.S. flyers were put aboard a train filled with regular German soldiers dressed in field gray. It turned out to be a local and the Wehrmacht men kept coming by to cadge cigarettes from the Americans and to chat. One German officer said, "Look, we Germans cannot defeat you. But neither can you Americans defeat us. Why don't we get together and fight the Russians?" At one stop, Andrews saw a girl collecting donations for the German Red Cross and gave her his last bit of Swiss money.

The train was ominously equipped with anti-aircraft guns, but was lucky enough to escape the attention of U.S. fighter bombers as it chugged across France. At the Spanish border, the Americans had the misfortune to cross at the same time as about 40 soldiers of the "Blue" Division, which fought alongside the German Army in Russia. The Spanish soldiers "yelled and screamed" at the Americans. Then a Swiss representative stepped up and took the airmen away in a waiting car.

Andrews subsequently reported Dulles' information to Washington and spent the rest of the war flying missions for Air Transport Command. It can never be ascertained how many lives he may have saved through his service for American intelligence. The information he carried had by any assessment been vital. Less than three months later, on D-Day, the Allies launched the invasion of France.

In response to overcrowding in the confines of Adelboden, which housed about 600 internees in summer 1944, and to reports that military discipline was breaking down, a separate officers camp was established at the resort village of Davos near Austria. Famous as a vacation spot for the British royal family, and since the war as the setting for world economic summits, Davos was then best known for its tuberculosis spas, which attracted large numbers of Germans. When the first contingent of U.S. officers arrived in town on June 22, 1944, they found the streets deserted and window shutters closed. The Germans had convinced the Swiss townspeople that "Chicago gangsters" were on the way.

When Jack McKinney first came upon Davos, he noticed how incredibly deserted it was at the time. He learned later how the Germans had attempted to frighten the citizens. The German Consulate also happened to be right across the street from one of the internees' hotels. As McKinney described, "We got even later by stealing the German swastika off the front of the Consulate wall. Not me, but someone did it and we all caught hell from [American Military Attaché] General Legge."

McKinney did not know it at the time, but the perpetrators were Lt. Oscar Sampson and Lt. John Garcia, who subsequently became the first American internees in Switzerland to escape. When the Germans protested the incident to the Swiss and the Swiss to General Legge, the two officers found themselves destined for a punishment camp. Sampson and Garcia were tipped off, however, and with the help of Swiss civilians were transported to the French border, where they passed into the hands of the local Resistance.

Of the necessity to open up more camps, Sgt. Francis Testa commented, "The Swiss were quite fair in their treatment of us at the time I arrived. The sudden influx of new airmen seemed too much for them though, and they couldn't be convinced that more personnel were needed in Bern to handle the situation. As a result, financial matters which were never handled any too well became quite a mess. This situation proved quite a handicap since with over five hundred men crowded into a space as limited as Adelboden, with little or no money to spend, life was anything but pleasant. I may add here that the men on the whole proved to be able to act and keep themselves under control."

In August 1944, the winter resort of Wengen was pressed into service as an internment site. Located approximately two hours by train from Adelboden and three from Davos, Wengen served both as an internment camp and as a quarantine center for new arrivals. At the peak of its activity in December, 14 hotels were utilized for internees. Hilda Graf, whose family owned a milk and cheese shop in Wengen, was 18 years old at the time and remembered, "The boys always wanted to hold your hand and go walking." Hotelkeeper Karl Fuchs recalled how the Americans would hand out candy to the children, mostly gum and Tootsie Rolls. He said the flyers were a source of amusement for children who attended a nursery school near the mountains. On many occasions, the students would be distracted from their schoolwork by the bumbling American skiers outside their window, barely surviving the Alpine slopes.

Karl Molitor, whose family owned a sporting goods store, tried to teach some of the Americans how to ski. He recalled that they always wanted to go straight down. They would take a tumble and then want to go straight down again. "It was very nice to look at," he said. Molitor recognized that the popularity of his family's store was partly due to the presence of his sisters, aged 17 and 19, who worked there. And his mother would take advantage of the airmen's enthusiasm. "If you want to see my daughters," she would say, "you have to come to the back of the store and sit down." She'd have them help prepare beans or do other chores. "They had a lot of fun doing it."

Adelboden, Davos and Wengen were the "big three" of the internee camps for the American airmen; however, a fourth location well remembered by internees—with decidedly mixed reviews—was the quarantine camp at Neuchatel. Located in western Switzerland near the French border, Neuchatel was the spot where airmen were most frequently held for about three weeks immediately after arriving in the country.

Charles Cassidy of the 303rd Bomb Group remembered his quarantine clearly. "The four of us were guarded by one Swiss soldier named Schell. At the top of the mountain, we were taken to a large chalet style lodge, not far from the funicular [cable car]. Here we would spend our three-week quarantine period. The area, called Chaumont, overlooks the city of Neuchatel and the lake of the same name. It is probably about 3,000 feet above the city. There are unpaved, single-lane roads snaking through the trees of the heavily wooded mountain. Having complete freedom, we walked the roads frequently. On Sundays, those of us who wanted to go to church were taken down by funicular to Neuchatel to attend services. On the first Sunday we were in Chaumont, we were taken by the townspeople to a cemetery where a memorial service dedicated to the memory of French people killed by Germans was held."

The quarantine was necessary for the Swiss to determine if the newly arrived airmen had any harmful or contagious diseases. This caused some friction between internees and the Swiss because part of the procedure was cutting the airmens' hair, which many Americans resented. Another aspect of Neuchatel was the "welcome" speech given to airmen by the American Legation, headed by General Bernard Legge, which informed airmen of their obligations. Many of the U.S. flyers were initially confused about their status as internees. Cassidy said, "First it was the Chaumont Hotel near Neuchatel where we spent some 10 days isolated from the world and being briefed by General Legge's staff. Although there were about 60 or 70 officers in the same hotel, we were a little suspicious of each other with the exception of our own crew members or those we knew from our group."

Such suspicion was further heightened by the sense that the airmen did not have the support of their superiors. That Switzerland, as a neutral, enforced different rules and regulations was difficult to grasp for many officers accustomed to the American army's way of doing things. According to many airmen, General Legge, for all his apparent professionalism, never addressed the essential confusion faced by arriving officers. Was the American Legation representing the Swiss, or was it representing the interests of its own airmen?

Legge was nevertheless firm on international military protocol. In one of several memos issued on the subject, he stated, "Since interned military personnel of the United States are in a position analogous to that of prisoners of war, the rendering of salutes to Swiss officers is mandatory and will be strictly observed."

On the whole, American officers seemed to regard their stay at Davos more favorably than did enlisted men recalling Adelboden or Wengen. As one remembered, "On June 23 we left Adelboden and went to Davos. Here the situation was greatly improved. For a while the food was rather poor but it did improve. I'm grateful for the fact that I never had the GIs while I was in Davos, which I did have occasionally

Swiss fighters frequently escorted American bombers to safe landing fields amid the Alpine nation's bewildering terrain. If fighters were not encountered, a bomber crew would often have to bail out or crashland.

Dubendorf airfield near Zurich during the winter of 1944–45. Of the 166 U.S. aircraft that arrived in Switzerland during the war, 96 were destroyed in crashes or later scrapped. Seventy were repaired after nearly 80,000 hours of work by Swiss and American maintenance crews.

Morane fighters at Magadino airfield. The Swiss manufactured Moranes under license from the French.

Prior to the Battle of France the Swiss purchased 80 Me-109s from Germany. During the war the Swiss enlarged the insignia on their planes so they would be easily recognized by Allied airmen.

General Henri Guisan emerges from the parliament building in Bern after being named the fourth general in Swiss history.
At his elbow is Minister of Defense Rudolf Minger and on the left is Federal President Marcel Pilet-Golaz.

The famous meeting at the Rütli Meadow in July 1940. At the place where medieval herdsmen had founded the Swiss nation, Guisan assembled his officer corps to reaffirm the principle of "no surrender."

At the Rütli, Guisan announced that the Army would neutralize blitzkrieg tactics by making the Alps its main line of defense.

At the end of 1943, Carl Spaatz was named commander of U.S. Strategic Air Forces in Europe, and Jimmy Doolittle was promoted to command of the Eighth Air Force.

Ford's assembly line for B-24s at Willow Run, near Detroit. At its peak efficiency, the plant was able to turn out one Liberator per hour.

77411-A 1-18-43

Death Dealer was the first American aircraft to land in Switzerland during the war.

Little Sheppard with all but its number four engine feathered. When an engine failed the pilot would feather the propellor by turning its blades in line with the wind so it would not spin uncontrollably, creating drag.

After the October 1943 Augsburg raid by the Twelfth Air Force, the Swiss held a mass funeral for 14 American airmen at Bad Ragaz.

Captain (later Major) Geoffrey von Meiss of the Swiss Air Force escorted a number of U.S. aircraft to safety during the war.

Part of *Lazy Baby*'s crew after crashlanding in Switzerland on "Black Thursday" in October 1943. From left: Ray Baus, Robert Cinibulk, Bernie Segal, Edward Dienhart and Christy Zullo.

Dazed but relieved airmen and Swiss civilians examine the wreck of *Lazy Baby* after the crash. The B-17 soon drew a larger crowd, below.

Lazy Baby's nose was shattered by a direct hit from a German fighter.

Major Noel Strader, at right, below, was the command pilot of an Eighth Air Force raid on Augsburg in March 1944.

The Germans converted their Focke-Wulf 190 fighters into "B-17 killers," adding additional armor and armament.

The 100th Bomb Group's *Battle Queen/ Peg Of My Heart* was crippled by fighters over Regensburg in August 1943.

Manchester Leader survived 45 missions before falling prey to flak in July 1944.

Note the chin turret added to "G" model B-17s to help fend off frontal fighter attacks.

Mount 'n' Ride, which lost two engines over Friedrichshaven in March 1944, sported a chin turret as well as other design enhancements.

Raunchy ditched in Lake Constance after the September 1943 Stuttgart raid. When the Swiss raised the B-17 a month later they found the body of ball turret gunner Joe Moloney, the first American airman to die on Swiss soil. The American internment camp at Adelboden was named after the fallen airman.

Christmas 1944 at the Palace Hotel, Wengen.

Internees pose outside the Regina Hotel in Wengen.

Swiss civilians flocked to the Wengen train station to say their farewells when airmen were repatriated in March 1945.

B-24 pilot Robert A. Long, pictured in Adelboden, lost 20 pounds during his stay in Switzerland.

Hilda Graf in Adelboden with an unidentified airman. "They always wanted to hold your hand and go walking."

Airmen recalled Swiss children as delightful. Swiss kids recalled that the Americans always had chewing gum.

Martin Andrews landed in Switzerland after the disastrous September 1943 Stuttgart raid. His B-17, *Est Nulla Via Invia Virtuti*, had 60 gallons of remaining fuel. Andrews would later be enlisted by Allen Dulles to carry vital intelligence back to Washington, DC.

Unbeknownst to Captain Edgar Woodward, his entire crew bailed out after their Fortress was hit over Stuttgart. He parachuted into Switzerland while his crew landed in Germany.

It took a Swiss radio tower to stop the crashlanding of Max Wilson's B-17 near Dubendorf in April 1944.

High Life, piloted by Donald Oates, was crippled by enemy fighters on the Schweinfurt-Regensburg raid of August 17, 1943.

During the last year of the war, nine U.S. aircraft other than long-range B-17s and B-24s landed in Switzerland. Above, Robert Rhodes's Mustang lies in the Rhine.

Ginny Gal crashed into a Swiss flak emplacement at Dubendorf on
July 21, 1944.

The Swiss city of Schaffhausen was accidentally devastated by U.S.
Liberators on April 1, 1944.

Touchy Tess was the last Eighth Air Force bomber to make it to Switzerland during the war.

In 1996, Cyril Braund (right) with a Swiss friend, Stefan Naef, climbed a Swiss mountainside to visit the wreckage of his B-17, *Champagne Girl*.

The American military cemetery at Münsingen in its early stages, above, and as it appeared on Memorial Day, 1944, below.

in Adelboden. [In Davos] we could go to movies, dances, and there were more women to go around."

Some airmen, like Lt. Russell K. Sherburne, recall being taken directly to Davos for quarantine, Neuchatel having become overcrowded. Sherburne describes his experience beginning after his plane crashlanded: "The officers and I were sent to Davos Platz by train. We were immediately taken to a hotel in Davos in which we were quarantined for 3 weeks. We had our meals in the hotel, and were able to get cigarettes, soap and other things, as earlier internees had set up a kind of traveling PX [Post Exchange] which came around almost every day."

Quarantine blended seamlessly into regular internment for this airman, and he remembers life in Davos as low-key. "Things got pretty boring just hanging around the hotel. We played cards, chess and practically anything we could remember to pass the time away. We finally got out at the end of three weeks and had the run of the town. However, we were still pretty well restricted since we could only get 45 francs a week and this didn't go far with the high prices. We also had to be back in the hotel by eleven o'clock each night. At the time I was there I couldn't get any passes for any other place in Switzerland. The food was good but seemed to come in very small quantities; there were only about two meals when I had enough to eat." Eventually, thoughts of leaving Switzerland surfaced: "When we heard on August 25th that the Yanks had reached Geneva, I left Davos to attempt an escape." Unfortunately for Sherburne, he was caught by Swiss soldiers and sent to Wauwilermoos. Others were more lucky.

Pilot Jack McKinney recalled, "The early days of Davos consisted of bridge games, golf, hiking, touch football games and meeting the Davos Swiss." Charles Cassidy said, "We had our freedom as long as we were present for bedcheck. Several times, to break the monotony, we hiked through the valley and over the pass to Klosters about three kilometers from the Austrian border, to eat at a small cafe.

"Our eating habits changed after we arrived in Switzerland. Having been used to plenty of everything, we were now in a country that was raising what it was feeding its own population plus very many displaced people from countries overrun by war. Thus our rations decreased. We had plenty to eat, but being bored from not doing very much of anything, we imagined that we were hungry all of the time." The experience of B-24 pilot Robert Long indicates that the airmen's reduced diet was more than a figment of imagination. He lost 20 pounds while interned in Switzerland.

Clinton Norby recalled the general cleanliness in one of the smaller internment camps set up toward the end of the war. Everything was sanitary and white, well ordered and without any unnecessary decoration. During his ten-day quarantine, however, "there was nothing to do. The guards would take us for walks around the little town [Munsingen] and show us the way the people lived and worked. We watched three men cut down a tree and not a thing was wasted; everything was used. The leaves were raked up and carried away, little twigs were bundled up and saved, and all the logs were cut the same length to be stacked around the house up to the eaves. All the roofs were constructed with a large overhang to keep the logs dry. The guard even showed us a butcher kill his own beef, in the open behind his meat market. He worked alone and all the time he worked the area was very clean."

The popular smoking habit among U.S. soldiers was made more difficult in Switzerland. According to Cassidy, "Smokers suffered, at least those used to American tobacco and cigarettes, which were very hard to come by and extremely expensive." Detrimental habits weren't altogether absent, however. "The beer was good. There were two types of beer that I was acquainted with, both made by the brewery in Chur: dunkel, a dark beer, and hell, a light. I preferred the light beer but only one bottle at a sitting because it was potent." Jürg Allig, whose father owned a bar in Adelboden, had frequent contact with the Americans. He remembered some of the airmen getting drunk, but also that the airmen had their own "police service," and if a man was too drunk other airmen would take him home and then as punishment the flyer had to do the police service for the next two weeks. "Even if they were drunk I never saw them cause trouble," he said.

Many Americans struggled with the fact of having little or no money. Karl Molitor's sporting goods store in Wengen would sometimes double as a pawn shop. At the end of each month airmen would come in and sell their watches while waiting for their next pay. At one point Molitor had 30 watches. "I was not worried," he recalled. "Ten days later or a few weeks later they would buy their watches again."

Hans Pieren, whose family owned a farm near Adelboden, said

that when the Americans were short of money they went out to the farms and sold their clothes. He remembered seeing farmers wearing flying boots. The airmen could make such transactions because the American Legation always replaced their "lost" uniforms. "Very different from the Swiss Army," Pieren commented. "If you lose something in the Swiss Army you have to pay for it yourself."

Lt. Earl W. Culbertson recalled, "We were treated very nicely by the main body of the Swiss people. The merchants seemed to want to make a fortune, but that was only natural." Prices were high, but so was demand. Switzerland was being squeezed from all sides during the war, and this caused not only low supply but also restrictions on commerce in order to preserve the economy's delicate balance. Adelboden storekeeper Peter Schranz recalled that he was unable to sell milk to the Americans because they didn't have ration coupons. On the other hand, according to Margrit Stiffler of Davos, "[The Americans] had a nice time and were paid very well from the States. They were drunk all the time because they had so much money to spend. They liked whiskey." Though the U.S. airmen were by no means flush with cash, as the only people in the country with discretionary spending money at all they were invariably considered rich by the Swiss. Teenager Hilda Graf from Wengen, the frequent target of hand-holding airmen, said their spending money impressed all the Swiss people at the time.

The Swiss tried their best to provide some entertainment, as in a physical education course given to internees by Swiss Army soldiers, and the airmen themselves killed time as best they could. But life in Switzerland for most U.S. flyers was frustrating. Distractions were few and far between, and, besides, there was a war going on. Partly spurred by a sense of abandonment that many felt from the American Legation, airmen inevitably began to plot their escape. About this time, many plans were being developed to leave Switzerland and get back into the fight. However, as Jack McKinney explained, "Most of these plans were placed on hold until the landings in southern France and the movement of the Allied forces up the Rhone Valley to the Swiss border. Some escape attempts were made before this, but most were unsuccessful." There was, in fact, little point in escaping a country that was itself surrounded by the enemy.

Although they were held in custody by the Swiss military, few American internees were privy to the activities of that army or to other events inside Switzerland. An exception was John Fanelli, who received a travel pass, and, instead of heading to a city as most men preferred, decided to take a train ride through the St. Gotthard Pass. After casually gazing out the window, he described "going through this valley, big haystacks on one side. Suddenly, this haystack opened up and an airplane came out of it. It was a concealed aerodrome." Near a town called Küssnacht he came upon a huge camp that he estimated held 15,000 Russians, escapees from German POW camps. For American internees, the war had suddenly slowed to a sluggish and usually boring pace. But for General Guisan's men on the border and in the Alps the war remained all too real.

11

AIR SUPERIORITY

After the titanic air battles over Germany in the spring of 1944, the Eighth Air Force was reined in to support Operation Overlord, the invasion of the Continent at Normandy. Howls of protest came from the bomber generals, who felt they had victory in the air war within their grasp; sighs of relief came from the bomber crews, who had been pressed to the limits of human endurance. Unlike Germany, France was within easy range of Allied fighters based in England, and the Luftwaffe had long since abandoned its forward bases. High-altitude bombers could still fall victim to heavy flak guns, but missions over France were far less dangerous than the deep-penetration raids over the Reich. The Eighth Air Force, along with Bomber Command and the U.S. 9th and British 2nd Tactical air forces, hammered the invasion coast, the French transportation network, and the still-elusive V-weapon launch sites. Eisenhower, as events proved, was correct in bringing all Allied resources to bear in support of Overlord, the most important military operation in modern history.

On June 6, 1944, Allied troops came ashore on the Normandy coast, winning a toehold on the Continent. The Germans massed panzer divisions to seal off the beachhead, and during the following weeks an inferno of tank battles seared the Norman countryside. The Allies couldn't penetrate the German cordon, while the Germans were unable to drive the invaders back to the sea. Then the "heavies" entered the battle. On July 25, over 1,400 Eighth Air Force bombers soared over St. Lo, a crucial hinge on the American side of the beachhead. The use of high-altitude bombers—blunt instruments by any measure—was problematic in the ground battle because of casualties that inevitably ensued from "friendly fire." On the morning of July 25, the Germans' first clue about what was to transpire came when American ground troops suddenly pulled their front back 1,500 yards from the path of the 80-mile-long bomber stream. A number of aircraft still mislaid their bombs, hitting Lieutenant General Lesley McNair, the highest-ranking American to die in the war, plus 500 others. Nevertheless, history's first successful attempt at carpet bombing also devastated the strongest division in the German Army, Panzer Lehr. The German commander, Fritz Bayerlein, said his front looked like a "moonscape." When American ground forces attacked they encountered scattered fire, assuming it came from advance German skirmishers. They soon realized that a few die-hard snipers were all that remained of Panzer Lehr. Two days later the U.S. 2nd Armored Division broke through and the enemy front in Normandy began to collapse.

In Switzerland, people anxiously kept an ear to their radios day after tense day for news from the invasion front. From the Swiss perspective, the rumbling in the East had grown louder that summer as the German front fell back from Russia. If the Allies did not succeed in their invasion, the Swiss would soon have the Red Army, in addition to the Wehrmacht, to contend with. Switzerland and the Soviet Union had always had an antagonistic relationship, beginning with the Swiss severance of diplomatic ties in 1918. Relations had been further exacerbated when the Swiss closed down two Soviet spy rings—Dora and Lucy—in October 1943. The Dora network, run from Geneva by a Hungarian emigré named Sandor Rado, consisted of ideological Communists with ties to what the Germans called the "Red Orchestra" in Berlin. According to historian Joszef Garlinski, Swiss intelligence moved against Dora after receiving specific information from Walter Schellenberg.

The Lucy network, run from Lucerne by an anti-Nazi German, Rudolf Roessler, was the more mysterious, and far more important, ring. Thanks to its pipeline into the highest councils of the Third Reich, Lucy is credited with providing the Soviets advance warning of the German offensive at Kursk, the battle that irrevocably turned the tide of war on the Eastern Front. Lucy's sources in Berlin have never been determined, though in the murky world of spy operations speculation continues. One theory is that Lucy was a front for British foreign intelligence, MI6, and used as a means of transferring Ultra secrets to the Soviets without having to reveal that the British had broken the Germans' top-secret Enigma code. When Germany was winning the war in the East, it was crucial for the British to help stave off a Soviet collapse. Once the Soviets gained the upper hand, however, it was just as essential that the Red Army not overrun Europe before Anglo-American forces could arrive on the Continent. After midsummer 1943 the Soviets no longer needed an advantage from Allied intelligence. According to this theory, Swiss Intelligence closed down Lucy after advice from MI6, and, many believe, Allen Dulles. (Throughout the war Dulles suspected that MI6 was riddled with Soviet agents, as postwar revelations confirmed.)

Meanwhile, the USAAF tried to forge a relationship with its Soviet ally with Operation Frantic, in which Eighth Air Force groups would bomb targets in Germany and continue east to land at Soviet bases. On June 21, 114 Flying Fortresses escorted by 54 Mustangs struck a synthetic oil plant south of Berlin and landed at Poltava in the Ukraine, the site of Swedish king Charles XII's climactic 1709 defeat. That night, some 200 German He-111 and Ju-88 bombers followed the American flight path and obliterated the air base, destroying 50 B-17s, 15 Mustangs and the airfield's entire quantity of carefully stockpiled fuel and munitions. The Americans wondered what had become of Russian radar, fighters or anti-aircraft defense. Operation Frantic, to which the Soviets had only reluctantly agreed, continued sporadically with additional missions until September, when the Soviets terminated it to prevent Allied air power from assisting the uprising of the Polish Home Army. Not only the Germans but the Soviets seemed to be intent upon preventing Western observers from seeing firsthand the kind of war that was being waged in the East.

To General Henri Guisan, Allied success in the West presented new dangers in addition to welcome news. On August 15, another American army invaded southern France, easily overcoming the coastal defenses, and began driving north. With the Germans falling back from two directions, the Swiss Army would have to be ready to meet a retreating Wehrmacht prone to desperate measures. Guisan ordered a mobilization with increased strength to the border units.

In May and June, only a dozen wounded U.S. aircraft had landed in Switzerland—a marked contrast to the deluge of March–April. (In June, Swiss fighters shot down a German Ju-52, whose crew of five died in the crash.) In July, however, the American armadas were freed from their D-Day tether and began streaming over Germany once more, in greater numbers than ever. Forty-five bombers landed or crashed on Swiss territory in July alone, together with a Mustang fighter, the bombers' new long-range companion.

On July 11, 1944, the Eighth Air Force launched nearly 1,200 Flying Fortresses and Liberators accompanied by about 800 fighters against targets in southern Germany. Of 20 bombers lost that day, eight landed in Switzerland. A B-24 of the 392nd Bomb Group, one of the formations that had accidentally attacked the Swiss city of Schaffhausen three months earlier, was the lead ship in a raid on Munich. Co-pilot James Green recalled: "Just after bomb release we took a 155mm hit in the number one engine plus assorted holes in the left wing including the fuel tanks. We dropped down through the other formations almost totally out of control until around 18,000 feet. When we began pulling out of the dive the airspeed was way past the red line and I'm sure we all felt the tail might come off at any moment. Fortunately the old girl held together. The engineer left his top turret to assess the damage and immediately reported a rapid loss of fuel from the left wing. Efforts to transfer fuel failed, and to compound the situation all radios went out."

Left with no communication and rapidly depleting fuel supplies, initial plans for a crashlanding were hastily made by navigator Ralph White. "With the fuel remaining the navigator calculated we could just make the French coast. The other alternative was to try for Switzerland. Prior to mission departure we had been briefed on the location of an emergency airfield on the southeast shore of Lake Constance. After assessing the possible courses of action, our pilot elected to try for that field."

As Green related, "There was a solid undercast that day and we were concerned that if no breaks in the clouds appeared, we would have to bail out prior to reaching the Alps. Fortunately, there was a fairly large hole over the southwest side of Lake Constance, so we lowered the landing gear and started spiraling down through the break. And those 'friendly,' 'neutral' Swiss anti-aircraft gunners sent up one helluva warm welcome of what looked and sounded like 20 and 40mm bursts! To this day I am convinced the Swiss put more holes in our B-24 than did the German gunners at Munich!

"We broke out at around 2,500 feet and started frantically trying to locate the airfield. The navigator found what he thought was it; a very small grass field, right smack on the Swiss-Austrian border." There was no time to worry about inches on one border or another, so the pilots began their descent. "We made one pass and decided it was this or nothing. At touchdown we knew we would have to collapse the nose wheel to stop or wind up in Austria. And that's what happened. We stopped with the nose of the plane right at the edge of a small ditch that we were later told marked the border."

Swiss troops immediately surrounded the plane and the American bomber crew was escorted to a building on the edge of the field. There, according to Green, "a Swiss Army major arrived, introduced himself, and said he needed to ask us a few questions. He informed us in a very friendly manner that his mother was an American and that he had graduated from Columbia University. Before he started the informal interrogation he demanded our escape kits. In particular he wanted the silk maps and money. The candy concentrate he let us keep. I attempted to hide my map by slipping it inside my long johns and letting it slide down to the top of my wool socks. When he didn't find the map in my kit he requested I drop my pants and underwear. He got the map! One of the first questions asked was if we had been on the April 1st raid that bombed Schaffhausen. I'm sure to a man we asked him, 'What is Schaffhausen?' I wonder what his reaction would have been if we had confessed that Schaffhausen had been our first combat mission!"

Each of the American flyers provided only his name, rank and serial number, plus his home address for the Red Cross to contact his family. Then, Green said, "At the end of the session the Major produced a map and informed us that we didn't need to give out any information as he already had all he needed. And with that he proceeded to show us the point where we left the British coast, the point crossing the French coast, route to the target, the primary target, the secondary target, return route, point where escort fighters picked us up inbound and where they left us."

The accidental bombings at Schaffhausen and elsewhere had increased the vigilance of Switzerland's air defense forces. That same day, a B-17 named *Manchester Leader* approached the Swiss border with serious engine trouble. The bomber had signaled for fighter escort and five U.S. P-51s accompanied the craft to Swiss airspace. This kind of show of force evidently sent the wrong signal to the Swiss. Pilot John Seilheimer recalled: "We were preparing to make a two-engine landing when Swiss fighters appeared and fired at us. We could see the tracers passing us. As they passed, the anti-aircraft barrage began. The first series took off the last three feet of the left wing. That was a jolting shock! The next series took out the radio room. As we turned onto final, the fighters reappeared, firing tracers all the way down. A landing was managed. The Swiss guards boarded the ship through the radio room with tommy guns and fire extinguishers and extinguished the oxygen-fed fire." As a rule, the Swiss welcomed U.S. internees, but if the American aircraft barged in with armed escorts, Swiss fighter pilots and AA gunners would not hesitate to assert their country's sovereignty.

In mid-July, while the remnants of the Luftwaffe were drawn into the battle of Normandy against Allied ground and tactical air forces, the strategic "heavies" poured into Germany on every clear day. Loss rates per mission had fallen below three percent, but given the great size of the raids—routinely numbering over 1,000 bombers per mission—the rates still represented hundreds of casualties. On July 12, 10 of 24 bombers lost by the Eighth Air Force made it to Switzerland, though some only partially or in pieces. One B-17 was severely damaged by flak over Munich and was picked up by two Mustangs who directed it south. Tail gunner Donald Boyle recalled, "When we got into the mountains, we were lower than some of the mountain peaks and we were flying in and out of snow squalls. The plane was sagging to the left as the two portside engines were the ones that were out. It was only through the great skill of our pilot, Lt. [Gerald] Kerr, that we had made it this far." Then the number three engine started pouring oil and Kerr ordered the crew to bail out. The aft crew, including Boyle, the waist gunner, ball turret gunner and radioman, jumped, but the plane was then over German territory and they spent the rest of the war in a stalag.

As Boyle later learned from top turret gunner Leon Finnerman, the weather had briefly cleared and the forward crew decided to stay in the air. But then number three went out completely and Kerr ordered another bail-out. Finnerman and the co-pilot jumped but pilot Kerr, the bombardier and navigator all crashed with the Fortress into a Swiss mountainside. The co-pilot's chute didn't open, so Finnerman was the only member of the crew to become an internee.

The number of U.S. bombers that tried but failed to make it to Swiss territory was never ascertained. On the afternoon of July 12, for example, a 492nd Bomb Group Liberator was hit over Munich by flak that set its ball turret on fire, killing the gunner. As recalled by pilot Herschel Smith, "I asked the navigator for a course to Switzerland. The only auxiliary maps we had were for northern missions, maps for Sweden and so on." Smith guided the craft south across miles of clouds until he saw the peaks of the Alps sticking out above the clouds at 16,000 feet. Finally he saw a break in the undercast. "I elected to spiral down through the hole. We broke out under the clouds heading downstream in a steep, narrow gorge. The next few minutes with clouds overhead and sheer rock walls right and left I stood that B-24 on first one wingtip and then the other as we followed that winding gorge downstream. Finally, we emerged, sweating, onto a plain and noted an airfield on either side of us at the base of the mountains."

When Smith flew over to check one of the airfields, a barrage of flak tore off chunks of the plane's wings. He flew to the other, only to see fighters with black crosses taking off. According to Smith, "The gunners reported enemy fighters all around us. We had three inoperative turrets, and a fighter fired a burst of 20mm cannon across my nose. I lowered the gear, signal of surrender, and followed him in for a landing in what turned out to be Northern Italy."

The next day, four B-17s and a B-24 made it to Swiss airspace, out of 10 bombers lost by the Eighth Air Force. The Liberator's crew bailed out near Solothurn just before their plane exploded. On the 16th, a B-17 with two damaged engines and a collection of flak holes crashlanded at Dubendorf.

On July 18, another huge fleet of U.S. bombers attacked Friedrichshaven and the Memmingen airfield in southern Germany, with only a single damaged plane reaching Switzerland. The plane, a B-17 of the 2nd Bomb Group, was piloted by Lt. Millard Pedigo, an experienced airman who had completed over 30 successful missions over Europe. The plane began to suffer mechanical difficulties halfway through the mission and was forced to drop out of formation. When the situation worsened, the crew made the decision to head for the nearest refuge. Radioman William Aeschbacher recalled: "Chances were that we could not get back to our base, so we changed course and headed for Switzerland. Ten or fifteen minutes later, I heard over the intercom, 'Look, coming in at 9 o'clock high, the Red Cross has sent us help. I didn't know they had an Air Force!' Sure enough there they were, three Swiss fighters who escorted us to fly to the Dubendorf air field. We landed with one good engine and were met with many armed Swiss soldiers. I did not know where we were for sure and at first I thought they might be German." The Swiss white cross on red background was often mistaken for the red cross on white background at first glance by nervous bomber crews.

One day later, a B-17 bomber named *Champagne Girl* took off with what pilot Cyril Braund called "one of the largest armadas of airplanes ever put into the air at one time." The size of the fleet would soon prove a detriment to Braund on this, his thirteenth mission. After fighters and flak, the third greatest danger to airmen was collision. Just as Braund lined up for his bomb run, another Flying Fortress suddenly careened into *Champagne Girl*'s right wing and tail. The other plane went spiraling down into Germany, but Braund was able to hold onto his: "We had just turned on our Initial Point at 28,000 feet when we were knocked out of the air with our right number four engine gone, number three prop damaged, and the right aileron gone. This was caused by another aircraft who had evidently been hit flying next to me and lost control and came up underneath my right wing and hit our starboard engines and our aileron.

"We went into a spin at 28,000 feet. I remember that during this time I called upon my co-pilot to put both feet on the left rudder and push, as I was doing with my left foot on the left rudder. He mentioned, 'I better pull the throttles back,' and I said, 'Hell yes.' I was thankful that he just beat me to it. But I was busy then trying to right the plane. At 11,000 feet we were able to pull the plane out of the spin and level off. The crew told me later that while in the spin they were flattened against the deck and they were trying to crawl to the escape hatches but couldn't move with the centrifugal force."

Despite recovering some control, Braund knew that the Fortress was barely able to stay in the air. "After the plane was flying straight and level we tried to assess the damage. The ball turret was bolted on with supposedly breakaway bolts. I ordered the waist crew and the ball turret gunner to use the tools provided to break away the bolts and drop the ball turret. That was 1,000 pounds that we could lose. However, no matter how they struggled, they could not drop it. I then ordered all flak suits and anything that was movable to be thrown out to lighten the weight." With the plane dropping from the sky, the pilot knew he had to look for other, more drastic solutions. "I asked the navigator to give me a heading to either Sweden or Switzerland. He informed me that we were nowhere near Sweden but we were not too far from Switzerland, so he gave me the heading to Switzerland. Prior to that time, I had turned around and tried to head back to England but was losing altitude too fast. We were only flying on two engines on the left side.

"At that time I tried to talk to my crew to give them instructions, but my mouth was so dry I could not speak. I remember getting a stick of gum out of the leg pockets of my flight suit and chewing on it until my mouth was moist enough to speak. I ordered them all to put on their parachutes and be ready to jump as we were losing altitude and could not seem to keep the plane on a level flight. As we neared Switzerland, my navigator was doing his usual excellent job in keeping us posted as to what location we were flying over. He said he was not sure but thought we were nearing the Swiss border. At this time I was flying between mountains and could see several miles ahead—mountains in front of me and to either side of me. At the time, I believed this was it!"

The airman realized that he couldn't land in such rough terrain, and ordered an immediate evacuation of the aircraft. However, his crew was reluctant. "I listened to a bunch of chatter over the intercom as one or two of them didn't want to jump, so I had the crew chief push them out. The bombardier and navigator opened the bombardier escape hatch and dove out head first. My co-pilot said, 'Well, we're alone.' I said, 'Yes, now you get going.' He replied, 'I can't leave you because you cannot hold the stick and rudders yourself.'" Knowing that his co-pilot was right, Braund came up with another solution. "I said, 'We'll set it up on autopilot the best we can. We have a rudder and an elevator and the left aileron.' So, I ordered him out and held onto the yoke as I stepped out of my seat onto the deck. I let go and started to back up and my chest chute caught between the seats. I had to come forward, turn a little sideways and free my chute and then I went down below deck and out of the bombardier's escape hatch.

"At this time the altimeter was registering 2,000 feet above ground. As I dove out and saw the tail of the airplane go by, I pulled the rip cord. I looked down, saw the pilot chute sticking out of my chest pack and thought it was not going to pull the main chute so I grabbed the pilot chute and pulled it out, threw it up in the air above my head and waited. It wasn't long until I got that sudden stop and there was that big white umbrella above my head."

Braund may have been lucky. Later that afternoon, Lt. Michael W. Ballbach died when his chute didn't open in time, or perhaps had been damaged. His crew had been forced to enter Switzerland as their number two engine failed and they were chased out of German territory by enemy fighters. The rest of the 456th Bomb Group crew, except for the navigator (who ended up as a POW in Germany), escaped the flaming plane with little injury.

Braund, too, escaped his aircraft alive, but couldn't help but look to see what happened to *Champagne Lady* after he had jumped: "I could see my plane still flying straight and level; wonder of wonders. Before I hit the ground I saw the plane crash into the side of a mountain and disintegrate. It was quite a sight!"

He twisted his leg on hitting the ground, and after getting out of his chute began limping in the direction of the crash. "I had not gone far when three farmers with pitchforks approached me. They just stood and looked at me and I tried to find out if I was in Switzerland. I kept asking them, 'Switzerland, Switzerland?' At the time I did not know they called it Suisse. So I thought I must be in Germany and I asked for the army. 'Army, army?' They did not understand me. Finally, I said, "Military" and this is a word that they did understand so they motioned for me to sit and wait." Allied flyers knew that if they made it safely to the ground in enemy territory, their next great threat could come from enraged civilians rather than military authorities, who followed the book. Passing into custody of the Luftwaffe, which ran its own POW camps for Allied flyers, was optimum because German airmen—almost exclusively in the Reich—viewed their counterparts with a degree of empathy. Alone in the countryside, Braund experienced some tense moments while waiting to see if his new acquaintances had summoned the military or more friends with pitchforks. He finally received proof that he had made it to Switzerland. "In about an hour, I was amazed to see the military drive up in a 1936 Chevrolet Cabriolet with the top down. An officer and five enlisted men were in it. They took me to a nearby town, I guess it was Chur, where they took me to a military house. There they gave me food and wine and called a doctor to attend to my hurt leg."

The relentless U.S. bombing of German industrial targets continued on July 20, though the most significant bomb that day was the one that exploded underneath the conference table in Adolf Hitler's East

Prussia headquarters. The German Army attempted a coup d'état in Berlin while Hitler's Nazi loyalists frantically tried to reassert control. Unaware of the crisis in the Third Reich, for Fifteenth Air Force, Italy, it was another day at the office: braving storms of enemy fire at 25,000 feet above southern Germany. The target that day was Friedrichshaven, on the German side of Lake Constance. To an experienced airman such as the 459th Bomb Group's Joseph Sinitsky, on his 49th mission, the target's proximity to the "safe haven option" was carefully noted in advance.

"En route to the target we lost first one engine, and then another one," Sinitsky recalled, "causing us to lose formation. At this point we were very low on altitude. We followed a valley with mountains on either side high above us, looking for a place to bail out. The plane kept dropping lower, as we found it impossible to gain altitude." Despite his airman's intuition, the appearance of the Swiss countryside produced more confusion than he or his crew had anticipated. "We did not know our exact location, and because of all the excitement and anxious moments, the navigator surmised we were near Switzerland, so the pilot just kept following the valley. Finally we saw an airfield, where we made a crashlanding on a short runway, ending up in a large ditch. Fortunately we all survived with no apparent injuries." Like many airmen before them, Sinitsky and his crew were a bit surprised when Swiss troops appeared seemingly out of nowhere to guide them away from the plane. "Suddenly the plane was surrounded by armed soldiers, and we were certainly relieved to learn that they were indeed Swiss. So we had made it into Switzerland, and the crew gave a sigh of relief." The site of their landing turned out to be Dubendorf, one of the most popular landing fields for crippled bombers on mainland Europe.

Another 456th Bomb Group Liberator barely made it into Switzerland that day. Sgt. Peter Lysek survived the harrowing experience of first suffering dangerous flak bursts to his B-24 *Rau Dee Dau*, then a nearly fatal jump from his dying plane, and finally a curious reception from the people around his landing area. Lysek was on his 50th—intended to be his last— mission of the war.

"We were on a bomb run over Friedrichshaven just minutes before 'bombs away' when we were hit by anti-aircraft shells. One blast knocked a gaping hole in the forward upper right hand bomb bay, and another direct hit was between the fuselage and number three engine.

Raw gasoline was pouring out onto the bombs and bomb bay, reaching us in the waist section of the ship. My position at the time was left-hand waist gunner. My duty as flight engineer was also to know the condition of our aircraft and at all times to keep the pilot informed on the condition." Those responsibilities forced Lysek to deliver the bad news to the cockpit. "With what must have been a shaky voice I informed the pilot of what had happened. He turned his head to look down into the bomb bay and what greeted him was raw gasoline in the face. Immediately he notified the bombardier to jettison the bombs." The situation was now critical.

The pilot, Lt. William Newhouse, began the sequence of events that would either save the crew, or, if he made the slightest misjudgment, result in their doom. Lysek said, "On the radio command intercom he notified all crew members he was turning off all electrical switches and power to the aircraft, and would rapidly drop down and out of formation. Then he said we would try to reach Switzerland across Lake Constance. He felt that we could clear the lake safely. Again he informed us that as soon as we cleared the lake, everyone should begin to bail out and they would be on their own—and, of course, 'good luck.'

"As we reached the Swiss side of the lake, we were at about 12,000 feet. Crew members began bailing out from the forward part of the ship. I informed all gunners in the aft section to begin bailing out." Lysek took a leadership role because, as he explained, "Too often on past combat missions I had seen aircraft get hit over a target, and raw gasoline trailing from the aircraft. Then all of a sudden a huge ball of fire explodes with nothing but pieces going down in flame. This fate I was trying to avoid. Quickly everyone was bailing out of the crippled aircraft."

When the rest of the men were safely out, Lysek followed his own orders and hastily left the aircraft. He continued: "After I bailed out and quit tumbling, I pulled the rip cord and was free falling, waiting for my chute to open. I looked at the 'D' ring and the two pins on the rip cord were pulled out okay. But my parachute was not opening." With time running out, Lysek's frantic instincts took over: "I dropped the 'D' ring like it was red hot and began clawing at my chest pack. All of a sudden the chute fully opened above my head. Looking up and seeing that beautiful white flower over my head remains to this day the most beautiful flower I have ever seen, for it saved my life."

Quick thinking on Lysek's part ultimately saved him future troubles. "When the chute opened, my flight-heated suit boots kept going. Before I bailed out I tucked my G.I. shoes under my chute harness. Otherwise I would have been walking in my socks." The ride down was nevertheless a long trip, and the airman remembered it vividly. "I had fallen from about 12,000 to 3 or 4,000 feet before the chute finally opened. This had given me just enough time to look about and see what was happening. As I looked toward the smoking target, I could see other bombers in formation dropping bombs on the target with flashes and noise from their explosions. Then I saw my crippled bomber crash and explode with a column of black smoke rising."

The presence of other planes and fellow crew members nearby seemed surreal. He remembers, "Swiss fighter planes were circling between my crew members floating down who were still about 5,000 feet up." Distracted by the scenery, Lysek suddenly realized he was about to land. "Then I looked down and saw I was falling in a large field with a lot of people working. I could see them smile up at me, and I figured right away this must be Switzerland; for no Kraut would be smiling." The workers were tilling a small patch of dried potatoes. Little did the airman suspect that the crops they were tending would become the staple of his diet for months to come.

For several weeks Lysek had nightmares about his harrowing fall from the aircraft, but for the time being Swiss hospitality was immediate and surprising. "Right away there were dozens of girls and children around me. Then a few Swiss soldiers came up and they told me that I was in Switzerland. They also said the war was over for me, which I could hardly believe right then. The soldiers carried my parachute and part of my flying clothes." Lysek was ushered away from the field toward a small village, perhaps half a mile away. There, he said, "Everyone in the surrounding field came and joined the parade. By the time I got into the village I was leading well over a hundred people. They claimed that I was the first one to bail out around there." After the war, *Rau Dee Dau*'s pilot, William Newhouse, recalled that, of the 17 crews in his original squadron, only five completed their tour of duty.

Hell's Bells, flown by Howland Hamlin and co-pilot Richard Newhouse (cousin of *Rau Dee Dau*'s pilot) ran into the same murderous wall of flak over Friedrichshaven, suffering damage to its flight controls and a massive gasoline leak. The plane couldn't make it over

Lake Constance and the crew bailed out over the water. Minutes later the aircraft exploded in mid-air, the tail landing in Switzerland and the rest of the debris in Germany. The top turret gunner, Donald Anderson, was the only crewman to land on Swiss soil, but local Swiss raced out in boats to retrieve gunner Tommy Tonnessen from the lake. They later found John Boardsen, who didn't survive his parachute jump. For the other members of *Hell's Bells* the fall would also have dire consequences. They all came down on the German side of Lake Constance where they endured a sample of enemy ruthlessness. Historians Hans-Heiri Stapfer and Gino Künzle related: "Several Swiss people had witnessed German troops across the lake firing on the crew as they parachuted to the ground. The same fishermen who rescued Tonnessen also attempted to rescue bombardier George Hunter, but were driven away by a German patrol boat. The bombardier was tangled in his parachute and drowned before the Germans could effect his rescue. This outrage was given considerable publicity by the Swiss newspapers and the local populace was greatly upset by this example of German barbarism."

While Switzerland was a viable and important option for endangered airmen, it certainly was not a risk-free destination. The proximity of German flak on the north side of Lake Constance was a danger every airman had to consider when trying to get into Switzerland. As a key landmark, Lake Constance was important, but it was crucial to remember that Germans were on the other side.

On July 21, Eighth Air Force lost 31 bombers in a "maximum effort" against southern Germany. Twenty-two of the losses were Liberators from the 2nd Air Division but eight of these, including *Ginny Gal*, whose story was recounted earlier, made it to Switzerland. All of the B-24s had suffered heavy damage and one, *Mary Harriet*, entered Swiss airspace unnoticed by Swiss fighter escorts. Disoriented and losing altitude, the crew bailed out as their bomber crashed into a mountain. Tragically, waist gunner Leo J. Hoffman was killed in the jump when his chute failed to open.

The last day of July 1944, the busiest month of the war for what one might term Swiss fighter "receptors," brought two final arrivals into the Alpine nation from the Mighty Eighth. A B-17 called *Twat's It to You*, piloted by Victor Lewis, was hit by heavy flak over Munich and made it to Dubendorf, whereupon it was deemed unrepairable and scrapped. The second Flying Fortress, piloted by Jay D. Ossiander, had two nicknames. On the right side it was called *Umbriago* and featured a headshot of Jimmy Durante; on the left it sported the name *Freckles* along with a painting of a beautiful girl. In his account of the day's events, gunner/engineer Penrose Reagan described a mission that began badly and only got worse.

"We blew a tail wheel on takeoff, which was the start of our problems. After we turned on to the IP, the number two engine began throwing oil, and our pilot, instead of dropping our bombs and going around the target and picking up the group on the way home, decided to take us across the target through heavy flak with three engines. Then the number two propeller would not feather and kept going back into high pitch. As a result, the number two engine lost all of its oil and seized. The propeller continued to rotate, stripping the propeller reduction gears, allowing the propeller to rotate freely which caused considerable vibration.

"By this time we had dropped out of the group and become a straggler, while the group went on to bomb the target. We had been flying the last ship, low squadron, commonly known as the Purple Heart Corner. As we went over the target and into the flak area, we were hit again in the number three engine, which started throwing oil. Ossiander by this time decided not to proceed through the target area and we salvoed our bombs and made a banking turn to the left." The split-second decision came not a moment too soon, as German air-to-air rocket fire had zeroed in on the Fortress. "As we made the bank, two rockets went by on the right side from 6 o'clock low to 12 o'clock high. If we had not made the bank, we would have been hit by the rockets.

"About 400 yards off to our right a B-17 exploded and no parachutes were seen. This ship was not from our bomb group and like ourselves was a straggler." Reagan's crew had escaped instant death, but problems kept piling up for the beleaguered ship. "The propeller on the number three engine duplicated the same sequence of events as number two. By this time we were having difficulty maintaining altitude because two of the propellers were frozen in the high pitch position, creating a lot of drag. Additionally there was a lot of severe vibration set up by the two windmilling props."

The pilots boosted power to emergency ratings on numbers one and four, the only good engines, but then four started to overheat. It would be only minutes before number one followed suit. At that point there was little hope that the bomber could make it back to England. The crew considered trying for Yugoslavia, which by that time had been largely retaken from the Nazis by partisan armies, assisted by the Russians and British. But the trembling Fort had become too weak to stay in the air. The navigator set a course for Switzerland.

By the time it reached Swiss airspace the aircraft was rapidly sinking. When German-made planes were sighted, the crew was initially alarmed. "By now we were 1,200 to 1,500 feet off the deck. Someone called, 'Me-109s at 9 o'clock!' I popped back into the upper turret and swung my guns on them." Ready for a bitter fight, only a quick move by one of the fighters prevented a disaster. "At this time the closest 109 flipped its wings up so we could see the Swiss cross. Then it proceeded to drop his wheels and motioned for us to follow him. The fighters took us to Dubendorf airfield. It was then that we found out that one of our main landing gear tires had been shot out. This tire, plus the tail wheel tire that had blown on takeoff, made the landing a bit dicey, since the aircraft wanted to ground loop. However, control was maintained and the powers that be smiled on us again." With the help of the neutral Me-109s and their own pilot's skill, the crew of *Umbriago/Freckles* landed safely at Dubendorf. The crew was questioned and eventually sent to officers' quarters at the airfield to await their internment assignment.

For the 45 U.S. planes that landed in Switzerland in July 1944, the little neutral country south of Germany proved to be a blessing. Operations against German targets had never been conducted on such a large scale, and many bomber crews were freshly trained newcomers from the States. When missions went wrong, as they inevitably did when up to a thousand heavy planes were dispatched at a time, knowledge of a safe place to land was critical to survival. Sgt. Kenneth "Bud" Youngren summed it up best when he called his crashlanding on July 13 the "highlight of my life." He said, "I never expected to survive the air war and land in that island of peace and beauty." Since his "near-death" experience in July 1944 aboard a crippled aircraft, he has been back to Wengen, where he was interned, several times simply to "enjoy the beauty and our dear Swiss friends."

The big news for Hap Arnold, Carl Spaatz and other American air chiefs after the July raids was that the Luftwaffe air arm had obviously been defeated. Even its flak arm, though perhaps stronger than ever, was increasingly overwhelmed by the size of the U.S. raids. Part of the Germans' problem was that over the invasion front in Normandy their pilots had been forced into combat within range of overwhelming numbers of Anglo-American fighters based in England. German ace Walter Krupinski said that in June he lost his entire group of 40 pilots. "They were not all dead, but in hospital or on the way back to their unit after bail-out." Fighter planes continued to pour off German assembly lines, but were often flown by hastily trained pilots who proved easy prey for the skillful, and increasingly experienced, American aviators. The burgeoning force of Mustang pilots was thirsty for kills, its greatest problem being a shortage of German fighters. Soon, Eighth Air Force would release its fighters from the bomber streams altogether and set them to maurauding the German transportation network and other targets of opportunity on an independent basis.

The sudden decline of the Luftwaffe, which can be traced directly to the brave persistence of American bomber crews striking at its material roots, was inversely paralleled by the ascendancy of U.S. industrial might. In high gear by mid-1944, American factories were turning out endless streams of aircraft; training schools more than enough capable airmen. In 1943, several hundred unescorted American bombers might have penetrated into Germany, only to be met by waves of experienced German fighters, but a year later over a thousand bombers were taking off on each mission, accompanied by an equal number of escorts against a fuel-starved Luftwaffe fighter arm shrinking into insignificance. A full 85 percent of Allied bombs dropped on Germany were delivered after D-Day, 72 percent during 1945, the last four months of the war. Air superiority had been won.

For American flyers already interned in Switzerland, reports of Allied success in the air campaign were accompanied by even better news from the ground war. By mid-August, the German front in Normandy had collapsed, its escape route through the Falaise Gap turned into a landscape of unspeakable carnage by Allied armor, artillery and tactical air. George Patton was leading the newly activated American Third Army in a breathtaking race across northern France. In the south the American invaders, together with a Free French army, quickly overran the bulk of Vichy France, where the Germans had been less prepared. In late August, U.S. Seventh Army touched the Swiss border near Geneva. The Axis encirclement of Switzerland had been broken.

For many U.S. airmen, the presence of American troops at the border proved an irresistible lure to escape internment. Adelboden, Davos, Wengen, and other smaller camps had been tolerable enough, but a poor substitute for the possibility of rejoining the now-triumphant Allied war effort. The only obstacles in the internees' way were an American legation in the Swiss capital obstinately obsessed with protocol and a Swiss Army firmly committed to doing its duty. "Armed neutrality" was not a policy of convenience Switzerland had adopted when the Nazi threat appeared in the 1930s. It was a historic position the Swiss had applied for centuries, and through strenuous efforts had carried out during the war with many thousands of French, German, Polish, Italian, Russian and Yugoslav internees. Swiss soldiers, of course, would continue to perform their duty as ordered by superiors who took seriously Swiss national policy and obligations. American internees who wished to join their fellow GIs who had arrived on the western border would face formidable resistance and a significant degree of risk. Nevertheless, it was a risk that nearly a thousand airmen were willing to take.

12

ESCAPE FROM SWITZERLAND

Switzerland had provided a safe haven for many airmen in dire peril, but there was no obscuring the fact that, once inside the country, the flyers were prisoners of war. Switzerland, in both policy and philosophy the opposite of a "hostile" power, still adhered strictly to the martial obligations assigned to neutral states by international law. In earlier centuries the Swiss Confederation had pioneered the principle of official nonalignment, and its location in the center of Europe required it to defend its status with a militance not required of countries more distant from the conflict. Turkey, Sweden, Ireland and Spain, as well as numerous South American states, could invoke neutrality with minimal fear of invasion or material involvement. Switzerland, which spent most of World War II completely surrounded by the Axis Powers, was involved whether it liked it or not.

The rules of war that designated internees in Switzerland as POWs in a neutral state were based on logic. If foreign combatants were able to enter Swiss territory and then leave at will, the concept of neutrality—as well as the national sovereignty of the neutral state—would be meaningless. The French corps that walked into Switzerland in June 1940, for example, could have evaded their German pursuers only to resume combat by returning to France on a safer sector of the front. The German Nineteenth Army, in August 1944, might have entered Switzerland to avoid Patch's American Seventh, then re-emerged in Germany to take new positions along the Rhine. Foreign airmen, if not interned, could have considered Swiss territory an extension of their base network. Instead, the rule was clear. Combatants entering a neutral state were disarmed and removed from the conflict—held as

173

internees of that country until repatriation was arranged, either according to the rules of international law or by mutual agreement among the combatants. The Swiss were not eager to be given military charge of the 102,000 foreign combatants who sought refuge in their territory during World War II, but they accepted their obligation. American airmen, often to their chagrin, were held as POWs in Switzerland, rather than being allowed to rejoin their units in Italy, England or France. The Hague Convention of 1907, in reference to the treatment of internees, stated in Articles 11 and 12:

> [The neutral] may keep them in camps and even confine them in fortresses or in places set apart for this purpose. It shall decide whether officers can be left at liberty on giving their parole not to leave the neutral territory without permission.

Neutrals were required to supply food, clothing and general humanitarian relief (medical care), as were combatant powers for prisoners of war. The Swiss didn't issue blanket paroles for officers (most of whom would have declined them in any case), but issued temporary ones to U.S. airmen for trips around the country or for visits to doctors. The parole, based on a centuries-old military honor system, was a signed paper stating that the internee would not escape while the term of the parole was in effect.

Most American airmen recognized Switzerland's precarious geopolitical position and respected its polices, but some expressed outrage after the war. One flyer asked, "If Switzerland was neutral, why did it have AA guns? Why were there bedchecks at 11:00 each night? Armed guards outside our rooms?" Many U.S. airmen, too, were curious about why Swiss officers interrogated them so thoroughly after they landed. What neutral would be so intent on operational intelligence and so interested in the technical developments of foreign aircraft? Just as the myth of Switzerland as a country club for downed fliers persisted in the outside world, many U.S. airmen were startled on arrival to find they had landed in an armed camp, and had fallen into the custody of an active foreign military.

Another source of frustration to American internees, who had arrived in the country aboard, or parachuting from, crippled aircraft, was the greater latitude granted by international law to "evadees" or "escapees." According to the Hague Convention, the latter two categories of personnel were unconfined and free to leave the country anytime they wished. Internees were considered combat soldiers who had sought refuge, while evadees were supposedly unarmed and separated from their units. Escapees were considered to be helpless former prisoners of war. Several thousand British Empire troops who had made it to Switzerland from Italian POW camps were simply put on trains out of the country once the Allies were ready to receive them. U.S. airmen could only watch the British depart in September 1944, though a number of enterprising USAAF flyers donned "Tommy" overcoats and joined them.

Escaping from Switzerland was not a high priority for most American internees as long as the country was surrounded by the Axis; however, when the Seventh Army reached the Swiss border following Operation Dragoon—the invasion of the French Mediterranean coast—the urge to escape became widespread. The reasons were various: many young airmen were bored to tears in their confinement; perhaps a greater number were influenced by the meager, unappetizing food (the same wartime fare the Swiss public, and army, was eating); some wished to rejoin their units and continue fighting; others wished more direct contact with their families or loved ones. An additional reason to escape Switzerland was that every American GI had been taught that it was his duty to escape from captivity, if at all possible. In Switzerland, where the public was overwhelmingly pro-Allied, escape was indeed possible. The only problem was the Swiss Army and the American Military Legation in Bern.

Brigadier General Bernard R. Legge, head of the American Legation in the Swiss capital, informed U.S. airmen on numerous occasions that they were absolutely forbidden to escape from Switzerland. Violators would be considered criminals under international law. Legge claimed that these orders came from Washington, although no record of such instructions has been found. Navigator Jack Mahaffey of the 351st Bomb Group remembered what he called the general's "Welcome to Switzerland" speech after his B-17 crash-landed in March 1944. "I'll never forget that pompous SOB Legge. Strutting around, dressed in his cavalry boots, swagger stick under his arm telling us how lucky we were, how nice Switzerland was and ordering us to make no attempts to escape. Of course this was contrary to our own Air Force orders to 'make every effort to return to your unit.'"

Pilot James Green learned of Legge's edict immediately upon checking into the Palace Hotel in Davos to begin his internment in July 1944. "One of the first things I recall was a briefing by our own camp commander. He informed us that our U.S. Military Attaché, General Legge, wanted us to understand that if we attempted to escape and succeeded in getting back to our respective groups, we would be court-martialed and sent back to Switzerland to serve out the war in Wauwilermoos! This was most puzzling to us as we had committed no crime, and certainly complying with the military order that specifical-ly stated the first duty of an American combat man if captured is to make every possible effort to escape and return to his unit, cannot be classified as a crime!"

The confusion was solved when the airmen heard from General Carl Spaatz, head of the U.S. Strategic Air Forces in Europe. "He sent word by the officer who came to Davos each month to pay us," Green said, "wanting all of us to remember the oath we took regarding capture. And also expressing indignation that very few had even attempted escape!" That settled it. The American Legation, which was not fondly viewed by U.S. airmen in any case, would henceforth be ignored.

Green continued: "I don't recall how I found out that there was a pretty good underground movement going on in Davos, and for the most part run by the Yugoslavs, but I kept dropping hints around until I was contacted by the Yugo major running the show. From there on it was just a matter of accumulating some money (not easy on $7 per month) and a plan that was acceptable to our camp commander."

Edward Winkle, a B-24 radioman quartered in Adelboden, stated: "The way to let the officers be aware of your intentions was to buy a suit of clothes. So I with my good friend S.R. Simms did just that and sort of flashed them around. Within a day or so, we were called into the officers' headquarters and asked if we were going somewhere. We answered that we were thinking about moving on. We were told to leave the camp in the evening." Airman Louis Joseph remembered that the American camp commander in Wengen warned the men each morning not to try to escape or they would be court-martialed. Joseph nevertheless decided to leave Switzerland and felt he should talk to the officer first. "I got the surprise of my life," he recalled. "He was all for it and told me to make sure I tell him the day I expect to go. And he then said, 'Say hello for me in the States.' Later, the same commandant who at roll call would preach 'do not attempt escape' said I would have to leave on the first cogwheel train, which left in early morning." Unknown to many airmen, U.S. officers had already made contact with a network of operatives, mostly Swiss citizens, connected to the French Maquis.

There were three basic choices for airmen who had decided upon escape. First, they could try it on their own, walking cross-country or hopping a train, perhaps relying on ad hoc help from Swiss citizens en route. Second, they could arrange a plan through their camp officers. The internees' main benefactor in these efforts was American Consul General Sam Woods, who enjoyed a good reputation among the airmen. Woods set up an escape network that connected the various internment camps to French Resistance personnel based in Geneva, and also supplied U.S. Consulate staffers to facilitate movement. Woods himself was omnipresent, especially when airmen were in trouble. The third option for escapees was to make careful plans of their own using freelance accomplices, though this method involved risks. Airman William Wilkey recalled:

"I had been in Adelboden approximately one month when I decided to escape. I contacted a Yugoslav, Captain Milos Karovic, who for $150 American money put me in contact with another Yugoslav who furnished me with civilian clothes and a passport. The escape plan was to walk to the nearest town and take a train from there to Lausanne and to Free France. We got to Lake Geneva without difficulties and were taken to a hotel in Lausanne and told to wait there until our Yugoslav friend came back to take us to the boat. We were in the room only a short time when Swiss police in civilian clothes arrived and placed everyone under arrest. I personally think the Yugoslavs had a money-making scheme going for them. They talked gullible Americans out of $150 per man, made what appeared to be an effort to help us escape, then delivered us to a pre-arranged place and notified Swiss police where we were and collected a reward from the Swiss for turning us in."

Eugene Metz had a similar close call with unofficial channels. Originally interned at Adelboden, he was transferred to Davos in late July. "It was a sad occasion when I was transferred to Davos," Metz said. "With only five of our original crew left, we were very close and leaving Adelboden was an emotional moment.

"At Davos my main involvement was the dance band, playing

tenor sax. Although I enjoyed this, I couldn't get it out of my head that I should not be there. Late in July I tried talking to the Military Attaché, who was on one of his visits from Bern. Requesting permission to escape and return to Allied control got me only a brush-off and a reminder that if caught I could expect six months of prison. I had also heard about a possible court-martial on return to Allied control. I could not bring myself to believe this was possible." Metz was soon approached by several other airmen who were in contact with a Swiss who ran an escape route to the south through Milan. According to Metz, "Ultimately we would go to Yugoslavia, joining Tito. The plan broke down when it was discovered that other evadees, upon successfully reaching the Milan checkpoint, ended up in German prisons. Obviously, the lady in Milan was playing both sides."

Other U.S. airmen who improvised their own escapes had better luck. One might suppose Cyril Braund had had enough excitement bailing out of his burning B-17 *Champagne Lady* in July, but internment in Switzerland did not sit well with him. "After a few weeks of eating cheese and bread for breakfast, I started to think about getting out of there," he recalled. "Due to the fact that you were not really free, and thinking a little more dangerous adventure might be in the offing, I began planning an escape. Just to see if I could do it, I guess!" In Davos, he needed to look no farther than the bar at the Davoserhof Hotel for an accomplice. "I started to query the barmaid to get her reactions on we Americans being penned up," he said. "After some weeks I was able to persuade her to buy clothing coupons on the black market and purchase some civilian clothes for me. This young lady spoke all the languages of Switzerland fluently, plus English, of course. I thought to myself, now if I could get her to guide me across Switzerland to the French border I might be able to make good my escape. I tried to get my co-pilot, navigator, or bombardier to go with me. I did not want more than one other person. To my surprise, it was my bombardier who chose to accompany me."

Braund saved his money until he had enough to pay the way for himself and his guide. "Several hundred dollars later, plus about $300 in her pocket, I had her buy train tickets for us to the French border and I planned it so we would change trains five or six times to make it harder to trace us. On the train she handled the tickets and spoke the different languages necessary to the conductor. She also said that Swiss soldiers on the train were making nasty remarks about me being a slacker in civilian clothes. She laughed and said if they only knew. But she told them I was her husband and I was very ill mentally and I was going to a special doctor."

"At the end of our journey we got off the last train and there was a group of soldiers lined up on the station platform. This had me worried. I thought, 'My gosh, I got this far and I'm going to get caught!' But no, I got off the train and walked right past them and on out to the edge of town. I was carrying a suitcase with my uniform in it because I did not want to get caught by Germans in civilian clothes as I could have been shot as a spy. At the edge of town, into a woods, the bombardier and I changed back into our uniforms, packed the civilian clothes into a bag, and gave them to the girl. There we bid a fond adieu to her and headed through the woods for the French border. We kept high on a hill in the woods for several hours and we saw a train rolling below us. We saw many lights then and the train stopped and was searched. We were observing this from a vantage point high on the hill. Soon we encountered barbed wire and knew this must be the border."

The two airmen managed to make contact with the French Forces of the Interior (FFI) shortly after crossing into France. After a few days they were driven to American lines near Lyon and from there put on a B-24 back to England. Like all airmen who escaped Switzerland after internment, they were given strict orders that they were no longer to fight in the European Theater of Operations. They could, however, be transferred to the Pacific Theater to participate in the war against Japan. The resourceful Braund, however, came up with still another diversion. After landing at St. John's, Newfoundland, in a C-54, he was sitting around the snack bar and heard two pilots talking about flying to Florida. "I asked them if we could go along," said Braund. "We had orders for New York but we did not want to go to New York. So they said, 'Sure, come on along.' We landed in Florida and were put up in beautiful hotels in Miami Beach. And that was the last I ever saw or heard from my bombardier!"

A less elegant escape was attempted by Harry Siemens and DeWitt Weir from Wengen. "We had stashed four hash sandwiches in the woods behind the Palace Hotel," Siemens recalled, "and in the early hours of the morning, when the guard at the door went to the next room, we went out the front door. We wasted a lot of time in the dark before we found the sandwiches." The pair made it to the cliffs that overlooked Interlaken, though sometimes had to hide on their bellies from Swiss soldiers along the way. At daylight, the airmen slid down a cliff, grabbing for any tree or brush that could slow their descent. After spending several hours hiding from Swiss sentries they suddenly heard the roar of motorcycles coming down the road. They had been spotted.

The airmen ran north, then doubled back and hid under some logs until the motorcyle troops gave up the search and left. They approached a train yard but found even more Swiss soldiers guarding the cars. That night, a freezing rain made the young men miserable. They had entered a woods for shelter when Weir found an answer to their problem. Siemens recalled, "As we stumbled into the grove he had put his hand out to a big tree to steady himself, and his hand touched cloth of some kind. It proved to be two heavy overcoats hanging on a stub that stuck out of the tree trunk. There could be no reasonable explanation for such good fortune. To this day I believe it was a Divine miracle placed there by our Guardian Angel."

The two young, now warmly-clad, flyers walked to Thun, dodging Swiss roadblocks, and then a few miles later down the road Weir shouted, "Hey, I know that guy!" They had reached Munsingen, where a crew of internees including Christy Zullo maintained the U.S. cemetery for airmen who had died in Switzerland. Soon, Siemens and Weir were in a cab headed for Bern, accompanied by three of the internees. They were given food, put up at a hotel and told to wait for a further contact. After several days hiding out in the hotel, another American, Rollin Looker, knocked on the door, having indiscreetly asked the desk clerk where the Americans were staying. Their cover was blown. Fortunately, their contact, a French cab driver, arrived minutes later. "The car ran on a mixture of alcohol and calcium carbide," Siemens recalled. "It had what looked like an old hot water heater fastened to the front bumper, and periodically he had to stop and remove a small, spent bag of calcium carbide and replace it with a new one. Top speed 35 mph."

Siemens and Weir, who had somewhat reluctantly allowed Looker to join them, were driven to Geneva, where they were introduced to three men of the FFI, or Maquis. The French said that the price of escape was carrying a backpack into France. Siemens said, "When I asked what was in the pack they said medicine. It was the heaviest medicine I have ever carried." The men had to wait until four in the morning for their next car and driver, during which time the Maquis practiced knife fighting. "We had a good omen," Siemens said. "The car was a 1939 Chrysler Royal Sedan running on gas. The car picked up speed and we roared past the sentry box at 70 mph." The three Americans and three French unloaded the packs while the driver took a gulp of wine and headed back to Geneva. After a strenuous climb up a ridge—at the top of which Looker decided, almost disastrously, to light up a cigarette—the airmen crossed the French border. One of the Maquis had run on ahead and procured a beat-up pick-up truck. Siemens recalled: "We passed a concrete rectangular building about 25 feet long by 15 feet wide. It had two windows and a door on the road side. Several weeks before the Mackies had trapped a bunch of German soldiers in it by barricading the doors and windows, then threw inflament into the window and burned them to death." By that afternoon, an American Army jeep had arrived to bring the tired escapees to the U.S. base at Annecy, and from there to Lyon and a plane back to England.

Louis Joseph prepared for his escape from Wengen, with his ball turret gunner, Howard Wellnitz, by collecting civilian clothes—including briefcases, derbys and glasses—from friendly Swiss. He said that when they were ready to go he and Wellnitz looked at each other and burst out laughing. "No more POWs, but a couple of Swiss businessmen!" They acquired tickets to Bern and easily passed through the railway station, but then, on the train, Swiss soldiers began moving down the aisle, checking IDs. As Joseph described: "The first thing that happened to me is my heart stopped and I thought I was going to pass out. I really thought they found that we were missing and were out looking for us. All this time we thought we had the perfect escape, but I never gave this part a thought. We were sitting in the center of the train. I said to myself, 'Here we go to Wauwilermoos.'" Joseph urgently whispered to Wellnitz to pull his hat over his face so they could pretend they were sleeping. With derbys over their eyes and briefcases on their laps, the guard, to Joseph's amazement, passed them by.

In Bern, the two young flyers met their contact, recognizing the man when he lifted a handkerchief and blew his nose. They were taken to a room where a dozen other British, Polish and American escapees were waiting. Eventually, a charcoal-burning moving truck arrived to pick up the entire group. Packed with the furniture in the truck in total darkness, Joseph's claustrophobia began to get the best of him. He said, "The charcoal fumes were gagging me and I wanted to scream 'Let me out of here!' At that point I wished I would have stayed in Wengen. We groaned up mountains and down mountains, I could tell by the growling of the engine. Four times the truck was halted. After 20 years in that truck we finally came to our destination and they let us out. Looking around, we were in the middle of a large field, the almost-full moon was at 12 o'clock high. The Maquis then gave us each a knapsack to carry—what was in them I don't know, probably smuggled goods from Switzerland. After the Maquis loaded us up we started to trek in the dark. We walked through dried streams, forests, bush area, up and down hills. It was such an ordeal that I really began to think I had made a mistake."

A few of the Allied soldiers couldn't match the pace of the Maquis and dropped behind. One man sprained an ankle and others took turns helping him to continue. The little column finally stopped at a farmhouse near Annecy, France. "Old lady, old man, mud floor, cow in the next shanty, dust on a half-cup of milk one-eighth-inch thick. I don't recall how we got to the American army," Joseph said, "but we wound up in Lyon in a makeshift headquarters. We were told to say nothing to no one and the CQ took our stories and a few days later Air Transport Command took us back to England. A few weeks in Prestwick, then to the Pentagon, then one month in Atlantic City for rehab. I should have stayed in Wengen."

Edward Winkle had a smoother time after the officers at Adelboden arranged his escape with the assistance of Sam Woods' Consulate and the Maquis. He and his friends, S.R. Simms and Jim Parker, met one contact, who drove them to a hotel in Bern. The next morning the hotel proprietress put them in a car to Geneva where they met half a dozen other U.S. airmen on the lam. A girl knocked on the door and ordered the airmen to follow her down the street. Winkle thought the procession seemed obvious, especially when he noticed the man in front of him was wearing GI shoes; nevertheless, after walking down a dirt road outside Geneva they came to a man with a pick-up truck that resembled an old Model T Ford. Winkle recalled, "He quickly crowded us guys into the bed of the truck, then he got out a crank and began to crank the engine. But it was stubborn and did not want to start. I don't know about the other fellows, but I was slowly dying. He finally got it started." He drove the airmen to a hill overlooking Lake Geneva, where fishing boats and pleasure boats leisurely floated in the center. Then, Winkle said, "All at once, one of the boats streaked toward the shore. We were told to run down to the boat. It was a large fishing boat, and as we boarded we had to lie down and were covered with a tarpaulin. The boat then took off along the shore for several miles, then darted across the lake to the French coast where a group of Maquis were shooting pigeons. We were handed over to them and they took us to a small town called Annecy, where we were turned over to an American officer. His first words were, 'You have to get out of those civilian clothes!'"

Ronald Grove, a B-17 tail gunner with the 95th Bomb Group, began his escape from Adelboden in a dentist's office. Grove and his friend, Joseph Piemonte, got their check-ups first and then evaded the guards by asking to use a bathroom. Then they slipped outside. Grove remembered: "As we were walking on the sidewalk toward the train depot, a Canadian man came up behind us and began to speak. He said, 'You two Americans should not go to the depot. Just follow me. Stay about 15 paces behind. Don't say a word, just listen to what I tell you. If you go to the depot and get on the train they will pick you up in Bern. They will be waiting for you when you get off the train. They know you are supposed to get on it. Just follow me but don't say a word to anybody. If I ask you a question, don't even answer. I'll do all the talking.'"

In a scene straight out of a spy movie, the airmen followed the stranger about fifteen blocks until they met additional accomplices: a Frenchman behind the wheel of a car with an Englishwoman in the back seat. The Canadian got in front while Grove and Piemonte piled in the back. "The woman told us to get out of our GI clothes and into civilian clothes," Grove said. "The Frenchman drove off and we hadn't gone but a mile when we ran through a roadblock and knocked it down. Of course, then the Swiss took out after us. We drove on with the Swiss chasing us." After plowing through a second roadblock, the car pulled up in front of the American Embassy in Bern and the airmen were told to run for the door. Under international law, the Embassy was considered U.S. territory, so Grove and Piemonte were given a good meal and a short night's rest.

It was still dark at 4:00 the next morning when another underground contact—either Polish or French—arrived surreptitiously at the Embassy to escort the airmen out of Bern. After walking across a bridge and some fields the men were left to hide in a woods, having been told a vehicle would pick them up. A half-hour later a truck filled with chicken coops parked near the woods and the driver constructed a makeshift cave for the airmen in the back of the truck beneath the chickens. At one point the truck was stopped by Swiss soldiers who shifted the coops around, but the escapees were not detected.

In the late afternoon they were dropped at a "safe house" and met by two Frenchmen who escorted them on foot across the countryside. "I'd say the snow was probably two inches deep," Grove recalled, "and I had on a topcoat and a set of slippers. You can imagine how cold it was in the snow." When they reached a lake, the entire party lay down on their stomachs for an hour. About midnight, the airmen were told to crawl to the lake's edge and get into a waiting dinghy. A rope was attached to the boat and two Poles on the other side of the lake pulled them halfway across. Then the Americans, as instructed, got out and waded through the freezing water the rest of the way, into France. According to Grove, "As soon as we got out of the water they told us we were free and gave each of us a little bottle of vodka. They said to drink it down to prevent getting a cold or pneumonia. I didn't drink at the time but we drank it down anyway and I'll tell you, it warmed you up in a hurry. We gave these Polish boys all the money we had with us."

The airmen were escorted to a French cottage where they were fed and given warm beds, and the next morning a U.S. Army jeep pulled up at the house to drive them to Annecy. The successful escape of Grove and Piemonte was a true multinational affair. During the collapse of France in 1940, an entire Polish infantry division had crossed into Switzerland to be interned. Though disarmed, they requested to be allowed to maintain their military formation to continue training. General Guisan actually figured them into his defense plans, assuming they could be quickly rearmed if the Germans attacked. In the meantime the Poles retained close connections with the FFI and involved themselves in more than a few escapes by U.S. airmen.

In Davos, Loren Merritt and Don Malloy of the 96th Bomb Group were, as Merritt put it, "like two dogs in heat. Home was what we wanted. He had a new baby he had never seen while I had gotten a picture of my wife in her tight little shorts. Plans, such as they were, were made. Local civilian friends got us some proper traveling clothes: suits, ties, hats and raincoats. To look official, two attaché cases. They also gave us a contact to meet in Bern." Toward the end of September the two started walking along the train tracks, changing out of their uniforms once outside town. "Our big plan was to find a railway station and get tickets to Bern, and to us it seemed quite simple," Merritt recalled. They found a small station with a ticket booth, but "We now realized we had better speak German and things did not seem as simple. I was chosen to do the honors. I approached the ticket seller and in my best German ordered "Dos Billets fer Bern, bitte." He said, 'Einfach?' [One-way?] I almost ran. What the hell did that mean? I stammered out 'Jawohl' and two tickets were stamped. Then he said, 'You English?' Our cover had been blown. I agreed that we were British, better that than American right then. He became very helpful.

"We followed his directions and sometime later we boarded the train for Bern. I don't think there were any civilians in that part of the country as everyone seemed to be in the army. We were surrounded by soldiers. Every little while the train would stop and another bunch got on." Merritt and Malloy pretended to sleep on the train and after arriving in Bern walked to a park to meet their contact. Midnight came and went, however, and the man didn't show. "By one o'clock we began to panic," Merritt said. By now the streets were bare and we stood out like two hookers. A young man passed and did a double take. He said, 'Hey, you Americans?' We confessed and he said, 'For Christ's sake, come on!'"

Their new friend, who worked for the International Committee of the Red Cross, called the American Consulate, which gave the airmen food and shelter for two days. Then they were given tickets and passes to Geneva, along with a rendezvous point at a hotel in Geneva and a password to use when they arrived. Sam Woods, the Consul General, reminded them that if they were caught the Consulate would deny any knowledge of their actions.

The next day, Merritt and Malloy, along with four other fugitive airmen, got on the Geneva train. They began to relax and even took their hats off—a big mistake. As Merritt recounted: "Before long the conductor was heard coming to collect our tickets. He approached us and, no doubt, meant trouble. His thick-lensed glasses glared at Don's red hair. It was like a red cape to a bull. Swiss do not have red hair.

He left the car and I soon saw him with a Swiss army officer at the glass door. He was pointing at us. They left, but a soldier took up a post guarding the door. I walked to the other end of the car and another guard was there. I went back to my seat and couldn't help but notice the four other escapees on the car. Their ill-fitting clothes and tense expressions were almost laughable. They were a dead giveaway."

When the train made its next stop, Merritt and Malloy opened a window and hopped off. They were soon captured by police, but then Merritt remembered the passes they had been given by the Consulate. The Swiss apologized and drove them back to the train station, waving good-bye as the Americans boarded another train. At Lausanne the airmen decided to leave the train and take a cab. Their driver got them to Geneva, after stopping several times to get gas from other cabs with a siphon. At Geneva, Merritt and Malloy met their contact and were placed with twenty other escapees. Two days later, a truck arrived to take the entire group into France. Merritt recalled:

"I have never had such a case of the shakes and been so cold as then. Even the Posen mission didn't hit me like that. We grabbed our clothes and quietly followed everyone down to a truck with a canvas cover over the rear. The guide rode in front and after an hour or so we lurched to a stop. The guide told everyone to stay together and follow him. Very quietly. After what seemed to be forever hiking over fields, we crossed a fence of barbed wire about four feet high. We were told we were now in France and safe. Laughing and joking we continued our trek. Suddenly, floodlights bathed us in light. Swiss guards with rifles were everywhere. Our guide had fled the scene. We had been snookered. I dove in the grass but soon felt three rifles in my back. Our whole group had been taken."

The men were escorted by a rather triumphant Swiss lieutenant and his men to a border post opposite the French village of St. Julien. However, Merritt remained determined to escape. "I began probing for a soft spot," he recalled. I had already tried offering a guard a wad of bills and only got a cocked rifle pointed at me. The lieutenant was holding court in his office at the edge of the building. We could look past the guards at the bridge that led to France. It was frustrating. I told Don, stick with me, I'm going to get out of here. He said, 'Sure.'" Merritt asked to use the bathroom, and on returning to the office slipped a matchbook over the lock on the door. While other airmen kept the Swiss officer occupied, he made a break out the back of the building. "The fence was ten feet away and some nice person had left a twelve-by-twelve-foot board lying there. I propped it against the fence, scaled it and leaped over to France. I scurried through the gully below, went to the other end of the bridge and looked back at my buddies.

"I turned and went into the black night of France. I walked along a lane with no plans or ideas of what lay ahead. A jeep-like car came along and stopped, and a voice called, 'Hey buddy, you American?' I almost fainted but managed to say yes. He said, 'Come on, you're the guys I'm looking for.' In the jeep were two other escapees from somewhere. We were taken to a house and told that in the morning we would meet the Maquis. We had two thoughts: eat and drink. The drink we found in abundance. Wine bottles galore. We drank, sang and laughed with abandon until too much vino put us to sleep."

In late September 1944, several thousand British Empire troops were put aboard trains and repatriated across the Swiss border to Allied lines in France. These troops had been captured by the Germans in North Africa and made it to Switzerland in the brief period between the fall of Mussolini and the German invasion of Italy. On September 25, the South Africans, mainly taken at Tobruk, went out as a group and took several American internees with them. Other U.S. flyers joined British or ANZAC (Australian and New Zealand) formations by the simple ruse of putting on a British overcoat. Swiss troops were instructed to inspect passes, but in practice the trains crossed the border unimpeded, the British cheerfully willing to let American internees hitch a ride.

Once the British were gone, U.S. escapees were once again left to their own devices. They had the advantage of Switzerland's small size, which meant relatively short geographic distances to cover. Even Davos, near the Austrian border, was only a seven-hour train ride from France on the route Zurich–Bern–Geneva. They also benefited from a population overwhelmingly sympathetic toward the Allies. After the war, Switzerland's Commission of Internees and Hospitalization wrote: "We did everything we could to prevent the escape of internees. Unfortunately, our efforts were hampered by the fact that a large part of the population felt bound to help internees escape in any possible manner." It is also true that many Swiss, despite their Allied sympathies, felt an even stronger allegiance to rule of law and

Switzerland's own historic national policy; however, a number of escape experiences indicate that even these Swiss civilians, if they didn't aid U.S. internees, felt little urgency to turn them in.

The great obstacle for airmen trying to escape was the Swiss Army. Even today in Switzerland one encounters soldiers frequently, young men in uniform coming or going from service in the country's universal militia system. During World War II, the army's presence was ubiquitous. While Henri Guisan's largest formations manned the Alpine redoubt, the border, and intermediate strongpoints in the north, other units guarded the transit routes. In Switzerland, there was no danger of an airman being executed after a failed escape attempt as sometimes happened in Germany. (In the famous "Great Escape" by British from a German Stalag, 35 men were lined up and shot after being caught.) But the Swiss refused to place failed escapees back in their internment hotels. Instead, the airmen were jailed as lawbreakers, and ultimately shipped to the special punishment camp the Swiss had set up for criminals among the country's foreign internees, Wauwilermoos.

James Misuraca, whose B-24 of the 448th Bomb Group landed in Switzerland in spring 1944, decided to escape internment in the fall. "Our daily routine was dull and we were bored," he wrote. "We followed the Allied invasion of Europe and advance of our forces with keen interest, especially as they neared the Swiss border. When the American armies had driven the Germans back from the Swiss-French border, a fellow internee and I made plans for an escape attempt."

"In early October, 1944, we made our way out of the hotel after midnight and walked down to the station. A friendly Austrian girl had purchased train tickets for us. We wore civilian clothes and traveled as Swiss internees using forged Swiss Army passes. It worked because we were checked by Swiss guards four or five times en route to Zurich, right where I had started from [Dubendorf].

"On arrival at Zurich, we were met by friends of my fellow internee, Irwin Schwedock from New York. We stayed overnight at their house and enjoyed their hospitality. The next morning, they bought us train tickets for Geneva. Our passes covered us until there. On arrival at Geneva, we went to a large hotel in the downtown area where our contact was the desk clerk, who took us to a room. Schwedock's friends had made these arrangements for us. The food was just great. Schwedock was taken out one night and he crossed the border."

At this point, the escape must have seemed almost too easy for Misuraca, slipping out of the country with a careful plan and little drama. He would soon, however, suffer the fate of 183 other American escapees.

"After a few long days I was taken out of the room and driven out of Geneva toward the French border. Our guides assembled about 25 people at a safe house. In the middle of the night we were led to the border fence, where we were all arrested by Swiss border guards. I had my hands on the fence and was just getting ready to climb over."

Misuraca and the others were driven to an empty building in Geneva, with only a large common room and a bathroom. "We were an assortment of American airmen and soldiers, rounded out by Swiss, Belgian and French smugglers. The next morning, an American paratrooper and I jumped out of the restroom window which we had pried open. As soon as we hit the ground we were apprehended. The Swiss officer was incensed; I can still see him fumbling to pull his pistol out of his side holster. The paratrooper and I were driven to the Geneva city jail, where we were booked in. Several days later I was separated from the paratrooper and three of us were put on a train under armed guard. We had no idea where we were headed—which turned out to be Wauwilermoos."

Pilot James Green, whose B-24 had crashlanded inches from the Austrian border in July, attempted to escape Switzerland in early October. He and two other airmen and a Swiss friend simply got on bicycles in Davos and pedaled almost the entire way to Zurich. "All of this at night," Green recalled. "No lights, and all downhill. I was picked up by the Swiss police the next morning when I boarded a train for Geneva. The others got away. Off to a Swiss jail for several days until I finally told them who I was. Twenty-four hours later I was in 'Wauwil.'" Later Green was transferred to another punishment camp, Les Diablerets, that had been set up to handle the overflow from Wauwilermoos. A guard told him his chances of escaping from Les Diablerets would be zero. "How right he was," said Green, "because I tried twice without success."

Dale Pratt, who parachuted into Switzerland on October 1, 1943 from the ill-fated B-17 *Sugarfoot*, spent almost a year in internment before deciding to leave. "At the beginning of September I had given very little thought to escaping from this country," he recalled. "We felt sure that very soon we would be going home through legal channels. By the middle of the month rumors and facts dispelled all hope from our minds of going out legally. Soon we were looking for ways and means of escaping and finally found a way. On the evening of September 26, we knew for sure that we could go. The next three days we worked hard getting rid of surplus articles of equipment, and packing things for our departure. In the meantime WIlliam Ballard and Wayne Fox joined us in our plan and the time was set to leave our hotels at eight in the morning on September 29."

The men put on as much civilian clothing as they could under their uniforms and began walking through Adelboden. "As we passed through the village we saw many of our friends, Swiss and American, and it seemed a shame that we couldn't even say goodbye," Pratt said. We had walked perhaps a mile from town when we came to a small barn filled with hay. Here we discarded all of our uniforms and finished putting on our civilian clothing. We buried the uniforms in the hay and started on again. From that moment we all began to feel like fugitives."

The men rendezvoused with a contact and acquired motor transport near Thun. There were poignant moments on the drive. "Going through Münsingen we passed the graveyard where all of the boys are buried. Some of the Americans were along the side of the road, but failed to see us." On the road to Lausanne, the car passed several Swiss military convoys and at one point, after passing a large convoy, the car developed a flat tire. Airmen hopped out of the car to change the tire in record time just before the Swiss trucks caught up. In Lausanne, the airmen made another connection and were placed in a "safe house" for a week. "Each morning," Pratt recalled, "when we got up we could look out of the window and see France across the lake; we were so near and yet so far from freedom."

The majestic beauty of Switzerland wasn't wasted on Pratt, and later he would be able to enjoy it. For now, however, he knew they had to leave at the first opportunity. "On the sixth of October we all went separately to the station and took the train to Geneva. I was sitting in the same seat with a friendly looking old gentleman who was reading a Swiss-German newspaper. I was in constant fear that he would start a conversation with me. I just sat there looking out of the window and pretended to doze, and he never said a word to me. When the conductor came through for the tickets I pretended to be as snobbish as possible and he took the ticket, punched it and walked on without a word.

"We arrived in Geneva without a mishap, but because of the many people there I got lost from the others and didn't know where to go. I just followed the crowd, and had to pass a military policeman who was stationed by the door watching for people like myself. Luckily I found my friends again and we were led to the place where we were to stay. That evening, we had a nice supper with steak and other things. We fortified ourselves with a couple of stiff drinks of cognac and started walking downtown. After an hour or so we caught a taxi that took us out of Geneva and to a farmhouse only a 10-minute walk from the frontier. Here we waited for another hour until it was quite dark and then we started down the road to the place where we were to cross.

"It was extremely dark that night. We could hardly see those ahead of us, and we passed several soldiers but they couldn't see us for that same reason. Then we were walking right along the fence that separates France from Switzerland. Suddenly we saw Fox and his companion stopped by someone, and because we couldn't distinguish who it was we stopped and turned back. We took a few steps and then looking back we saw that they had gone on.

"We turned again and started to follow. All at once one of the men bumped right into a Swiss guard. The guard asked us in French for our passports. We pretended we didn't understand, so he asked us in German. All we could do was pretend not to understand and this gave Fox and his companion more time to get away. The guard was getting suspicious and had his rifle ready. He stepped away a couple of steps so to be safe from us. We then told him we were American soldiers, and he ordered us to march ahead of him down the road. One of the other men told me that the guard had the gun pointed right at our backs, so we knew we would not be leaving Switzerland that night. The guard marched us down the road to a customs house right on the border. We were taken into an office and were questioned.

"Soon a Swiss officer came in. He was a nice young fellow who said he was very sorry he couldn't let us go on over. We were there for more than an hour while the soldiers made out papers and asked a lot of questions which we either refused to answer or answered misleadingly. During the time we were in the office it had begun to rain very hard and when finally the young Swiss officer told us he was taking us back to town it was pouring down. He furnished me with a canvas cape that the Swiss soldiers use for raincoats and we started out."

The Swiss officer led Pratt's group to a bare room where they were treated as prisoners rather than internees, with considerably worse conditions than they had escaped from. "We were searched and everything was taken away from us. Then they took us to a large room where we were to sleep. When we entered this room my heart sank; there were about thirty men and all were lying around the walls on straw, sleeping. In this room I saw several boys I knew. They had all the blankets, so the guard went around and took two or three from them. I was cold, wet and very discouraged.

"The boys were waking up and we started discussing experiences. Finally two of them said that the only way to keep warm was to double up with the others and share the blankets. I put my blanket with theirs and crawled in beside them, clothes and all." The airmen found companionship despite their bad fortune, and were soon taking their minds off the cold and their bleak immediate future. "We did have quite a lot of fun talking over stories and our experiences, so it wasn't completely bad." However, the friendships were short-lived. Five days after their arrival, they were taken to the railway station and put on a train, destination: Wauwilermoos.

Before the war, the Swiss had never bothered with erecting an extensive or elaborate penal system. There has never been, after all, much crime in the country. When American airmen were captured during escape attempts or arrested for other matters such as drunkenness or disorderly behavior, they were generally thrown into town jails that resembled (or were) medieval dungeons. In terms of light, sanitation and bedding, the facilities were often terrible, or at least far below U.S. prison standards.

Such temporary stays in local jails would pale, however, before experiences endured in Switzerland's special punishment camp, built in 1941 to confine serious lawbreakers among the country's scattered "city" of over 100,000 foreign military internees. The camp housed a number of truly dangerous characters who had formerly served in the German, Russian, Polish or other armies. Unfortunately it would also become a temporary home for many U.S. airmen who had only tried to rejoin their units.

13

WAUWILERMOOS

On July 15, 1941, Swiss authorities appointed Captain André-Henri Béguin commander of Wauwilermoos, the newly erected disciplinary camp for lawbreakers among Switzerland's growing population of foreign military internees. They could not have chosen a shadier character. At the time of his appointment, Béguin was under surveillance by Swiss Counterintelligence for spying, adultery, improper use of uniform and embezzlement. Born in Neuchatel in 1897, Béguin had trained as an architect, but then joined the French Foreign Legion, serving as a non-com in Tunisia 1930–32. He then lived in Munich from 1933 until the German invasion of Poland, during which time he signed his correspondence, "Heil Hitler." He had been arrested in Switzerland in 1937 for illegally wearing a Nazi Party uniform.

After moving back to Switzerland in 1939, he became an ordnance officer in the Swiss Army, translating artillery manuals from French to German. At the time of his promotion to prison camp commander, he was deeply in debt. A major reason for his financial insolvency, according to Swiss journalist Jean-Pierre Wilhelm, was that he kept four mistresses, including a Spanish dancer and a barmaid named Dolores. As camp commander, Béguin not only took bribes, he strong-armed loans from men under his command and confiscated or looted packages meant for prisoners.

In February 1942, over two years before the first American airman was sentenced to Wauwilermoos, Béguin's stewardship of the camp was under investigation. A Major Humbert, head surgeon of the

Bunen Military Hospital, found that 37 percent of his internee patients had come from Wauwilermoos even though the camp housed only 5 percent of the internees in his district. He made a personal visit that confirmed his suspicions of physical and mental abuse of prisoners. In a report to the Swiss Commission on Internment and Hospitalization, he stated that Béguin was psychologically unfit for his task and recommended that patients from Wauwilermoos be transferred elsewhere rather than be returned to the camp. Despite Humbert's report, however, Béguin retained his command.

Since Béguin's character and sympathies were well known, it is difficult to explain how he was able to maintain his commission in an army led by General Henri Guisan. One suspects that the Swiss officer corps, unable to dislodge a man who obviously had patrons somewhere in the army or government, decided upon the only logical place for him. If Switzerland had to have a disciplinary camp, and if the army had a Nazi-sympathizer in its ranks, why not put the two together? According to growing evidence from Germany, running camps was a particular Nazi forté. Since Wauwilermoos was intended to house criminals, there may also have been the uncharitable sentiment, "it takes one to know one." In any event, the Swiss Army divested itself of a questionable character, much to the detriment of many American and other foreign internees. After the war, the decision would cause the Swiss Army, and people, a significant degree of shame.

Straflager Wauwilermoos, or, in English, "prison camp at the swamp of Wauwil," was located in the center of the country, northwest of Lucerne. U.S. airman James Misuraca, who had been captured near Geneva just as his hands had grasped the border fence, recalled: "When we were driven through the gates, we could see barbed wire, armed guards and dogs. We were assigned to a single-story wooden hut that was heated by one stove. We each had a wooden bunk filled with straw. Food rations were soup, potatoes, cabbage, black bread and ersatz coffee. We never worried about the menu because it was the same every day. No letters were permitted and we were allowed a daily walk around the camp. The guards were coarse and crude. The officers treated us like scum. This was pure and simply a concentration camp."

According to a report from U.S. Sergeant Edward Cunningham, the camp at Wauwil was "rated worse than the normal POW camp in

Germany. Conditions there were almost intolerable. Officers and men were jammed in overcrowded barracks. The GIs were forced to sleep on loose straw strewn over planks, while officers were accorded the comparative comforts of straw mattresses. Food at the camp was barely above subsistence level. Barracks were located in the mire of ankle-deep mud and there were no recreational facilities. Vicious dogs and guards with machine guns patrolled the barbed-wire enclosure."

B-17 navigator (later Colonel) James Mahaffey recorded: "Surrounded by a high barbed-wire fence it was commanded by a Swiss who had formerly been a sergeant in the French Foreign Legion, with all the worst characteristics associated with that type. Not only were Americans imprisoned there, but French, British, Russians and Poles. Enlisted men were placed on work details, officers were in a separate compound guarded by armed soldiers and police dogs." B-24 pilot Uriah Hartman recalled that, on his arrival at Wauwilermoos, "Our next door barracks was filled with Germans. [We] were in with Poles, Russians, French and Italians. After about two weeks we were moved to a new barracks across a creek—Americans only, but still with guards and dogs."

American airmen began arriving at Wauwilermoos in May 1944. A few of the initial prisoners were violent or alcoholic and were not overly missed by their compatriots at Adelboden. After the great surge of escape attempts that began in September 1944, however, the camp began to see many more American GIs—not criminals but simply men who had been caught trying to escape to Allied lines. Béguin's dark, private fiefdom subsequently became infamous to U.S. internees, prompting outrage from flyers forced to spend time there. James Misuraca, for one, stated: "This was an incredible situation in a neutral country. We didn't know if the American Legation was aware of this camp. They knew that internees like myself had escaped from Davos and had not made it to France where they had contact with American forces."

American Military Attaché Bernard Legge could indeed have objected vigorously to the conditions at Wauwilermoos. But Legge was the foremost U.S. authority in Switzerland urging men not to escape. Wauwilermoos buttressed his advice rather than contradicted it, and the American Military Legation did not make a serious attempt to ameliorate conditions in the camp.

Dale Pratt, whose attempted escape had been foiled at the French border, jotted down his experiences at Wauwilermoos just after he had been released back to Adelboden. "Wauwil is a dirty, filthy prison with miserably small barracks with many men in each," he wrote. "Double barbed wire fences surround it, with an armed guard every few feet. When we arrived there we were searched and everything was taken except the cigarettes and matches.

"The first two nights in Wauwilermoos I slept in a barracks with nothing but Polish soldiers, then I was moved into a barracks with Americans. There were forty of us there, and our beds consisted of a small bundle of straw and two blankets, and it was necessary to sleep together to keep warm. I made my bed with a Spanish boy from the Dominican Republic who had fought for General Franco during the Spanish Civil War. We all knew that we could expect about three months in this concentration camp and the prospect was very discouraging."

American Lieutenant Russell Sherburne recounts: "The food was brought to us in milk cans and the diet consisted mostly of soup, potatoes and bread. The beds were straw and I had to sleep with my clothes on to keep warm on most of the nights. The toilet facilities consisted of an old fashioned back house where odors were pretty bad at times, and a water faucet. This faucet was outside of the barbed wire enclosure and we had to call the guard whenever we wished to use it. Newspapers were used for toilet paper. During the four weeks I was there I didn't have one change of clothing. We were allowed 21 francs a week for cigarettes and other things. That is, you were allowed that if they got around to give it to you."

According to James Mahaffey: "The food was horrible and was poured from slop pails into tin pans and cups. Those who experienced solitary confinement reported worse conditions. No sanitary facility except a slit trench next to the building, hosed down weekly. Food was put into a trough from the outside. Dysentery, pyorrhea and boils went untreated."

Dale Pratt confirmed in his journal: "The latrine and washroom at one end of the camp was about the worst of all. It was a long low brick affair with the washroom in the back and was fixed with a long pipe with holes in the bottom. The water came from the pipe, ice cold, and fell into a wooden trough. The trough was exactly like a hog trough and about as clean. The latrine was used French-style and one had to watch his step or he might come up missing.

"The angriest I got while in Wauwilermoos was one night as I left the latrine a guard set one of the dogs on me just to train him. I was walking back to the barracks when suddenly the dog coming silently from behind leaped at my left arm. He missed and landed about four feet in front of me; he turned with a growl and started for me again when the guard called him off. I used some language on both dog and guard that I must never write here . . ."

In September 1944 there were 278 inmates at Wauwilermoos, a number that would grow to 376 by February 1945. Some airmen reported practically no contact with the outside world, even the International Committee of the Red Cross (ICRC). Others received mail or packages. Movies were reportedly shown twice a week; however, many airmen deny that films, or any other form of entertainment, was provided. Evidently, conditions varied from month to month, and, for Commandant André Béguin, perhaps according to developments in the war. On October 26, a Swiss journalist, Albert Adler, visited Wauwilermoos after hearing disturbing stories about the camp from American internees. He spent four hours talking to Béguin and to prisoners, and found his worst suspicions confirmed. Afterward, Adler described the unsanitary conditions and decried the fact that Red Cross parcels were not distributed. During the war the Geneva-based ICRC had sought to alleviate conditions at countless prisoner or punishment camps in foreign countries; yet, ironically, in the center of Switzerland the camp at Wauwilermoos failed to adhere to humane standards.

Pratt recorded in his journal: "Finally though things began to get better. Friends hearing of our being there began to send us packages with food and other necessities. I had to wear the same socks and underwear for a month before I received a package with these things in it. A young lady in Geneva sent me a pair of hand-knitted socks and I received a letter or package from her nearly every day after that. Other friends sent cigarettes, chocolate, socks, underwear, sardines, and many other things. The Red Cross gave us more blankets and clothing, and I received two more packages from home with cigarettes, candy and cake. On our arrival at Wauwilermoos the Swiss had given us only a pair of ragged trousers, a jacket, a small piece of soap, and a small towel."

Despite the harsh conditions prevailing at the camp, perhaps the worst aspect of Wauwilermoos for U.S. airmen was the uncertainty of their term of imprisonment. The Swiss Army's own code of regulations (Article 26) called for 20 days of imprisonment for attempted escapes; the Geneva Convention, to which the Swiss were not signatories, called for 45. Instead, Americans were thrown into Wauwilermoos without due process and often endured a month or longer in the camp before being brought before a court. Sherburne recalled: "We were given no trial or sentence at the time we left, so we still had no idea how long we were supposed to stay. The only way we could contact the outside was by letter and those were all censored so I don't know how much got out."

In addition, Swiss officials could be capricious in sentencing airmen. Waist gunner Dale Ellington, who had been captured with three other men by Swiss troops near Basel, spent 30 days in Wauwilermoos before being summoned to appear before a court in Bern. "They usually sentenced you to the thirty days you had just served," Ellington said, "but in our case they were not as lenient. During the trial, one of our foursome smarted off. A court officer asked him what he was doing so far from the camp at Adelboden and he answered that we were 'chasing butterflies'! The officer was upset, and when it came time for the sentencing he said, 'You have served thirty days at the detention camp, and now you will return there to serve forty-five more!'"

When Ellington and his friends finally returned to Adelboden they escaped again, this time with the help of the U.S. Consulate, and were able to rejoin their 385th Bomb Group in England for Christmas.

Although Wauwilermoos was the most notorious punishment camp in Switzerland, overcrowding there led to the establishment of additional camps at Hünenberg, Les Diablerets and, briefly, Greppen. Les Diablerets, a deserted hotel, was intended for officers but soon housed both officers and enlisted men. Its location near the French border prompted numerous escape attempts and the Swiss found the population of the camp difficult to contain. Hünenberg, located northwest of Lucerne, not far from Wauwilermoos, was a tougher nut to crack.

B-24 turret gunner Peter Lysek, who had experienced a harrowing parachute jump from his gasoline-soaked B-24, was nabbed on a train to Bern while trying to escape from Wengen. "They put me into a prison cell that looked like it must have been built during the Middle Ages," he wrote. "A sort of dungeon-looking stronghold." A court-martial at Wengen subsequently sentenced him to Hünenberg where he witnessed a dramatic episode. "While I was at Hünenberg there was an escape attempt from that barbed wire hell-hole. With all watches hacked into the second, at precisely the pre-set time, a dozen men with blankets rushed the barbed wire fence, threw the blankets over the barbed wire and bolted over the fence. The Swiss guards began shouting 'Halt! Halt!' and firing into the air.

"Some men did make the pre-planned rendezvous point, but the people that were supposed to be there to pick them up were late getting there due to the dense fog. The Swiss police dogs quickly tracked them down and in a few hours they were back and put into solitary confinement." The Swiss officer in charge took the opportunity of his success to impress the remainder of his prisoners. "The next day the Commandant of the camp had all of us fall into formation and informed us that all those who escaped were quickly caught and thrown into solitary confinement and that it was futile to try to escape from Hünenburg."

At Wauwilermoos, daring young airmen continually tested André Béguin's ability to keep them confined. Uriah Hartman recorded: "The guards marched us to the main compound to watch an old movie. On the way, we decided to dive into a row of lilac bushes bordering the path. We set it up so that others would cover for us." At one point a Swiss guard approached within feet of Hartman, but only to answer nature's call in the bushes. When darkness fell, Hartman became separated from his companion, so he started away from the camp by himself. "Our information on escape was to follow the stream until hitting a road, follow the road to the first town, then go through the town to a small lake on the other side. This I did and came to the lake and saw the island off shore with a walkway out to it. Lights all over so I went to a field and as I came to a large tree a voice whispered, 'Hey—in here!' I did as asked and lo and behold it was Bob Simpson, who had jumped the fence at the barracks and arrived here ahead of me." (Simpson had been the navigator on *Death Dealer*, the very first U.S. aircraft to land in Switzerland.)

Hartman continued: "After several hours walking we came to

another town. We saw a church and decided to try to call the Zurich consulate from there. As we entered the driveway, two men rose from a row of bushes, and we were relieved to see Jack McKinney and Ed Weyer! They had seen Simpson jump the fence with no trouble, so they followed." The airmen placed their call and soon a car arrived from the American Consulate in Zurich. Two days later, Consul General Sam Woods drove Hartman and his friends, plus another airman who had walked all the way to Zurich, to Montreux. Woods bought the airmen mountain boots and handed them over to Frenchmen, who served as guides on the hard climb across the border.

While at Wauwilermoos, airman James Misuraca wrote, "We had one motivation—escape and return to friendly forces. After several weeks of imprisonment, two other Americans and I decided to make an escape attempt. By this time we knew approximately where we were located. To the best of my recollection, the only other nationals there were two Russian pilots who had been shot down and somehow escaped to Switzerland. Everyone in our hut helped us plan, including the Russians. The Russians taught us to cut thin slices of potatoes (bribed from the guards) and stick them to the hot sides of the stove and they would brown very nicely. The plan was to time the rounds of the guards and dogs. Spotlights were at the building corners, so we exited out of a center window, one at a time, keeping to the shadows and then climbing over two wire fences. We moved as fast as the terrain permitted and crossed many streams."

The airmen covered about 10 miles before cold and exhaustion forced them to stop and build a fire. After a short rest they continued walking until they came to a country inn. Misuraca was elected to investigate. "A friendly young lady was inside and I purchased a beer. She knew I was an American and I was wondering whether she was going to turn me in. I could see the telephone and asked her if she would make a phone call for me to the American Legation. She made the call and in a few minutes I was talking to the captain who sat in on our interrogation at Dubendorf aerodrome. I explained our situation and he said, stay put, don't move and I'll be there as soon as I can."

After an excruciating wait, the U.S. officer arrived at the inn and drove Misuraca and his companions to Zurich, where they were given food and baths. The next day they were driven to Geneva and joined a group of other American escapees. The twenty men waded a deep, icy stream and climbed two fences along the border. "I asked the French guards if we were in France. They grinned and said 'Oui.' Just a short distance away we could see the Swiss guards. One of the French got on the phone and then told us that the American soldiers would be there in a couple of hours. They suggested that we go to a taproom down the road and have a drink while we were waiting. We walked in and bought drinks for the house and toasted the French."

Of course, many escapes from Wauwilermoos ended in failure, either just outside the camp or elsewhere in Switzerland. Dale Pratt noted: "One night three Germans and an American escaped through the wire. They were later caught in Lucerne, sentenced to ten days solitary confinement, fed soup and bread, and were allowed no cigarettes. When an escape succeeded, the remaining prisoners felt repercussions. "Another night," wrote Pratt, "four Americans escaped and were never caught. After that we were guarded by the Swiss armed with submachine guns."

Although many American airmen complained of inactivity during their internment in Switzerland, such was not the problem for James Mahaffey, who escaped from Wauwilermoos twice. He had arrived in Switzerland on March 18 aboard the *Battlin' Cannon Ball*, a B-17 crippled by Focke-Wulfs over Munich. At Davos he was quartered in the Palace Hotel (now the Europa), across the street from the German Consulate. "We celebrated the 4th of July with fireworks and bombarded the consulate with sky rockets," he wrote. Soon he fell in with companions who were not risk averse.

"I had met up with an American Lieutenant named Jack [Christenson] from Tallahassee. Well, Jack was quite a daredevil; he was also a big guy and handy with his fists. One of our favorite pasttimes was to come in late at night after curfew and evade the Swiss guards. Jack liked to play the evasion game. Unfortunately, he got caught—so what did he do? Jack clobbered the guard." Christenson knew he was headed straight for Wauwilermoos, so he persuaded Mahaffey to join him in an escape. Using fake passes they reached the U.S. Consulate in Zurich where Sam Woods set them up with an American civilian, George "Tony" Page, an executive of the Borden Milk Company. Unfortunately, Mahaffey noted, "The Swiss are very nationalistic. One of Tony's servants turned us in to the authorities, and the local gendarme came to pick us up." They were jailed on the sixth floor of a building in Zurich. That night, Jack Christenson kicked out the window of their room and the two airmen climbed to the roof, hanging onto the gutters. They leapt to the balcony of a building across the way, but on breaking into the building discovered the stairwells blocked with iron mesh. They had no choice but to jump back to their jail, and the following day arrived at Wauwilermoos.

"Five days of sleeping on straw and eating food that was brought to us in slop cans was enough for me," Mahaffey recalled. He, along with a German Army deserter, crawled under the barbed wire one night and hiked back to the Consulate in Zurich. They asked Sam Woods to arrange for a car to park near Wauwilermoos to abet another escape scheduled for two nights later; meanwhile, Mahaffey was instructed to walk three blocks to the home of the American Vice-Consul. He was only yards away from his destination when he turned a corner and bumped into the same Swiss guard who had originally escorted him to Wauwilermoos. Mahaffey was taken back to the camp; however, as he put it, "The Swiss didn't realize the reason I was smiling was that I would escape again two nights later.

"I was welcomed back to Wauwilermoos by a Polish prisoner whom I had met earlier. He worked for the Commandant and hated his guts. The Pole confided in me that he had a knife and asked if I would like to go with him. He was going to kill a guard and escape over the fence. How do I meet these people? First it's Jack who clobbers a guard and gets thrown into prison camp. Then it's this Pole who wants to kill a guard. Not for me. The Swiss played it for keeps. I had heard that while I was away the Russian barracks had been raising hell, shouting, etc. To quiet them down, the Swiss lined up outside the barracks and shot a few volleys into it. Reputedly, several Russians were killed. The Swiss had no great love for the Russians. Incidentally, we did have a Russian officer in our compound. He would talk to no one. He just sat in a corner on his bunk all day long saying nothing and very expressionless."

Two nights later, Mahaffey and four other airmen crawled under the barbed wire and met the car the Consulate had arranged. In Zurich, Sam Woods gave them civilian clothes and put them on a train to Geneva, where hundreds of British troops were on their way across the border. According to Mahaffey, "On arrival at Geneva, I was hidden out in a wine cellar, given a British 'great coat' and told to wait there and get on the troop train the next morning. Swiss wine certainly fortified my courage. Next day I got on the train without a hitch. The Brits covered up for me when Swiss inspectors came around at the border.

"I detrained at Annecy, France, and waited there a few days until a C-47 flew in and picked us up. As I recall, there were about 25 of us waiting at Annecy to be brought back to the UK. Even at Annecy some were inclined to have their fun. A couple of them went up to the front lines to fight with the troops. It was in Annecy I saw female prisoners with shaven heads. I visited the prison where those French who had been collaborators were being held. The guard offered me any woman who was to my liking. Somehow a woman with a shaven head doesn't have much sex appeal. I declined the offer."

Aside from André Béguin, the man who most enraged the American internees in Switzerland was their own Military Attaché, Brigadier General Legge, primarily for the "no escape" orders he issued. Unbeknownst to most airmen, however, by mid-December 1944 Legge was in the middle of complicated negotiations to have all U.S. airmen released from internment in a group. His problem was that the constant escapes kept shifting the basis for negotiations.

When talks began between American, Swiss and German diplomats, there were an estimated 3,000 German internees in the country and 800 U.S. flyers. The German government did not seem very anxious to retrieve its personnel, many of whom were deserters, and the German internees, understandably, were even less eager to return to a Third Reich in its death throes. The Americans, on the other hand, were all highly trained specialists, many of them officers. Still, the U.S. would not accept such a steep exchange rate.

The Swiss stepped in and recounted the Germans, finding 2,500, 1,200 of whom were customs or other civil officials while 1,300 were army, SS or military police. Minister Walter Stucki then presented a revised Swiss position: "German customs officers, who have entered Switzerland in the course of events, are considered by the Federal authorities as officials whom a neutral state in compliance with international law is neither forced to receive nor to intern in its territory if they are received." In other words, the Swiss decided to release the non-Wehrmacht Germans from internment (whether they wanted to be released or not) and consider only 1,300 German soldiers available for exchange with the airmen.

The count of Americans provided by Legge began at 800 but soon changed to 600–800, and then 600–700. The American State Department agreed to a two-for-one exchange with the Germans, but by then due to a surge of escapes the number of U.S. flyers had fallen to 550. As talks continued, Legge continued to lose his leverage. The State Department would call off the deal if the ratio became considerably greater than two for one. A plaintive Legge wrote: "While I have ordered that all attempts to escape cease, there may be some who will doubt that an exchange is imminent and who will attempt to escape. I estimate this morning that we have about 500 aviators at present in Switzerland." It was suggested that 45 RAF airmen be included in the exchange to beef up the total, a proposal to which the British heartily agreed.

Legge also wrote to U.S. airmen imprisoned in Wauwilermoos and other punishment camps, requesting that they sign 30-day paroles in exchange for release back to their regular camps. "Rather than have you confined again, I have agreed to ask you not to attempt to escape until arrangements for an exchange, which I hope will come to a head within ten days, are completed. The alternative solution is to accept what the Swiss internment authorities decide to impose upon you in the way of imprisonment, confinement or restriction."

Dale Pratt noted: "The General came to see us three times, and the American Minister [Leland Harrison] once. They told us they were working hard to get us out, but it came as a complete surprise when we were told on the twelfth of November that we were leaving the next day." Some airmen refused to give their word not to escape, but Pratt didn't hesitate. "We signed a thirty-day parole and left the next morning for our camps. Eighteen of us returned to Adelboden that day. We arrived to find about three feet of snow and everyone skiing or preparing to ski. The next two days I spent getting clothing and trying to recover some of the things I had left behind." After Wauwilermoos, Pratt was satisfied to take it easy for a few weeks at Adelboden. In his journal, written in December 1944, he jotted: "I bought ski boots and rented a pair of skis. This afternoon I came down the Boden ski run twice. I am out of practice, but I believe I am going to have a good time, at least until my thirty-day parole is over."

As weeks passed, Legge became frustrated that his grand trade for all the airmen in his charge had still not reached fruition. On January 31, 1945 he cabled Washington urging the exchange:

(1) our men need to get home and back under military control
(2) lack of discipline and supervision is having telling effect
(3) conditions at two confinement camps Diablerets and Hünenberg becoming more severe. Ration there cut down to bare subsistence level over my protest to Swiss Federal Military Councillor. Swiss are well aware that I, members of my Staff and Consulates are engaged in escape activity. Foreign Minister so stated this morning. He also stated that Federal Council had had this under advisement and that they would have to protest formally against our activities if matter were not liquidated in near future. . . . Much depends upon what value Arnold and Spaatz place on these 515 men who are left.

On February 17, 1945, the deal was struck and Legge was able to find 473 U.S. airmen to transfer as a group over the border to Allied lines in France. The U.S. earned a "credit" of about 100 more internees they could repatriate in the future to meet the required two-for-one ratio. The airmen were flown to England and then back to the States. The German military personnel who were simultaneously repatriated had a more difficult time after returning to their homeland. There, one of their first priorities was to evade the USAAF bombers and fighters which by then owned the skies over the Third Reich.

As for André-Henri Béguin, commander of Wauwilermoos, justice did not slumber long for the man who had mistreated some of the bravest fighting men America has ever produced. In September 1945, he was arrested by Swiss authorities and charged with administrative crimes, adultery, embezzlement, withholding complaints from prisoners and dishonoring Switzerland. His sentence consisted of numerous fines, a dishonorable discharge from the army, loss of civil rights for seven years, and three-and-a-half years in prison.

14

DOWNDRAFT

The best chance for a rational solution to the war in Europe was lost on July 20, 1944, when the German Army only wounded Adolf Hitler in its elaborate "officers' plot." Count Claus von Stauffenberg placed a bomb just feet away from the Führer, but the heavy map table and wood of his headquarters absorbed much of the explosion. A simultaneous coup attempt in Berlin failed ignominiously. Under mysterious circumstances, Stauffenberg and other plotters were quickly lined up against a wall and shot, although the Gestapo would have preferred to have taken them alive. Thereafter, the entire Wehrmacht was forced to adopt the "Heil Hitler" salute, and the Nazis enjoyed new freedom to execute any member of the traditional German officer class suspected of disloyalty.

The Army had attempted its coup after seeing clearly what the German public could not: that the collapse of the Atlantic Wall, combined with advances by the Red Army and the steady attrition of fuel and industrial plant inflicted by Allied bombers, had placed the Third Reich in a hopeless strategic situation. The army plotters, however, had underestimated the grip the Nazis still held on Germany. Hitler continued to profess an unshakable belief in victory, and his fanaticism, misinterpreted by the German public as confidence, earned him a surprisingly high degree of public support until the end of the war.

Hitler's hand had been strengthened by the "unconditional surrender" demand announced by the Allies as early as the Casablanca Conference in January 1943. Although following the successful Allied invasion of France widespread support in Germany could be found for an armistice with the Anglo-Americans, very few in the country could countenance laying down arms on the Eastern Front. In addition to the traditional European fear of invasion from the East, many within the Third Reich were aware of the devastation German armies had wreaked on Russia and feared revenge. After the unconditional surrender demand, Hitler could claim that surrender in the West was identical to capitulation in the East, and that the Germans needed to hold on against both sides. In September 1944, the "Morgenthau Plan," named after U.S. Treasury Secretary Henry Morgenthau, was leaked to the press and bolstered further German determination not to surrender. The plan called for Germany to be turned into a pastoral, agricultural territory divided among the occupying powers—a Carthaginian solution to the German problem.

Despite the dampening effect news of Allied intentions had on German resistance movements, and its energizing effect on German will to resist, the unconditional surrender policy was vindicated by events. The Soviet Union had carried the greater burden of the ground war since mid-1941, making the Allied invasions of Sicily, Italy, Normandy and southern France possible. Stalin's great subsequent fear was that the Western powers, once on the Continent, would make a separate peace with Germany and combine with the Germans to resist the Red Army—including the Communist system that would follow behind. The fear in the West was that if Stalin suspected betrayal by his allies, he would immediately settle with Hitler, allowing the Wehrmacht in the East, as well as Germany's entire industrial output, to be re-directed to the Anglo-American front. With Western democracies invading on one side, and Soviet Communists on the other, such a break between the Allies was, in fact, the Nazis' most realistic remaining hope.

Instead, Roosevelt and Churchill made clear that German surrender had to be total: to the Russians as well as to the Anglo-Americans. Although this left the Nazis no option except to fight to the bitter end, it was also the glue that held the East-West alliance together. The Nazi phenomenon had far exceeded the Kaiser's militarism in brutality. And both were fresh in the memories of Allied leaders in 1945. The armistice in 1918 had been a half-measure, while the verdict in 1945, revealed as necessary by the Hitlerite resurgence, would have to be more complete. For the Germans, then, the "Gotterdämmerung" phase of the war had commenced. The Wehrmacht regrouped and fought stubbornly on all fronts. Meanwhile, the Allied strategic air forces attempted to pound the German homeland into submission.

In August 1944, as the German Army retrieved its remnants from France and, in the East, fell back grudgingly from White Russia and the Ukraine, only one Eighth Air Force bomber and three from the Fifteenth Air Force landed in Switzerland. American fighter groups were by now flying from airfields on the Continent and had become a greater scourge than ever for enemy movement during daylight hours. With the loss of advance airfields and ground controllers in France, Germany had also lost its buffer against air raids. The Germans could track incoming formations by radar, but Eighth Air Force had grown increasingly skillful at deception, dispatching its bomber streams on zigzag routes that often resulted in targets being hit by surprise. The Luftwaffe fighter arm had in any case been gravely weakened; only the ground anti-aircraft system, to which two million Germans—including boys, women and older men—would be committed by the end of the war, continued to operate at greater strength than ever.

Somewhat shaken by the arrival of 45 B-17s and B-24s in Switzerland during the massive July raids, the USAAF command inquired about the matter to the head of the OSS in Switzerland, Allen Dulles. Based on his own observations and after consultations with General Bernard Legge (code-named "520") and General Henri Guisan, Dulles replied to Colonel Edward J. Glavin in an August 11 communication:

> No case of any nature has come to the attention of myself or 520 giving the least credence to the report that American airmen are attempting to evade any more combat by landing here. I believe this nothing but ill-willed propaganda inspired by Nazis, since I learned in a confidential talk with General Guisan a short time after many U.S. planes landed here, that under his orders each case was investigated and determined that none of the planes could possibly have returned to its home field. A complete report has been forwarded to [Hap] Arnold by 520. Naturally, the information from General Guisan should not be disseminated.

The myth of bomber crewmen—who by definition rank among the bravest men of World War II—landing in Switzerland to avoid combat persists, without factual basis, to this day. Turning to non-fiction, one is reminded of the hero of Joseph Heller's famous novel,

Catch-22. A B-24 crewman who flew with the Fifteenth Air Force, Heller knew enough not to plant his protagonist in a country that spent most of the war surrounded by Axis powers. At the end of that story, readers may recall, Yossarian went to Sweden.

On September 5, John Fanelli, piloting a Liberator called *Lonesome Polecat,* took off with over 700 other American bombers to support the epic battle George Patton's Third Army was waging at Metz. On overflying German rail marshalling yards, Fanelli saw the ground lined on both sides with flatcars mounted with AA guns. There was also a thick mass of clouds directly ahead of the bomber stream, and formations naturally loosened up as they entered the soup. While flying blind, *Lonesome Polecat* and other planes ran into a downdraft and began to plummet earthward. After falling from 21,000 to 4,000 feet, Fanelli finally regained control of his aircraft and began climbing to regain his previous altitude. By that time, the tight box formations had fallen apart. "There were B-24s coming through that area in all different directions," he said. "What a mess." Fanelli made it through the clouds to find a beautiful day on the other side, but the bombers had become disorganized. "I broke radio silence—someone had to break it because no one knew where the leader was. Way out front was this little speck that started shooting off flares—that was the leader."

Fanelli caught up and and had started his bomb run when the plane was hit by flak in its number one engine. "You look down," he commented, "and you can see the cannon winking at you like fireflies." The plane took a near-miss under its bomb bay which caused four of its 1,000-pound bombs to get hung up. Then, "another near hit under our right wing flipped us over and down we went." The B-24 made another harrowing plunge toward the ground, this time in a spin. Fanelli began ringing the alarm bell for the crew to put on their parachutes. At 9,000 feet he was able to level out but number one had quit and number two had caught fire. The top turret gunner kept up a running report on the engine fire until Fanelli finally yelled, "What do you want me to do, go out there and spit on it?"

The crew started tossing every object they could pry loose out of the plane and finally dislodged the hung-up bombs. Two roaming Mustangs flew over to provide escort. The plane was down to 4,000 feet and approaching the Vosges Mountains, which were considerably higher. At that point Fanelli announced over the intercom, "Would anyone like to go to Switzerland?" He later found that the second ship in their squadron had also been hit and had tried to return to England. The crew had had to bail out over France, and two men died when their chutes didn't open.

When *Lonesome Polecat* crossed the Rhine it was down to 1,000 feet and the navigator reported he didn't have a map. Fanelli snapped, "Why the hell don't you have a map?" He didn't realize he was already over Swiss territory but the top turret and waist gunners did. Two Swiss fighters had approached the aircraft from the rear and had begun to execute pursuit curves. As the Liberator churned on into Swiss airspace, the Swiss Me-109s reportedly opened fire. Suddenly, the pair of P-51 Mustangs that had been guarding the stricken bomber dived on the Swiss fighters and shot both of them down. One landed on its belly at Dubendorf while the other was destroyed in the air, its pilot killed. Swiss fighters, by that point in the war, had escorted over 150 American bombers to safety. The new presence of aggressive U.S. Mustang fighters over Swiss territory, even though they were not damaged, meant a new challenge for the Swiss air force and its flak units along the border.

Fanelli, oblivious to the action going on behind him, continued to concentrate on setting the bomber down. Finally, when only 100 feet high in the air, he spotted the airfield at Dubendorf. On his approach, a man with a red flag attached to a long pole attempted to wave him off. Fanelli said, "At this point I was sweating spigots. 'Get out of the way you son of a bitch—I can't go up. I gotta go in!' The guy dropped the flag and ran like hell." The plane had lost its brakes and skidded across the field, finally stopping when it careened into a drainage ditch, its tail sticking in the air.

For some reason, after the chaotic landing Fanelli's first instinct was to look around the cockpit for a glove he had dropped. He was in the process of searching when he was poked in the rear by a Swiss bayonet. "I thought I was in Germany," he said. "Outside there were people running around with buckets trying to catch the gas dripping out of the airplane."

Eight more bombers arrived in Switzerland in September 1944, a month in which General Eisenhower relinquished control of the heavies, allowing Spaatz, Doolittle and Eaker to resume their strategic offensive. Their primary target was oil. The Third Reich had already lost its largest oil center, Ploesti—first bombarded into a ghost town during the summer by the Fifteenth Air Force and then overrun by Soviet troops at the end of August. Now Germany relied on a few natural resources in eastern Europe and on 56 synthetic manufacturing plants. Crude refineries in Hungary, Czechoslovakia and Silesia were struck by the Fifteenth Air Force while the synthetic plants scattered throughout Germany were attacked by the Mighty Eighth. By the end of the month, only three installations were undamaged. Ironically, German fighter production—over 3,000 aircraft—reached an all-time high in September. However, fuel production was running at only 23 percent of its spring level, and production of aviation fuel had stopped almost completely. For the rest of the war the Luftwaffe was forced to rely on its rapidly diminishing stockpiles.

The successful American targeting of a German industrial nerve center had a cascading effect. German training schools lacked fuel to provide new pilots with air hours, since the remaining supplies needed to be funneled to frontline service. As experienced pilots became casualties, there was an increasingly acute shortage of replacement flyers. As the U.S. bomber streams encountered weaker opposition, the destructive effects of their raids increased. The only factor that ameliorated the Third Reich's catastrophic situation was the fall weather that closed in during October, along with fewer hours of daylight. In winter, American heavies based in England were unable to reach the plants and facilities Albert Speer had safeguarded in the east and southeast of the Reich. Targets in western Germany, including the Ruhr and Saar industrial regions, and cities such as Emden, Hamburg, Cologne and Aachen, were meanwhile blasted beyond recognition. A solution to the Ruhr was finally found when the Allies targeted its surrounding transportation network: coal could still be gotten from the Ruhr's deep mines, but by demolishing railroads and canal traffic, the USAAF made sure the fuel would just sit there in immense piles.

While the USAAF cut the legs from under the Luftwaffe, the RAF's "Bomber" Harris, throughout the late summer and fall, adamantly resisted suggestions that the British strategic force attack industrial targets, abandoning its practice of area, or terror, bombing. Of Germany's 60 largest cities, he noted, 18 had still not been obliterated. Bomber Command's practice of flying at night meant that its planes didn't have the option of seeking refuge in Switzerland if they were crippled in the air. Of 13 RAF aircraft that did make it to Swiss territory during the war, nine crashed in the countryside and barely half the crewmen survived. The better option for British flyers, except in mid-winter, was to ditch in the sea or Channel, whereupon they could be retrieved by the crack Air/Sea Rescue Service of the Royal Navy. By the last year of the war, southern Germany and Austria, the region containing the Reich's most vital industries, had become almost exclusively an American target area with daylight raids.

During the last three months of 1944 only seven American aircraft arrived in Switzerland. These included a Stinson L-5 liaison plane, a Thunderbolt fighter and five bombers from the Fifteenth Air Force. The Italian-based bombers had a greater hurdle to overcome than their counterparts based in England when they were hit by enemy fire. While a plane from the Eighth Air Force could conceivably return to its base at low, or even tree-top level across France, craft from the south had to return at 17,000 feet, or not at all. The Alps stood as an immense immovable barrier in front of stricken craft from Italy that could not maintain altitude. For hurt Fifteenth Air Force bombers, Switzerland represented the last refuge before crashing into the mountains they had more easily overflown en route to their target.

On Christmas Day, an Italian-based Liberator called *Maiden America* lost both its port engines to flak during a raid on Innsbruck, Austria. The crippled ship headed for Basel in northern Switzerland but couldn't find a landing field through the dense undercast. After turning around and heading for Zurich, it came under fire from Swiss AA guns at the village of Würenlingen, and the crew was forced to bail out. Tragically, the co-pilot landed in the Aare River and drowned; another crewman's chute got hung up on the tail section of the plane; and a third man couldn't (or wouldn't) jump and went down with the plane. The three flyers were buried at the American cemetery in Munsingen. In 1965, the Swiss citizens of Würenlingen erected a memorial to the airmen in their village.

By December 1944, American troops realized they would not be "home for Christmas," but they still considered the war as good as won. They were thus surprised on December 16 when the Germans launched a gigantic counteroffensive spearheaded by two panzer armies against the American front in the Ardennes. Although the Red Army was the greatest threat to Germany, both militarily and in terms of the consequences of Russian occupation, Hitler opted to strike at the opposing front he thought was weakest. It was one of his greatest mistakes. American combat troops, though outnumbered, held on to strategic points with a ferocious tenacity the Germans had not anticipated. At Bastogne, St. Vith, Marche and other battlefields, U.S. GIs proved themselves equal to the best the Nazis could send against them. Responding quickly to the offensive, combat-hardened U.S. divisions from north and south counterattacked the "Bulge."

At first the Wehrmacht was aided by dismal weather that grounded Allied planes. But when the skies cleared, the full weight of American air power descended on the enemy's lines, its transportation network and supplies. Like the German Army, the Luftwaffe saved its last great effort for the offensive, launching a surprise attack of 700 fighters against Allied tactical airfields on New Year's morning. Several hundred Allied fighters were destroyed, but those losses were quickly made good. In the process, the Luftwaffe fighter arm had shot its bolt. The Battle of the Bulge lasted well into January as American ground forces first stopped and then pushed back the initial enemy penetration, severely reducing Hitler's last operational reserves.

By the turn of 1945, the Thousand-Year Reich was still persisting in history's most calamitous war, but its chances for survival had nearly disappeared. Adolf Hitler still anticipated a political break between the Western Allies and the Soviet Union because, from his limited perspective, he couldn't imagine Britain coping with the Red Army by itself once German power had been destroyed. Throughout the war he underestimated the United States, not imagining that for half a century after World War II the Americans would maintain formidable forces in Europe. His other hopes had become pinned on the "wonder weapons" his scientists were frantically trying to develop.

In fall 1944, the Germans launched the world's first operational jet fighter, the Me-262, but it proved too little and too late against the proliferating numbers of Allied aircraft. U.S. fighters found that the jets were most vulnerable when they were landing, so swarmed the German airfields when Me-262s had run out of fuel or ammunition. In the U-boat war, which can be considered Germany's counterpart to the Allied strategic air campaign, new "schnorkel" boats that could stay submerged indefinitely arrived only as American armies were occupying the French Atlantic ports. The Type XXI U-boat, which could move faster underwater than most ships on the surface, appeared only in 1945, too late to have an impact on the war. Additional "wonder weapons" that failed to live up to expectations were the German rockets, which the Allies had long feared and that finally came into operation on June 13, 1944.

The impact of the "Vengeance" weapons has often been underestimated in American, if not British or Continental, histories of the war, despite the massive German development effort and the equally intensive Allied efforts to pre-empt or resist them. The V-1 "robot bomb," or, as the British called it, "buzz bomb," was the predecessor of the modern cruise missile. Flying at nearly 400 mph on a flat trajectory, it could fly in any light or weather, but could also be knocked down by fighters or by radar-guided AA fire. The British constructed an elaborate aerial defense line called the Diver Belt southeast of London and eventually succeeded in destroying a majority of the incoming. The far more frightening V-2, which appeared in September, was a precursor to the Saturn rocket that would eventually carry men to the moon. It soared into the stratosphere, then plunged to earth without warning at four times the speed of sound. Once in flight, it could not be defended. Fearing public panic, British officials tried to explain away the first attacks as "exploding gas mains." This soon became absurd and Churchill publicly admitted what Londoners already knew: they were under attack from a novel and sinister new weapon.

Reactions to the V-weapons were diverse. In contrast to the dismay felt by British civilians, and later those of Antwerp, Liege and other cities, some Allied officials were privately relieved. Despite rumors that the rockets would carry unprecedented explosive power, the Germans had only been able to fit the weapons with one-ton warheads. This was less payload than carried by a single bomber, and, in fact, the total weight of explosives delivered by the V-weapons during the war barely exceeded that of a single 1,000-bomber raid.

Nevertheless, among those same officials the appearance of the V-weapons prompted additional worry. If the Germans had been able to make such a leap beyond their Allied scientific counterparts in rocket technology, who could be sure what other inventions were coming to fruition in the Third Reich's secret laboratories? Before the war, Germany had been the world's leader in the study and application of nuclear physics. A select few Allied leaders realized that Hitler's obstinate belief in a potential "wonder weapon" that could turn the war around was not misguided. In Los Alamos, New Mexico, at that time, American scientists were secretly in the process of perfecting just such a war-winning weapon.

Though much maligned as a waste of resources, particularly by Allied scientists caught unaware by Wernher von Braun's breakthroughs, the V-weapon campaign had both tangible and intangible benefits for Germany's war effort. In the first half of 1944 the Allies made over 25,000 air sorties against V-weapon preparations, expending 36,000 tons of bombs in Operation Crossbow. Most of the damage was inflicted on 96 suspected "ski sites" for the V-1 which were hidden in French orchards or farmyards. While the Allies bombed away, the Germans switched to pre-fabricated launch catapults that could not be spotted from the air. The ski sites became, though not by design, one of the more successful deceptions of the war. Observing Operation Crossbow, Hitler commented, "Every bomb dropped on France is one less dropped on Germany." The very novelty of the robot bombs prompted a response out of proportion to their numbers. If the same payload eventually carried by the V-weapons had been delivered by conventional bombers, the British would not have insisted on such urgent defensive and pre-emptive offensive measures.

Intangibly, for a German public whose cities had been methodically destroyed or incinerated by Bomber Command for two years, the V-weapons provided a boost in morale. Despite the degradation of the Luftwaffe and the massive growth of the Allied air forces, Germany was suddenly hitting back at Britain with revolutionary means. Widespread German fear that the Allies would escalate the scale of carnage by employing poison gas or napalm (introduced by the Americans at Normandy) was partly alleviated by the rockets. The V-weapons provided a degree of security to the Germans, through deterrence. If the Allies employed unconventional or forbidden weapons against German cities, Britain itself could suffer the same fate.

Perhaps the most positive aspect of the robots and rockets from the German point of view, however, was that they provided a means to bomb the enemy without risking the lives of airmen. This was in marked contrast to the Allied effort, which still entailed dispatching large bombers each with ten vulnerable airmen aboard deep into enemy territory, where many were shot down in flames.

Not a single foreign aircraft landed in Switzerland during January 1945, but in February 16 crippled American planes sought refuge as the return of good flying weather brought thousands of U.S. bombers and fighters into action over the Reich. Flying from airfields in France and Italy, the new arrivals in Switzerland included two twin-engined B-25 Mitchells, a P-47 Thunderbolt and a Mustang. Swiss Air Force Captain Geoffrey von Meiss was dispatched to pick up the Mustang pilot, who had come down near a woods in the countryside. The two men flew back to Dubendorf in a Fiesler Storch observation and ground liaison plane. Von Meiss recalled that when the American pilot emerged from the passenger seat of the small craft he looked green, as if he were about to be sick. He stammered, "I have never flown so low and so slow!"

On February 5, the crew of a B-17 flying from Italy was forced to bail out in a snowstorm over the Alps. The forward crew of the plane, including the pilots, bombardier and top turret gunner, landed in Austria, whereupon they were seized by Wehrmacht soldiers. The aft crew—ball turret gunner, radioman, waist gunners and tail gunner— was found ten days later by Swiss soldiers, huddled in a small hut just half a mile from the border. The navigator died at the end of his parachute jump, having cracked his skull on a rock.

U.S. strategic air commanders had by now run so short of vital industrial targets that they committed the Eighth Air Force to assist in the destruction of Dresden, resulting in the highest death toll of any bombing raid in Europe. (Author Kurt Vonnegut, who was in a POW camp near the city, later described the attack in his book *Slaughterhouse Five*.) After the RAF's Bomber Command attacked the city with 855 planes on the night of February 13, about 400 American heavies soared in to drop more bombs into the spiraling pillars of smoke the next day. The process was repeated on the 14th, killing anywhere from 40,000 to 100,000 civilians. A more accurate number was difficult to determine because no one knew how many refugees from the Eastern Front had been packed into the city, and since all the victims' remains were hurriedly buried in mass graves to prevent disease.

The success of the attack was due to the RAF's use of incendiary bombs which ignited the medieval city and created one of the firestorms in which "Bomber" Harris placed great pride. The raid was of questionable military value since Dresden had no vital war industries and its railyards were then being used to move civilian fugitives. The city's 88mm flak guns had been transferred to the front to hold off Russian tanks, and what few German fighters took to the air inflicted only a half-of-one-percent loss rate on the attackers.

American participation in the attack reflected a shift in strategic priorities in the last few months of the war. During the first two years of its bombing campaign, when the Germans mounted formidable defenses, the USAAF had waged war against the enemy military, refusing to participate on a significant scale in the British war against civilians. Historian Geoffrey Perret wrote: "The morality of heavy bombing in residential areas, where large numbers of civilians were sure to be killed and mutilated, was a long-running debate among AAF commanders. It was conducted *sotto voce*, like a family dispute you wouldn't want neighbors to know about." Now that the end was in sight, however, a few devastating blows might possibly end the war, thereby saving lives. The reasoning was that if Germany needed just one last push, the USAAF was willing to give it to them.

The other motive for destroying Dresden was the impression it was certain to make on the Red Army, which was then about 50 miles from the city. While Albert Speer termed the Allied strategic air campaign a "second front" which opened long before D-Day, Stalin had been unimpressed throughout the war and had continually demanded a greater Western effort against Hitler. The Soviets, like the Germans, had not developed a strategic bombing force and may have been unconvinced of the efficacy of that form of warfare. Prior to 1945, with the exception of Berlin, the greatest devastation had fallen on German cities in the west rather than in the future Soviet-occupied zone. The attack on Dresden, which was approved by both Roosevelt and Churchill, provided an opportunity to demonstrate Western strength to the Soviets firsthand. Or, as aviation historian James P. Harrison opined: "The Allied intention was to create a 'signpost' for the rapidly advancing Red Army, in the event that Stalin, flush with his recent success, had any doubts about the effectiveness of Allied air power."

Although Dresden brought into relief a certain revulsion that had stirred in Britain toward the RAF's targeting of civilians late in the war, the Red Army had overrun Auschwitz the preceding month and Allied forces were soon to encounter Dachau and other camps piled with evidence of Nazi atrocities. Had the German population been made to suffer too much or not enough? The moral dilemma would remain, the only indisputable logic being that anything that might shorten the war—rather than just rendering it more horrible—had to be tried. In the following months, the USAAF would actually exceed the ruthlessness of Bomber Command with its incendiary and atomic attacks on Japan. Air power quickly ended that conflict; however, public shock at the casualties, and subsequent fear of similar events during the Cold War, forced a postwar reappraisal of air strategy away from the concept of area bombing.

With the Third Reich in precipitate decline in 1945, Swiss armed neutrality, an intense irritant to the Nazi leadership throughout the war, came to be viewed as an asset by more practical Germans. At least there was one direction from which Germany was not being attacked. Some businessmen and Nazi officials attempted to move their families to Switzerland to avoid the approaching debacle, or even tried to cross the border themselves. In addition, a number of Germans who had accurately read the handwriting on the wall attempted to transfer money out of the country into Swiss banks. Though people could be executed for this activity if discovered by Hitler's loyalists, to the degree that even the dictator relied on institutional support for his decisions—in industry, the military and government bureaucracy— rousing national bloodlust against Switzerland in 1945 would have been difficult. During the last months of the war, in contrast to the crisis years when German power was greatest, Switzerland's independence, and consequent stability, was appreciated by some Germans, if not by the fanatics who held power.

The Swiss, who were aware of the Third Reich's growing desperation, resolved to prevent Nazi fugitives from entering the country. They also agreed in February 1945 with an Allied commission headed by Roosevelt's representative, Lauchlin Currie, to decline suspicious bank deposits and to suspend their bank secrecy laws for German transfers. The Swiss bank secrecy laws had been enacted in 1934 partially in response to Nazi attempts to identify Jews and other opponents of Hitler who transferred wealth from the Third Reich. The Nazis had made such transfers a capital crime, but the Swiss responded by refusing to name depositors. The laws were willingly revoked when the new clients were likely to be Nazis themselves. Nevertheless, after 1933 many transactions were made by intermediaries who masked the true identity of the depositors and who afterward had access to the funds. After nearly 50 million people died in the war, Swiss banks found themselves holding a large number of dormant accounts, as did banks in all other European countries as well as the United States.

By 1945, the American government had come to view Switzerland with a curious disparity. Henry Morgenthau's Treasury Department pressured the Swiss to cease all commerce with neighboring Axis states, including trade for food and fuel. The U.S. State Department and military, on the other hand, backed by the British government and its chiefs of staff, opposed forcing Switzerland to sever its commercial ties and become, in effect, a belligerent against the Axis. Switzerland was by then acting as Protecting Power for 32 nations and was the sole conduit to Allied POWs held by the Nazis (and Japanese). The Geneva-based International Committee of the Red Cross had become a restraining factor amid the scorched earth policy that the Nazi leadership seemed intent on implementing. An impulsive "Führer order" to massacre Allied prisoners could not be ruled out; the physical presence of Swiss ICRC delegates in the POW camps helped to ensure that no German commander would obey such an order.

With Allied forces in close proximity, the Swiss could now benefit from massive Allied support if the Germans were to attack. However, demands from the U.S. Treasury Department, which unfortunately seemed to resemble in their arbitrary tone demands from the Reich's Economic Ministry, were unwelcome. "Armed neutrality" meant not caving in to one power after successfully resisting another. The Swiss, after six years of defying Nazi Germany—in a strategic situation not of their making—had no wish to be bullied by U.S. civilian government officials in Washington, DC.

When Switzerland stood as the sole remaining democracy in Europe, its trade negotiators—in a sense, the country's "front line" against Nazi intimidation—had repeatedly faced up to their counterparts in the Reich. Their primary goal was to acquire enough basic sustenance for the nation to survive. General Guisan had made certain that, if not negotiating from strength, they were at least not negotiating from weakness. As hundreds of American airmen could attest, the Swiss public made do with a bare minimum of life's necessities during the war, relying on their own resources to the highest degree possible. Politically and militarily, for example by denying the Luftwaffe access to Swiss airspace and the Wehrmacht permission to move troops through their Alpine transit routes, the Swiss refused to concede an inch of their sovereignty.

Part of the success of the Currie Mission, which included not only Roosevelt's assistant but British and French representatives, was that afterward the Swiss no longer felt they were being pressured by the new victors in the war to abandon their cherished principle of neutrality. The Swiss placed great importance on even-handed treatment of belligerents and were not ones to jump on a bandwagon. Nevertheless, it turned out they were entirely willing to accede to nearly every Allied request, using the pretext that Germany had fallen in arrears on prior agreements. The Allies, in turn, promised that essential Swiss trade could be allowed through their naval blockade of the Continent. As the first nation in Europe, along with perhaps Poland, to take the Nazi menace seriously, Switzerland was fully inclined to assist the Allies to the degree allowed a neutral by international law. On a grass-roots level, of course, the Swiss public had hoped and prayed for an Allied victory for years. The Currie Mission had not discovered a new "ally," but it found as much cooperation as it needed.

Swiss banks, which had established a strong international presence over the centuries, were utilized by both sides during the war. During the years 1939–45 the Swiss traded gold to the amount of approximately 1.8 billion in Swiss francs with the Allies and 1.2 billion with the Axis. The latter transactions included national reserves of countries conquered by the Germans, particularly Belgian gold that in 1940 was unwisely safeguarded in France (the French shipped their own to North Africa). According to international law these were legitimate prizes of war. Over half a century after World War II, however, accusations came from America that some of the Axis gold derived from more sinister sources and that Swiss banks were wrong for having conducted any gold trades with Germany during the war. A number of U.S. publishers and headline writers, upon finding that the phrase "Nazi gold" had the same titillating effect on the public as "pirate treasure," provided enormous publicity for the charges.

Individuals who view such titanic events as World War II through the prism of economics alone have a difficult time with the Swiss, who endured the war on a subsistence level and who in 1940 devoted 62 percent of all government expenditures to their army. A few Swiss businessmen, and even bankers, may have profited from the war, though not remotely on the scale of fortunes that were made in the United States during and immediately after the conflict. A distinction between Swiss businessmen and those in other countries, however, was that in Switzerland every able-bodied male was also a soldier, trained in marksmanship or heavy weapons, and subject to instant mobilization for frontline service if an attack were to occur. The fact that the Nazis did not choose to invade Switzerland during the period when their power was unrivaled on the Continent owes more to the martial preparedness of the Swiss—from bankers to farmers—than to trade the encircled Alpine nation was compelled to conduct in order to sustain its people and its strength.

In January 1945, the Battle of the Bulge, along with intermittently brutal weather, managed to curtail the strategic air campaign. In the ground war, meanwhile, the Allies delivered hammerblow attacks. By mid-month the German assault in the Ardennes had been utterly defeated by U.S. infantry and armor, as was a subsidiary offensive, Operation Northwind, that Hitler had launched in the Saar. On January 12 and 14, respectively, Soviet Marshals Konev and Zhukov launched gigantic offensives from the line of the Vistula River in Poland, their ultimate destination Berlin. Hitler, as if in denial about the Red Army juggernaut that had begun to stream across the flat Prussian and Polish landscape, ordered 6th SS Panzer Army to be transferred from the Ardennes front to Hungary, where it launched an attack at Lake Balaton near Budapest. Hitler continued to fight for his few remaining oil resources.

In his dispersal of essential German industry, Armaments Minister Albert Speer had moved as many facilities as possible to the east, away from Allied bombers. Now those installations were among the first in the Third Reich to come within range of Red Army tanks and artillery. The move of Germany's last remaining striking force to the southeast can in retrospect be attributed to the USAAF's successful targeting of Hitler's oil and synthetic gasoline resources. However, at the time, the sudden transfer of the SS panzers away from the defense of Berlin reinforced Allied concerns that the Nazis were reorienting south, planning to make their last stand in a "National Redoubt" in the Alps. Dwight D. Eisenhower wrote:

> If the German was permitted to establish the Redoubt he might possibly force us to engage in a long-drawn-out guerrilla type of warfare, or a costly siege. Thus he could keep alive his desperate hope that through disagreement among the Allies he might yet be able to secure terms more favorable than those of unconditional surrender. The evidence was clear that the Nazi

intended to make the attempt and I decided to give him no opportunity to carry it out.

The type of Alpine Redoubt strategy that General Guisan had adopted in July 1940 became a major concern to the Allies—if such a strategy were pursued by the Germans. American XIIth Army Group commander Omar Bradley wrote: "Concern over the Alpine redoubt had a decisive impact on my thinking and planning. My concern intensified in mid- to late March, when Ultra indicated that certain German military headquarters were moving from the Berlin area to the Bavarian Alps." In the controversy that raged within the Allied high command over whether to race the Russians for Berlin, the specter of a Nazi Alpine redoubt ultimately decided the issue. While the Russian focal point remained Berlin, the Americans would race for Prague and farther south, cutting off any potential flow of German forces to the mountains. The quick destruction of Nazi Germany was the only development that could end the war with amity between the Soviets and Anglo-Americans, along the lines most recently agreed upon at the Yalta Conference of February 1945. If a rump Nazi state continued to exist, forcing Western and Soviet armies to jostle for territory in a devastated central Europe, the prospect of a break between the Allies—over occupation of German, Polish, Czech or other territory—would dramatically increase.

In early 1945, the ground war converged on Switzerland from three directions as the Wehrmacht fell back through Italy, France, and before (increasingly skillful) Soviet attacks from the east. Airman Bert Pollock, while an internee, received a pass to visit Basel on the Rhine where he could look across at both Germany and France. "I could see German tanks racing for the border—then American tanks—they had hundreds, chasing them like dogs." Pollock heard rumors that the French Maquis, many of whom were Communists, were being rounded up by DeGaulle's Free French and were thus trying to get into Switzerland. Swiss border troops were keeping them out. At one point a woman handed Pollock a note that read: "No escapes this week. Maquis on the border killing anyone who tries to keep them from crossing."

For General Guisan, and the 800,000 men he could by then mobilize, rumors that the Nazis would make their last stand in the Alps prompted an ongoing alert. Eisenhower cited "the mountains of southern Bavaria, western Austria and northern Italy" as the project-ed location of a German national redoubt. These areas formed a semi-circle around Switzerland, where Alpine fortifications, guns and enor-mous stockpiles of food and ammunition were already in place. Guisan could not assume that the Germans would respect Swiss neu-trality if forced into a desperate, last-ditch enclave in the Alps. Instead he would have to anticipate an attack.

During the "gold" controversy of the late 1990s, or, as many who observed the arguments between Zurich and New York termed it, "the battle of the banks," the bizarre charge appeared in U.S. newspapers and in one official U.S. State Department report that Switzerland had intentionally prolonged World War II. This was the most far-fetched in a sudden series of accusations that led to the conclusion Switzerland could only have escaped the wrath of postwar American lawyers if it had surrendered to German arms or threats as all of its neighbors had done. In truth, Switzerland's only means of prolonging the war would have been to collapse, morally and militarily, thus allowing the Swiss Alps (and the country's industrial infrastructure) to become part of Hitler's domain. Kesselring's Tenth and Fourteenth armies in Italy, which by 1945 were the most intact of Germany's large forces, were in the best position to initiate an Alpine strategy. They could later be joined by whatever army or SS forces the Nazis were able to retrieve from the Balkans or the north. The Swiss General Staff recognized that their vast Alpine fortifications would be invaluable if the Nazis attempted to construct a national redoubt of their own. It was Henri Guisan's task, unaided by allies, to make sure the Germans would not even try in those parts of the Alps that flew the Swiss flag.

15

MISSION TO MUNICH

On February 22, Carl Spaatz launched Operation Clarion, a new approach to bombing the Reich. Instead of aiming large bomber fleets at a handful of major objectives, 9,000 U.S. fighters, medium bombers and long-range heavies took off to hit hundreds of targets along the German rail network. The wide-ranging operation brought the war home to previously undamaged towns and villages throughout Germany. High-level bombers roamed the width and breadth of the Reich. Low-level fighters and tactical bombers followed railway tracks to strafe stations and marshalling yards. Unfortunately, some of the U.S. pilots, given more or less free rein, lost their bearings or became overzealous.

President Roosevelt's assistant Lauchlin Currie, along with British official Dingle Foot, were making progress in their series of economic talks in Bern, during which the Swiss agreed to halt German trade and transit in exchange for the Allies' loosening their sea blockade. Enormously pleased with the discussions, on February 22 Currie, along with Allen Dulles, was en route to Schaffhausen to lay a wreath on the mass grave of Swiss civilians killed in the worst of the preceding year's accidental bombings. As the American delegation neared the city, air raid sirens went off, explosions were heard and U.S. aircraft were sighted in the sky. Operation Clarion had spilled over into Switzerland, with tragic results.

The town of Stein-am-Rhein, just 12 miles from Schaffhausen, was ripped by explosions and machine-gun fire, with 7 dead and 16 injured. Another 8 civilians died at Rafz, and in the town of Vals a small child was killed. Twelve Swiss locations were bombed or strafed, resulting in 20 deaths and numerous injuries. Currie was outraged that the USAAF, with its supposed precision in daylight bombing, was hitting targets indiscriminately, and not even in the right country. After conveying his regrets for Schaffhausen, he drove to Stein-am-Rhein to deliver more apologies. He also cabled Roosevelt and Acting Secretary of State Joseph Grew, who expressed "profound shock" at the attacks. Repercussions flowed through the U.S. chain of command, from Chief of Staff George Marshall to Eisenhower to Hap Arnold and Carl Spaatz.

Although it is tempting to picture the USAAF as a finely-honed machine—and in systems and command it did improve enormously throughout the war—veteran crews were a minority as the force expanded, having fallen as casualties or having transferred stateside after completing their missions. At this point in the war, most U.S. flyers were replacements or fresh crews assigned to newly created bomb groups. Over Germany, when an aircraft or even an entire wing became lost (as often happened), the mission could be retrieved by unloading bombs on a target of opportunity. In practice this meant virtually any sighting on the ground that would give aircraft the chance to return to base before running out of gas. When disoriented pilots and navigators hit targets of opportunity in Switzerland, the mistakes were publicized. There is no evidence, however, that bombings of Switzerland by U.S. aircraft were anything but the tip of the iceberg of countless other mistakes happening nearly every day over the Reich. German civilians located far from a group's target, after all, could never claim they were bombed by error, though they often were.

On February 25, the Eighth Air Force launched 1,200 heavies against southern Germany, with a remarkably low loss of five planes, three of which landed in Switzerland. Even though the percentage of bombers downed by German defenses had fallen, the terror of the air war had not abated for those crews who fell victim to enemy fire.

Ball turret gunner George Hintz described the demise of his 95th Bomb Group B-17: "We were at 20,000 feet, approximately eight minutes from the target, when we were hit in the number four engine, which began to disintegrate. Losing altitude, we turned back toward Colmar, France. We were surrounded by heavy flak and part of the nose was shot away. The wingtips were gone and the tail gunner, Wilbur Schraner, had his guns shot out of his hands. We dropped our bombs on some town, then there was a direct hit on the number three engine and we feathered the prop.

"The oxygen bottles below the flight deck were hit and the escaping air sounded like leaking tires. The hydraulic tank above the oxygen tanks was also leaking. We prepared for a crashlanding, stowing the ball turret, etc., when holes appeared in the radio room walls. The radio table was hit, the number two engine caught fire and flames were blowing back over the wing and the fuel cells were leaking. The word came to bail out, even though we were at low altitude." The crew parachuted safely and were picked up by Swiss soldiers. The abandoned aircraft meanwhile continued flying level across the countryside as Swiss AA gunners tried to bring it down. Incredibly, the B-17 eventually descended on an open field in what resembled a perfect crashlanding.

On the morning of that day's raid, bombardier Frank Bush of a Flying Fortress called *Dinah Mite* was approached by his radioman, Robert Shepherd, who told him, "Lieutenant, this is going to be a bad one today. If I do not get back, have somebody go talk to my girlfriend, OK?" Hours later, over Munich, *Dinah Mite* was rocked by flak and Shepherd was killed, two other men badly wounded. The crippled craft crossed Lake Constance but was unable to stay in the air and made a rough landing in a cow pasture. According to historians Hans-Heiri Stapfer and Gino Künzle, "Their landing place was only 400 feet inside Switzerland and soldiers from both sides came towards the ship. The Swiss were there first and took the crew into custody."

The crew of *Touchy Tess*, a 351st Bomb Group B-17, was flying only their second mission and turret gunner/engineer Clinton O. Norby remembered it vividly. "The day began being awakened at 2:00 A.M. with breakfast at 2:30 A.M. and briefing at 3:00 A.M. After the main briefing, as gunners, we went to the gun room to pick up the guns for the plane and clean them and put them on the truck to be taken out to the aircraft."

They then proceeded to the dressing room to prepare for their mission: against rail marshalling yards outside Munich. Their cold weather attire included shorts, undershirt and long underwear; a wool olive drab shirt and pants; a heated suit (including electrically heated boots and gloves); a one-piece wool coverall; the flying suit; a Mae West life preserver; and parachute. Norby and the other gunners were also required to wear silk gloves underneath their heated ones to prevent their hands from sticking to the frozen metal if they had to work on the guns or open fire. After dressing, Norby and the other crewmen went to the equipment room to get flak suits, helmets and oxygen masks. At the aircraft the bombardier passed out emergency rations and escape maps. As Norby remembers, "the escape maps were made of silk and were stored in small-rubberized containers."

Norby felt as excited as every other airman on that busy morning, but he also had a premonition. "On this particular morning, for some reason I had a feeling that this mission would be different, so I laid in bed and said a silent prayer and asked for protection for that day. I took all my personal belongings and locked them in my footlocker." (It was a rather morbid practice in the Eighth Air Force to divide up an airman's belongings if he was reported missing in action.) It seems that co-pilot Harold Gividen had had a similar inkling of fate. "After the plane had been checked and we were going aboard, Harold came up to me and asked me if I had said a prayer that morning; I told him that I had and he said that he had also."

Touchy Tess was among the last of the 36 planes in its group to take off. Norby recalled: "As we left England and headed out across the English Channel, the excitement, anxiety, or fear seemed to take hold. The formation was climbing for altitude, which for this mission was 27,000 feet. Our flight plan took us out and over the North Sea so that we would approach Europe by way of Holland. Right after that, we picked up our fighter cover. They never flew too close to us but we could follow them by their contrails. This, to me, was a very beauiful sight, as the trails were above us, to our right and left and below us." Over the North Sea the gunners test-fired their guns and then (except for the turret gunners) donned their flak suits. On crossing into Germany they began to search the skies for Luftwaffe interceptors. "By listening on the radio we could hear the fighter pilots talk to one another and also by following their contrails we could watch their action. On this day, I did hear the fighter pilots talking of spotting enemy planes and calling for support, and by watching their contrails, they did engage with enemy planes. I don't know what the outcome was. All this happened very fast and with your assigned duties you cannot follow the action."

As engineer, one of Norby's tasks was to check the bomb bay

doors to see if they opened when the bombardier, Ernest Ogden, tested them. Ogden called on the intercom to say the doors were open, but Norby could see they remained shut. The pilot was asked to try opening the doors with his switch, but that didn't work either. Pilot Charles Abplanalp (who was of Swiss descent) ordered Norby to crawl down to the bomb bay and crank the doors open by hand. He had to lie on his belly and he found the crank harder to turn than expected. The doors were a third of the way open when the aircraft was hit by flak.

"I heard an explosion and the bomb bay filled with black smoke. Out of the corner of my right eye, I could see a lot of the wires which lead to the bomb shackles dangling and smoking. The next thing I knew," Norby recalled, "someone was shaking my feet, so I crawled back into the cockpit area and there was the navigator, Brown, standing between the pilot and co-pilot. The sight almost turned me sick. Brown was wearing his flying helmet and oxygen mask but not his flak helmet. All across his forehead was blood; it was running down over both eyes and the bridge of his nose and then onto his oxygen mask. The blood was freezing and building up over his eyes so he could not see. (The air temperature gauge in the nose at the time showed minus 67 degrees Celsius.) Brown also had a number of head wounds that were bleeding and looked very messy with blood running down his neck in front of his ears. Brown was such a mess I didn't know what to do."

Brown, however, had his senses about him. He was the plane's first-aid man and told Norby to sprinkle sulfa powder over his wounds and apply a compress bandage. Norby then looked around to assess the effects of the flak burst. "Most of the damage was on the left side of the plane. The pilot's windshield, both front and side, was damaged, so he could not see out. The pilot's rudder controls were shot away, so the co-pilot now had to do the flying. By this time we had dropped out of formation and were all alone, so we asked the radio operator to call for fighter support; however, the radio was shot up and not working. Our No. 3 engine had stopped, and our No. 2 was running away, so the co-pilot feathered it. We had an oil leak in No. 4. This leak was such that, as the oil went into the engine, it leaked going out, so we were using up our oil supply for that engine. No. 1 had an oil leak going into the engine, which meant it was not getting proper lubrication, so eventually both Nos. 1 and 4 would freeze up on us and then we would have no power for flying."

Of the plane's four oxygen systems, two had been knocked out so that the nose and waist crew had to use walk-around bottles. *Touchy Tess* was losing altitude as the pilots struggled to maintain control of the craft. The flight instruments were damaged so the pilots and navigator could only estimate a general direction to the west (it turned out to be southwest). Norby continued:

"Not long after Brown was bandaged he returned to the cockpit and said that Ogden was giving him a bad time and asked that I give him a hand. Ogden was about 6 feet tall and 190 pounds; Brown was 5 feet 6 and about 150 pounds. We went down to the nose of the plane to see what was wrong with Ogden. This was the first time I had been in the nose since we were hit. It was really a mess. Part of the plexiglass was shot away and holes were all over the left side. Ogden had a wound in his left arm just above his elbow. Brown told me to sprinkle sulfa powder into the wound, and then he bandaged it. This took some doing because when we were hit Ogden's mask was blown off his face and his gloves were off, so he was suffering from lack of oxygen. Ogden was out of his head but didn't pass out. He was trying to get to me to keep his hands warm. With Brown's help we were able to get some spare gloves on his hands. Why he thought I could get his hands warm was not explainable. It was just one of those things that happens when someone is out of his head."

Norby and Brown were able to get the bombardier stretched out in the radio compartment and tried to reattach his oxygen mask. At that point they realized the tube of the mask had been severed by shrapnel and it couldn't even be attached to a walk-around bottle. Brown and Ogden alternately shared a mask while Norby went back to the flight deck. Pilot Abplanalp asked if the bombs were still sitting in the bomb bay and Norby found them still there: 500 pound bombs on the bottom with incendiary clusters on top. He was trying again to turn the crank by hand when suddenly the bomb bay doors opened by themselves, ripping the crank from his hands. Ball turret gunner John Genetti, who was watching, thought Norby had been hit by flak. Unfortunately, only the bombs on the right side salvoed. Norby and Genetti had to manually dislodge the others, first by pushing off the incendiaries, which would crash against the 500-pounders before falling.

"While Genetti and I were doing this," Norby said, "one of us would hold on to the other so as not to fall out. About this time, someone started to fire their guns. It turned out to be the chin turret, so I got out of the bomb bay to see what was happening. All I could think of was that we were being attacked by an enemy fighter. The co-pilot told me to check to see what was going on in the nose. As I went into the nose, Brown told me that Ogden had gone out of his head and started to fire his guns. He had fired so long that he used up all his ammunition. Apparently the walk-around bottle had run out of oxygen and neither Brown nor Ogden realized it. So again, I gave them my bottle and then refilled their bottle so I could use it while I was in the bomb bay.

"Between Genetti and I, we finally released all the bombs. This does not sound like much of a job, but when you are lying on a cat-walk about 10 inches wide and reaching down to try to release 500-pound bombs with nothing to really hold on to, just someone else holding onto you so you won't fall out, somewhere between 15,000 and 20,000 feet in the air with no parachute, it becomes pretty scary."

After the bombs had all been released, Norby tried the switch to see if the bomb bay doors would close. Now the switch worked perfectly; no cranking was necessary. When he returned to assessing damage to the aircraft he noted a number of shrapnel holes that had entered the plane on the left side and gone out the right. Several of these holes had passed through his top turret. If he had been standing at his station instead of being on his belly in the bomb bay trying to work the crank, he would have been wounded in his lower trunk and legs. "I can't help think," he said afterward, "that prayers are answered in many different ways."

Other damage was found to the ship's flare gun, which had shrapnel lodged in its trigger mechanism, and the hydraulic tank and some of the lines. If the plane did manage to land, the brakes and flaps would be inoperable. The good news was that the plane had lost so much altitude that oxygen was no longer necessary. The bad news was that the pilots were unable to control the descent. They were also frantically trying to determine where they were. The B-17 had been hit over Munich and tried to head west, but the expected landmarks on the ground had not appeared.

"At this time," said Norby, "someone called on the intercom that there were four enemy fighters at three o'clock high, so I got into the top turret, turned on the power, gun switch and gunsight, and hand-charged the guns." Then he saw four fighters at nine o'clock. He called back that the report was in error, but again someone yelled that the fighters were at three o'clock. Norby looked again and saw a total of eight aircraft approaching the plane from two sides. "They were out of range, so I test-fired my guns and nothing happened. I hand-charged the guns a second time; still they would not fire." They had been damaged by the flak that tore through his turret. "The eight fighters were going into a pursuit curve. I was so afraid that my knees were actually knocking together. As the enemy planes came closer, I was still trying to fire my guns but with no success. I recognized some of them as German Me-109s. I knew also that the chin turret was use-less because Ogden had used up all the ammunition when he was out of his head. When the enemy planes came closer and still didn't fire on us, I wondered why they had a red square with a white cross painted on the fuselage."

Touchy Tess had been surrounded by Swiss Messerschmitts and Moranes—two each above, below and on either side. A Swiss fighter in front lowered its landing gear as a signal for the Fortress to do the same, but the bomber's wheels wouldn't go down. Norby recalled: "We thought we were over Switzerland, but were not sure. The pilot told me to get down in the nose and tell Brown and Ogden to get ready to jump and for me to open the emergency hatch in the nose. Then the pilot called the men in the rear of the plane and told them the same thing. When I kicked the hatch out in the nose and looked out, the ground appeared to be very close. In fact, too close to jump, so I told the pilot, but he said get ready just in case.

"I picked up my parachute to have ready in case we had to jump. As I picked it up I discovered more damage—personal—my chute had holes where pieces of shrapnel had torn into it. I didn't know whether the chute would open or not, and another shot of fear went through my nervous system."

The co-pilot went on the intercom to tell the crew not to jump, but in case the aft crew didn't get the message Norby went back to tell the radioman to get everyone into crashlanding positions. Tail gunner Gene Bullock found waist gunner Herb Berlin standing at the waist door with his parachute on, about to leap. Bullock had to wrestle him back into the aircraft. By now they were at almost tree-top level. Brown and Ogden settled beneath the turret, Brown's damaged head pressed between Ogden's legs to prevent further injury. Norby went up to the cockpit to see if the pilots needed any help. "This is when I first noticed how close we were to the gound and nothing but mountains all around, and no airport to be seen. At this time the number one engine started to sound noisy and the RPM gauge was fluctuating, so I knew it wouldn't be long before we would lose it.

"I noticed the pilot reached over and turned on the switches for Nos. 2 and 3 engines. When the co-pilot feathered numbers two and three I remembered him turning the switches for those engines off, so I reached over and turned them off again and explained that if we crashed, I didn't want any fire. The only reason I could think of why he did this was because we were experiencing some tense moments.

"By now I could see that we were going to crash, and not on a flat piece of ground, so I stood up behind the pilot's seat and braced my head against the armor plating which is at the back of the seat. Just before I put my head behind the armor plating, I looked at the air speed, and we were indicating 140 mph. Three things came to my mind: one was that it would be a bad crash, two was that we still had over 1,000 gallons of gas, and three was fire. As I could not see out the windows on the pilot's side, I was looking out the window behind the co-pilot and was very amazed to see tops of trees going over the top of the wing. It reminded me of a knife cutting them down. Also, for the first time, I was aware of no noise from the engines. I don't know when they quit running. The only noise was from the plane hitting the trees below."

Surprisingly, when the plane hit the ground on its belly the ride seemed smooth. But it lasted too long because the aircraft had no means of stopping, and ended suddenly with a crash. *Touchy Tess* hit a large tree with its left side and swung 180 degrees, the crew thrown against the glass or fuselage to the right. Norby said, "There is one thing that I will always remember and that is just before we hit the last tree the pilot yelled 'don't!' and I often wondered what he was referring to."

Smoke was pouring out of the plane on the left, and Norby's fear of fire was heightened by the realization that his foot was stuck in something and wouldn't move. A mass of wreckage blocked his view of the pilot and co-pilot, though an arm was dangling between their seats, dripping with blood. Norby called out to the co-pilot, Harold Gividen, and received a positive response. But the dripping blood was coming from the pilot, Charles Abplanalp, and Gividen said that it didn't look good. Norby recalled, "I asked if Harold could get out and he said yes—out through the top of the plane. The top of the plane from just below the windshield clear back to the top turret dome was sheared off. This in itself should have got the pilot, co-pilot and me. It did kill the pilot."

The B-17 had broken in two just forward of the wings. Brown and Ogden crawled into the bomb bay and walked out through the torn right side of the plane. Norby finally freed his foot from the wreckage and saw smoke coming from the wings. It turned out to be powder from the life rafts. He went to help Brown and Ogden, who were on the ground in front of the nose. Co-pilot Gividen was lifting the pilot under his arms through the hole where the windshield had been, gently dropping him down to the men below. When Abplanalp was on the ground, they cut off his parachute harness with a knife and then popped a chute to cover him for warmth. He was bleeding from his eyes, ears, nose and mouth. The co-pilot had suffered a nasty bump on the head.

Norby and Brown decided to collect the B-17's maps and charts that were scattered all over the field. They could hardly believe the amount of wreckage that was strewn for 200 yards leading back to the point of initial contact. A machine gun was hanging from a tree; an intact gas tank sat by itself on the slope; a propellor blade was sticking straight up from the ground. Ammo belts, oxygen masks, parachutes and other items covered the hill. They could see soldiers and civilians hurrying toward the crash site, so they knew time was limited. They quickly buried the maps because there were no matches to burn them. When they returned to the main wreckage, the rest of the crew and a civilian were huddled around the pilot. It was then that Norby realized the co-pilot had suffered a serious concussion. He walked over to Norby and said, "I know you—you dated my girlfriend while we were in high school." Norby tried to reason with him but finally realized that Gividen wasn't listening. The co-pilot suddenly began smiling and started walking around the plane in a daze.

Local Swiss Army troops had already arrived. "When I first saw the soldiers, all I could think of was that we were in Germany," Norby recalled. "Their uniforms looked German; they all talked German; and they were men in their 50s or above, which fit the idea that they were members of the home guard and too old for regular service." A crowd of about 100 civilians had gathered from the nearby village of Muswangen. "Had we traveled another 100 yards forward and about

50 yards to the left, we would have crashed into the village," Norby noted. The pilot, Abplanalp, had made a good landing after all, even though it cost him his life.

Minutes later, younger soldiers in different uniforms arrived, and the surviving airmen were escorted to an inn in the village. They were brought dinner, and a Swiss Army doctor told the airmen they would be examined one at a time, the most seriously wounded first. Norby remembered: "After the doctor left, three more guards came into this small room, one to guard each door. That made eight crew members and four guards in one tiny room. The doctor came back in and told us that those with head injuries could not drink any alcohol. This announcement made Ogden happy as he liked to drink and he didn't have a head injury. Ogden immediately tried to con the bottle from the guard that was sitting with us. This is when we discovered that none of the guards spoke English. Then Ogden reminded us that we were to give only our name, rank and serial number. Also that we were allowed to say, if asked, that we were on a training mission." When Norby followed this advice in the perfunctory interrogation that followed, the Swiss officer replied, "Sure, we know."

A steady flow of Swiss civilians came in and out of the inn to look at the airmen. Gividen, who was sleeping after his concussion, attracted the attention of four young Swiss girls, one of whom asked, in English, how a man so young could possibly be a pilot. Eventually the crew was taken to two vans waiting outside the inn, which were surrounded by civilians as if the downed airmen were more celebrities than soldiers. The wounded men were taken to the hospital in one van while Norby and the others were put in what he termed a "paddy wagon." They were driven to Lucerne where they joined the crew of the B-17 *Dinah Mite,* which had landed earlier that day. To their surprise, the group was taken to a large modern hall where a dinner for them had already been prepared.

During their two days in Lucerne the airmen were furnished with rooms, which Norby noted as being exceptionally clean and orderly. He continued to be somewhat unnerved by the intense curiosity of Swiss civilians, though he admitted: "I guess we were quite a sight with our flying clothes all covered with blood, dried of course, which we got on us while helping to get Charles [Abplanalp] out of the plane."

Of all the people Norby met in Switzerland, one stood out in his memory. As he tells it, "A young boy, about 11 years old, came walking over and started to talk with us one day. We recognized that he was speaking French, and none of us could understand him and he didn't understand English, but he pointed to a scar on the back of his head and the calf of his leg and said what sounded like American '*boom*!' He kept repeating it and then would laugh at us. About this time, an older man carrying a briefcase came along. When the boy saw him, he pointed to the older man and said something like 'Professor' then went running down the lane. When the man reached us, he looked us over, then said in good English that we must be the American airmen that had recently arrived in Switzerland. Then he asked about the boy who we had been trying to talk to, I suppose because he had heard some of the conversation just before he left. When we explained that we could not understand the boy, the 'Professor' sat down on a bench and told us about the program the Swiss were conducting for the young children of Europe."

The Swiss government had been running a program throughout the war that brought a number of sick or undernourished children, mostly from France, to Switzerland to be schooled and brought back to health. The services usually lasted about six months for each child, and then a new group would be brought in, to treat the largest number of children possible. Norby said, "The young boy who had tried to talk to us was from the Normandy area during the invasion. The scars on his head and legs were caused by shrapnel from American bombs, and he was very proud of them. The reason he was laughing at us was because he thought we were great warriors and fighters and we couldn't understand a little French boy. The professor said that the boy looked up to all American soldiers and thought they could do everything and anything—even understand French."

A week after the crew of *Touchy Tess* came to a screeching halt in the Swiss countryside, its brave pilot was laid to rest in the cemetery at Munsingen. He was to be buried along with *Dinah Mite's* radioman Robert Shepherd, who had said before the day's mission, "This is going to be a bad one."

Norby was introduced to Sgt. Christy Zullo, who had been shot down on Second Schweinfurt in 1943 and who had been put in charge of the American cemetery. The Swiss life had apparently been good to the downed airman, who had married a Swiss girl and had one child by 1945. He informed the airmen of their role in the ceremony. "The enlisted men from the crews in which a man had been killed would be pallbearers and were to dress as uniformly as possible. All other crew members were to march behind the coffins. Leading the funeral procession was an American Protestant minister by the name of Tracy, followed by the men from [pilot] Donald Proctor's crew and then from our own crew." American Ambassador Leland Harrison marched in the procession along with eight officers from the Embassy and a Swiss officer. Swiss civilians attended the ceremony, observing solemnly. It ended with a three-gun salute by a Swiss honor guard.

On March 1, the crew of *Touchy Tess* was transferred to Camp Moloney at Adelboden, the guards on the train pointing to areas of interest to the airmen en route. According to Norby, "One that I particularly remember was a very well camouflaged airfield in a very narrow valley with one runway. The hangars were built into the side of the mountain. The valley was about 200 to 300 yards wide and two miles long, and just the train tracks and runway were visible to us. The runway was grass, so really only the train tracks were visible. We saw one plane land, taxi and go into the mountain and another plane come out of the mountain, taxi and take off."

Upon their arrival at Adelboden, the crew of *Touchy Tess* learned of some good news. As a result of General Legge's trade of American airmen for German internees, additional U.S. flyers were to be repatriated to achieve the agreed-upon two-for-one ratio. This included all airmen arriving in Switzerland through February 25. The airmen were each given $50 to purchase souvenirs before they left, and Norby quickly took advantage. He recalled, "I bought a good watch, a nice ladies watch for my mother, a good leather wallet, and a $5 American bill for $3.75—all for $50. When I returned to London, I could have sold the watches for $200 each, mainly because watches were just not available in England."

The Swiss limited the amount each soldier could take with them. Five watches were the maximum for any individual, as well as $50 currency and three cameras. Many of the men had been purchasing Swiss objects throughout their stay, especially currency for its lower value, and some asked the newer internees to help smuggle their goods out of the country. A large party was held on the night before repatriation, but Norby, as a member of the Church of Latter Day Saints, stood apart from the crowd. By doing so, he caught the attention of a woman. "There was a lady standing there, and she asked me why I wasn't drinking. I told her I didn't drink, and then she asked me where

I was from. When I told her Salt Lake, she asked if I was a Mormon. When I replied yes, she asked me my name. When I said Norby, she asked if I knew Ann Norby. I told her that Ann was my mother, and she told me to tell my mother that I had met Lola Beers. Lola and my mother had served in the Relief Society together. Her name was now Lola Legge—the wife of General Legge, who was the American Military Attaché."

The next day, the men were walked to the French border, had their identity confirmed by guards, and then were picked up by trucks to be driven to the U.S. base at Lyon. Norby, with a tailgate seat, had a clear view of the destruction Germany had inflicted on France during the war: "As we traveled to Lyon, we could still see burned tanks. We also saw an area where trench warfare had been used for a short time at the beginning of World War II.

"In one small town, every other house had been burned down as the German army retreated. A cone-shaped hill was honeycombed with tunnels that the Germans had built, and the entrances were very well camouflaged. When the Germans had retreated, a few soldiers were left as a rear guard in this hill, and they held out for two months. On the road we traveled, there was very little damage to the countryside; most of the damage was centered on small villages. When we reached Lyon, we saw more damage. For the size of the city, there were few people on the streets. The trucks took us to the airport, which was damaged but being repaired, and we were told that all the damage was done by Allied planes while the Germans had control of the airport."

Norby was soon put aboard a C-47 bound for England. His Flying Fortress, *Touchy Tess*, had been the last Eighth Air Force plane to seek refuge in Switzerland during the war.

Accidental air attacks on Switzerland continued in February 1945, prompting testy exchanges within the American high command. On the 25th, General George Marshall cabled Eisenhower, insisting that "everything within our power" be done to restrict the USAAF from attacking targets within 50 miles of the Swiss border unless positively identified; no targets within 10 miles of the border were to be attempted. Eisenhower agreed, but not without rising to the defense of the airmen under his command. "Our air forces are performing thousands of successful missions daily in weather conditions that would normally prevent all flying," he answered back. "We will continue to make every effort to prevent recurrence of these incidents." Roosevelt's representative, Lauchlin Currie, had already assured the Swiss that no further errant attacks would occur.

The straw that broke the camel's back came four days later, when disoriented U.S. Liberators not only hit Basel, which is in the north of Switzerland on the Rhine, but Zurich, deep within the country next to an easily identifiable landmark (the large lake of Zurich). Over 16 tons of explosives landed on the former, and 25 tons, split between explosives and incendiaries, fell on the latter. By now American apologies had worn thin. Regret had given way to humiliation. The Swiss, who suffered 6 dead and 50 wounded, were in good position to observe that American precision bombing was clearly not as accurate as claimed. The only positive note was sounded by the American Consul at Basel, who reported that the citizens of that city told him, "such accidental bombings appear to be unavoidable in modern warfare." As the Swiss buried or tended to their casualties in the attacks, the Americans made a last great effort to solve the problem.

On March 7, Carl Spaatz, commander of the United States Strategic Air Forces in Europe, traveled to Switzerland on orders from George Marshall, conveyed through Eisenhower. He and his staff changed into civilian clothes before crossing the border, only to be met by General Guisan and other Swiss military leaders in full dress uniform. At a general meeting, attended by Swiss Federal Councillors, Spaatz attempted to explain the USAAF's difficulties, and once again apologized for the mistaken bombings.

In a subsequent meeting with Guisan and Swiss air force commander Rihner, he was more specific. From that day forward, the territory around Switzerland prohibited to U.S. aircraft for targets of opportunity would be 150 miles rather than 50. He cautioned the Swiss commanders that if the Germans learned of the cordon sanitaire and attempted to take advantage of it, the USAAF would have to revise its plans. Guisan and Spaatz saw eye-to-eye at the meeting, and afterward even the unrestrainable Swiss press was somewhat mollified that such a high-ranking American officer had come to Bern to take responsibility for the tragedies.

On the same day Spaatz met with Guisan in Bern, another, even more secret, assignation was taking place in Zurich between the commander of the German SS in Italy, General Karl Wolff, and Allen Dulles. In the meeting arranged by Swiss Military Intelligence Major Max Waibel, Wolff offered the unconditional surrender of all German forces in Italy—23 divisions, or nearly half-a-million men. A week later, on March 15, generals Lyman Lemnitzer and Terence Airey, chiefs of staff, respectively, of the American 5th Army and British 8th Army, arrived in Switzerland to meet Wolff and hammer out the details. It was agreed that the surrender would take place on March 21 at Caserta, headquarters of Allied commander-in-chief of the Mediterranean Theater, Field Marshal Harold Alexander. On that day the British invited Stalin to send a representative to witness the surrender. The response, from Soviet Foreign Minister V. Molotov, was immediate and blunt:

> In Bern for two weeks, behind the backs of the Soviet Union, which is bearing the brunt of the war against Germany, negotiations have been going on between representatives of the German military command on the one hand and representatives of the English and American commands on the other.

It turned out the Soviets had been well aware of the secret talks, which seemed to confirm their darkest suspicions that the Western Allies and Germans would conspire to keep the Red Army out of Europe. Churchill, professing umbrage at Molotov's response, refused to reply. His silence only fueled Soviet suspicions. Roosevelt, however, stepped in. The President, who was then only a fortnight away from death, wrote to Stalin to allay his fears and to defend the integrity of the Western Allies. "It would be one of the great tragedies of history," he stated, "if at the very moment of the victory now within our grasp such distrust, such lack of faith, should prejudice the entire undertaking."

Stalin, in turn, took the opportunity to vent frustration over what he perceived as a German Army fanatically resisting in the East while surrendering in droves in the West. He wrote Roosevelt on April 7:

> The Germans have 147 divisions on the Eastern Front. They could without prejudicing their own position detach fifteen to twenty divisions from the Eastern Front and transfer them to reinforce their troops on the Western Front. Yet the Germans have not done and are not doing this. They are continuing to

wage a crazy struggle with the Russians for an insignificant railway station like Zemlyanitsa in Czechoslovakia, which is as much use to them as hot poultices to a corpse, and yet they yield without the slightest resistance such important towns in the center of Germany as Osnabrück, Mannheim and Kassel. You will agree that such behavior on the part of the Germans is more than curious and unintelligible.

Stalin was misinformed about the tremendous battles (and casualties) taking place in the West as Allied troops surged across the Rhine. Nevertheless, a sudden German surrender in Italy would have been a disaster for the Soviets, negating their hard-fought advances in southern Europe and subsequent postwar plans. While the Red Army fought for every mile of ground, Anglo-American forces could have poured unopposed into Austria, Yugoslavia, Hungary, Czechoslovakia and Germany itself, perhaps to Berlin. Churchill's "soft underbelly of Europe" theory would have been vindicated. By any reckoning, it was distinctly not in the Soviet interest that German armies opposing the Western forces in Italy prematurely lay down their arms.

As urgent letters among Allied heads of state were exchanged (Churchill soon broke his silence) and clandestine meetings took place in Lugano, Lucerne and Bern, General Karl Wolff was called to Berlin to consult with Hitler and Himmler. Italy, like North Africa before it, was not an "SS theater," and Wolff did not command troops there except in a behind-the-lines capacity. Albert Kesselring, the German Army commander in Italy until March 10, and his successor, Albert von Vietinghoff, would have been executed had they tried to surrender. Italy was, in fact, Germany's most successful front and the least likely to capitulate while the rest of the Wehrmacht fought on. Wolff's offer to surrender had been, at best, a probe; at worst, a deception. While the SS initiated "secret" talks with the Anglo-Americans in Switzerland, it simultaneously made certain that the Kremlin could covertly follow their progress. It was the closest the Nazis came to provoking irretrievable discord among the Allied coalition arrayed against them.

Swiss intelligence, encouraged by General Guisan, persisted in trying to facilitate a German surrender in Italy, and by late April Wolff, who by then had his sights set on the postwar era, warmed to the task. Vietinghoff agreed that if Berlin, which was surrounded by the Red

Army on April 25, were taken and Germany's cause lost, there was no point in perpetuating further bloodshed and ruin. Delays ensued because the Germans demanded full military honors and other conditions incompatible with unconditional surrender. Historian Richard Lamb noted, "Both Vietinghoff and Wolff believed that they still had bargaining power, being under the mistaken impression that the Allies would want to use the German army to contain the Russians in the east."

On April 29, after the spectacular success of the U.S. 5th Army and British 8th Army in crushing the Germans' Po River line, the enemy in Italy finally surrendered with terms effective May 2. The Italian front thus closed down almost a week before the official end of the war, saving many lives. By that date, however, Hitler had been dead for two days and Benito Mussolini had been captured and executed by Communist partisans. President Roosevelt, too, had died, on April 14. Unlike his Axis counterparts he succumbed to natural causes and could reflect during his final moments on the truth that his leadership in history's greatest armed conflict had not been in vain.

The USAAF continued flying missions during the last two months of the war, with decreasing loss rates as flak emplacements were overrun by Allied troops. The once-formidable Luftwaffe was severely crippled and starved for fuel. In mid-March, Adolf Galland summoned Germany's surviving aces to fly the Me-262 jet fighter in a group called "Jadgverband 44." By this time the jets appeared more as a phenomenon than threat to the USAAF, and more than one Luftwaffe legend was killed by Mustangs while trying to land at camouflaged airfields near Munich.

In March 1945, only one American bomber, a 15th Air Force Liberator, landed in Switzerland, and a German Me-109 crashed after being shot down. In April, the last full month of the war in Europe, the Swiss hosted a variety of foreign craft, including a British Spitfire, an Me-262 jet, and several other Italian or German planes. Two Italian-based American Liberators limped in on April 8, and a damaged B-26 Marauder arrived on the 12th, providing the Swiss their first look at that excellent tactical support craft. On April 20, 1945, the very last American bomber, a Flying Fortress named *Princess O'Rourke*, arrived after being hit by flak over northern Italy. It landed safely at Dubendorf.

On that day the USAAF ended its strategic bombing campaign in Europe. Most of the Third Reich was covered with advancing Allied troops, surrendered German soldiers and countless displaced persons and refugees. However, up until May 8, 1945, the day of Germany's unconditional surrender, and for months afterward, thousands of American bomber crews would continue to fly missions to the Continent. Their new task was to deliver food and other necessities of life to the devastated population of Europe.

16

SEPARATE WAYS

The Second World War concluded more decisively than Americans have witnessed in many subsequent conflicts. In Europe in 1945, Hitler chose to join the Gotterdämmerung he had created, simultaneously shooting and poisoning himself in his Berlin bunker as enemy soldiers approached above. A few days later, the United States celebrated V-E Day: "Victory in Europe." In Japan, the following August, America's atomic weapons forced a similarly abrupt capitulation, prompting V-J Day. On both occasions, households, towns and cities throughout the United States fairly burst with pride over their young men who had courageously pitted themselves against aggressive militaristic empires. The New World—as Churchill had hoped during the darkest days of 1940—had indeed come to the rescue of the Old. Postwar revelations of enemy barbarism confirmed that American GIs had truly fought a noble crusade.

In Switzerland, the brief period of relaxation after World War II prompted a general feeling of relief. The Nazi state that the Swiss had prepared to fight since 1933 had finally been destroyed. Switzerland did not emerge from the war with combat heroes, aside from fighter pilots, but even today one can detect a certain proud bearing in men and women of a certain age—those who served under General Guisan. It was their martial skill and determination, purposely joined with the immovable strength of Switzerland's ancient ally, the Alps, that played a major part in deterring the Wehrmacht from attempting an invasion. Guisan's army, which included every able-bodied man in the country during the war, as well as tens of thousands of women, maintained its readiness to fiercely resist an attack until the very end.

During the Cold War that commenced shortly after the destruction of the Nazi state, the Swiss, as their historic practice required, took measures to enhance their ability to resist foreign invasion. In December 1944 Switzerland offered to renew diplomatic relations with the Soviet Union, primarily because of over 12,000 Red Army internees living in Swiss camps. At first the Soviets refused. After the war, while the United States organized Western Europe into the NATO defensive alliance and the Soviet Union formed the more menacing Warsaw Pact, Switzerland adhered to its policy of armed neutrality. If a World War III in Europe had occurred, the Swiss would once again have relied on their own defenses to maintain their democratic way of life. It can only be a matter of speculation whether the Soviets, viewed in Switzerland as hardly more palatable totalitarians than the Nazis, would have tested Swiss defenses and resolve.

Today in the United States, the "boys" who fought World War II are disguised as retirees. Many of them have passed away after careers in insurance, retail, the fuel industry, manufacturing, or other jobs that would offer few clues about what they experienced during their youth. Some men remained in the military and fought through Korea and Vietnam, though accolades for service in those conflicts, on the home front, were few. Studs Terkel described World War II as "The Good War," and Tom Brokaw has termed the men and women who fought it or served in supporting roles "The Greatest Generation." Both terms are easily accepted by one who is even marginally aware of what U.S. GIs braved during the greatest conflict in America's history. A tail gunner at Second Schweinfurt could be the familiar older fellow who sits at the local diner. A pilot who once cheated fate between Alpine peaks with the fate of ten men at his fingertips could be your father-in-law. The heroes of World War II are scattered throughout the country but have largely become anonymous—at this writing, senior citizens—and are often reticent to speak to strangers about the drama they experienced when younger.

A private movement is under way in the U.S. to create a World War II Memorial in Washington, DC. Proponents may realize that until now an elaborate structure in the capital has not been necessary because since 1945 the entire world has existed as a monument to the heroism of the World War II generation. Nevertheless, in the new millennium a tribute to those heroes is called for. As veterans of the conflict become fewer, replaced in the population by babies who will not gain firsthand knowledge of the great struggle from their fathers or grandfathers, the time for an enduring memorial has come. One trusts that the enormous resources of the American government at the turn of the century—made possible in large part by the generation that fought World War II—will stand fully behind the project's planners.

No nation has thrust as many of its citizens into air warfare as did the United States in World War II. Hundreds of thousands of recruits were hastily trained and thrust into combat far above the clouds on a scale that we will never see again. The young flyers who emerged from the deadly maelstrom over the Third Reich into Swiss airspace not only deserve our admiration and gratitude but also through their recollections provide a unique view of "near-death" in the air war. Their experiences stand as testimony to the heroism of thousands of other airmen who did not have a refuge nearby when their planes were crippled by enemy fire.

The resolve of the small Alpine nation to resist Nazism during the war—despite encirclement and intimidation—amounts to another form of heroism. If Switzerland had been weak or indifferent, willing to succumb to the "New Order" during the years when German arms possessed an aura of invincibility, the fate of over 1,700 U.S. airmen would have been dismal to contemplate. Instead, a small, extremely stubborn democracy held on to its sovereignty in the center of the Continent. The spectacle of fighting men from the world's most powerful free nation, the United States, finding refuge in another free enclave in German-held Europe has been the fascination underlying this work. For the Swiss, the refuge they provided to U.S. airmen is only one aspect of the pride they can assume for their successful and, in the context of central Europe, singular resistance to the Third Reich.

The fact that nearly 1,000 U.S. airmen embarked on daredevil escapes from neutral Switzerland in order to rejoin their units invites further admiration—not least for the Swiss who felt obligated to confine our young airmen in internment. Switzerland, though it presented a united front and determination to defend itself against a German onslaught, proved unable to resist the flow of American airmen trying to rejoin their fellow GIs. Most were assisted by empathetic Swiss civilians and by U.S. Consular officials against whom the Swiss government only considered making a formal protest. In the escapades that took place throughout the Alpine nation, the final tally was 184 airmen caught by Swiss soldiers (some of them more than once) against 764 successful escapes.

After the war, the Sister Republics—one which defied the Nazis against great odds and one which projected its air power to gain total victory—once again went their separate ways. Switzerland has retained its historic neutrality throughout the Soviet era and its aftermath. The United States has engaged in other conflicts, in East Asia, Latin America and the Mideast. All the while, Adelboden, Wengen, Davos and other Swiss towns and villages have had occasion to welcome American veterans and their families who desired to revisit the country that once gave them refuge. Airmen, in turn, have hosted Swiss visitors in the States, and many long-term friendships have ensued.

During World War II, the United States and Switzerland—together with Great Britain, the world's oldest democracies—withstood Nazism, each in its own way, according to separate traditions. In the American air campaign over Germany, 1943–45, their histories intersected and merged, leading to one of the more stirring human dramas to unfold in the war. Most people today are unaware of the role the Swiss played in the lives of almost 1,700 American airmen who flew Flying Fortresses and Liberators in combat against German defenses. But for those young American airmen it was a vital benefit that Switzerland stood firm in the heart of Axis Europe, offering refuge when they were most in need and their lives hung in the balance.

BIBLIOGRAPHY

Air Forces Escape and Evasion. Paducah, KY: Turner Publishing Co., 1991.

Anderton, David A. *Aggressors, Vol. 3: Interceptor vs. Heavy Bomber*. Charlottesville, VA: Howell Publications, 1991.

Bailey, Ronald H. *The Air War In Europe*. Chicago: Time-Life Books, 1981.

Bericht des Commandanten der Flieger und Fliegerabwehrtruppen an den Oberbefehlshaber der Armee über den Aktivdienst, 1939–1945. Bern, Switzerland: Eidgenossichen Militärbibliothek, 1946.

Boyne, Walter J. *Clash of Wings: Air Power in World War II*. New York: Simon & Schuster, 1994.

Bradley, Omar N., and Clay Blair. *A General's Life: An Autbiography by General of the Army Omar N. Bradley*. New York: Simon & Schuster, 1983.

Brooks, Thomas R. *The War North of Rome: June 1944–May 1945*. New York: Sarpedon, 1996.

Brookes, Andrew. *Fighter and Bomber Squadrons at War*. Shepperton, Surrey (UK): Ian Allan Publishing, 1980.

Chant, Chris. *Aircraft of World War II*. New York: Barnes & Noble Books, 1999.

Churchill, Winston S. *The Second World War*, Vols. I–VI. Boston: Houghton Mifflin Co., 1948–53.

Dame, Frederick William. *Continuity and Change in Swiss Neutrality from 1815 to 1980: An Analysis*. Saarbrücken, Switzerland: Schweizerische Landesbibliothek, 1981.

249

Eisenhower, David. *Eisenhower at War 1943–1945*. New York: Random House, 1986.

Eisenhower, Dwight D. *Crusade in Europe*. New York: Doubleday, 1948.

Freeman, Roger Anthony. *The Mighty Eighth*. London: Jane's Information Group, 1986.

Garlínski, Józef. *The Swiss Corridor*. London: J.M. Dent & Sons Ltd, 1981.

Gautschi, Willi. *General Henri Guisan*. Zurich, Switzerland: Verlag Neue Zürcher Zeitung, 1989.

Gibbs, Steve. *A Green Hill Far Away: The Story of Lazy Baby*. Ligston, Leicester (UK): Buccaneer Distributions, 1995.

Glines, Carroll V. *The Compact History of the United States Air Force*. New York: Hawthorn Books, 1963.

Grose, Peter. *Gentleman Spy: The Life of Allen Dulles*. New York: Houghton Mifflin Co., 1994.

Guderian, Heinz. *Panzer Leader*. New York: E.P. Dutton, 1952.

Halbrook, Stephen. *Target Switzerland: Swiss Armed Neutrality in World War II*. Rockville Centre, NY: Sarpedon, 1998.

Halder, Franz. *The Halder War Diary, 1939–1942* (Charles Burdick and Hans-Adolf Jacobsen, eds.). Novato, CA: Presidio Press, 1988.

Hingley, Ronald. *Joseph Stalin: Man and Legend*. New York: McGraw-Hill, 1974.

Harrison, James P. *Mastering the Sky: A History of Aviation from Ancient Times to the Present*. New York: Sarpedon, 1996.

Harvey, Maurice. *The Allied Bomber War, 1939–1945*. Staplehurst, Kent (UK): Spellmount Publishers, 1992.

Hutson, James H. *The Sister Republics: Switzerland and the United States from 1776 to the Present*. Washington, DC: The Library of Congress, 1991.

Keegan, John. *The Second World War*. New York: Viking-Penguin, 1989.

King, Benjamin, and Timothy Kutta. *Impact: The History of Germany's V-Weapons in World War II*. Rockville Centre, NY: Sarpedon, 1998.

Lamb, Richard. *War in Italy, 1943–1945*. London: St. Martin's Press, 1993.

Mason, Herbert Molloy, Jr. *The United States Air Force: A Turbulent*

History. New York: Mason/Charter, 1976.

Newby, Leroy W. *Target Ploesti: View from a Bombsight*. Novato, CA: Presidio Press, 1983.

Oman, C.W.C. *The Art of War in the Middle Ages*. Ithaca, NY: Cornell University Press, 1953.

Overy, R.J. *The Air War 1939–1945*. New York: Stein and Day, 1981.

Perret, Geoffrey. *Winged Victory: The Army Air Forces in World War II*. New York: Random House, 1993.

Ries, Karl. *Deutsche Luftwaffe über der Schweiz 1939–1945*. Bern, Switzerland: Verlag Dieter Hoffman, 1978.

Schwarz, Urs. *The Eye of the Hurricane: Switzerland in World War Two*. Boulder, CO: Westview Press, 1980.

Siegfried, André. *Switzerland: A Democratic Way of Life*. New York: Duell, Sloan and Pearce, n.d.

Shirer, William L. *Berlin Diary: The Journal of a Foreign Correspondent, 1934–41*. New York: Knopf, 1941.

———. *The Rise and Fall of the Third Reich*. New York: Simon & Schuster, 1990.

———. *This is Berlin: Radio Broadcasts from Nazi Germany*. Woodstock, NY: The Overlook Press, 1999.

Snow, Crocker. *Log Book: A Pilot's Life*. Washington: Brassey's, 1997.

Stapfer, Hans-Heiri, and Gino Künzle. *Strangers in a Strange Land, Vol. II: Escape to Neutrality*. Carrollton, TX: Squadron/Signal Publications, 1992.

Thomas, Roy J. *Haven, Heaven and Hell, Part I: The United States Army Air Force Aircraft and Airmen Interned in Switzerland During WWII*. Monroe, WI: Puka Press, 1991.

Urner, Klaus. *Switzerland Has Yet to Be Swallowed*. Zurich, Switzerland: Verlag Neue Zürcher Zeitung, 1990.

USAAF: 50th Anniversary in Great Britain, 1942–1992. Hadleigh, England: The Winchester Group, 1992.

Weigley, Russell F. *The Age of Battles: The Quest for Decisive Warfare from Breitenfeld to Waterloo*. Bloomington, IN: Indiana University Press, 1991.

Wildblood, Richard. *What Makes Switzerland Unique?* Sussex, England: The Book Guild Ltd., 1990.

Wood, Raymond. *Or Go Down in Flame: A Navigator's Death Over Schweinfurt*. New York: Sarpedon, 1993.

ARTICLES

Anderson, Douglas, and John Zmirak. "No Way Is Impassable to Courage: The Wartime Experiences of Lt. Martin Andrews, USAAF," Occasional Paper, American Swiss Foundation, February 2000.

Cunningham, Ed. "The Swiss Stake," in *Yank, The Army Weekly*, August 1945.

Helmreich, Dr. Jonathan E. "The Diplomacy of Apology: U.S. Bombings of Switzerland During World War II," in *Air University Review*, May–June 1977.

Hutson, James H. "Bombing the Sister Republic," in *Swiss-American Historical Society Review*, February 1995.

Ketchum, Richard M. "They Can't Realize the Change Aviation Has Made," in *Military History Quarterly*, Autumn 1989.

Stüssi-Lauterburg, Jürg. "Switzerland and the Three Totalitarianisms, 1917–1945," n.d.

This book owes much to the newsletter of the Swiss Internees Association, Inc., *The Swiss Internee*. Published for fourteen years, its latest issue, number 84, is dated February 2000. Members of the Association have also been encouraged over the years to record their experiences in detail for the Association's archives. Many of the first-hand airmen's accounts in this book derive from this rare and fascinating collection.

The archives of Maxwell Air Force Base, Alabama, as well as the National Archives in Washington, DC, have been a valuable source for Missing Aircrew Reports, Questionnaires for Escapees and Evadees, Operation Reports, and countless other documents and official correspondence pertaining to United States internees in Switzerland.

INDEX

253